LinkedIn®

for dummies®

A Wiley Brand

LinkedIn®

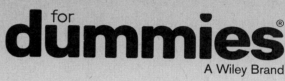

for
dummies®
A Wiley Brand

4th edition

by Joel Elad, MBA

LinkedIn® For Dummies®, 4th Edition

Published by: **John Wiley & Sons, Inc.,** 111 River Street, Hoboken, NJ 07030-5774, www.wiley.com

Copyright © 2016 by John Wiley & Sons, Inc., Hoboken, New Jersey

Published simultaneously in Canada

For general information on our other products and services, please contact our Customer Care Department within the U.S. at 877-762-2974, outside the U.S. at 317-572-3993, or fax 317-572-4002. For technical support, please visit www.wiley.com/techsupport.

Wiley publishes in a variety of print and electronic formats and by print-on-demand. Some material included with standard print versions of this book may not be included in e-books or in print-on-demand. If this book refers to media such as a CD or DVD that is not included in the version you purchased, you may download this material at http://booksupport.wiley.com. For more information about Wiley products, visit www.wiley.com.

Library of Congress Control Number: 2016935256

ISBN 978-1-119-25113-2 (pbk); ISBN 978-1-119-25115-6 (ebk); ISBN 978-1-119-25114-9 (ebk)

Manufactured in the United States of America

10 9 8 7 6 5 4

Contents at a Glance

Table of Contents

Introduction

Relationships matter. Ever since the dawn of time, when Fred Flintstone asked Barney Rubble whether there was any work down at the quarry, human beings have always networked. We're social creatures who like to reach out and talk to someone. As the Internet developed and grew in popularity, people rapidly took advantage of this new technology for communication, with e-mail; instant messaging; personal web pages sharing voice, video, and data with each other; and lots of other applications to keep everybody connected. But how can the Internet help you do a better job with your professional networking? I'm glad you asked! Welcome to *LinkedIn For Dummies,* Fourth Edition.

LinkedIn was founded in 2003 by a guy named Reid Hoffman, who felt that he could create a better way to handle your professional networking needs. He saw lots of websites that let you build your own page and show it to the world, extolling your virtues and talents. But a lot of the popular websites that Hoffman came across at that time focused more on the social aspects of your life and not that much on the professional side. LinkedIn changed all that with its approach of augmenting all the professional networking you do (or should do) on a daily basis. You don't have to be looking for a job to use LinkedIn, but if you're looking, LinkedIn should be a part of your search. As Hoffman put it, LinkedIn was designed to "find and contact the people you need through the people you already trust."

In short, LinkedIn allows you to coordinate your professional identity on the Internet and make you more effective in your career. The site is designed to make the aspects of networking less time consuming and more powerful, so you can open doors with your professional connections and tap the connections of people you know who make up your extended network. LinkedIn doesn't require a huge amount of time or usage to be effective, and is focused only on providing tools that help your professional career.

Perhaps you've heard of LinkedIn, but you don't understand fully what it is, how it works, and most importantly, why you should care about it. Maybe you got an invitation to join the LinkedIn website. Perhaps you've gotten multiple invitations, or you keep hearing about it and want to find out more. Well, you're taking the right first step by reading this book. In it, I talk about the *whys* as well as the *hows*. If you're looking to enhance your professional life, I truly believe you need to look at LinkedIn. If you want to go straight to the beach and retire, though, maybe this isn't the book for you!

This book covers LinkedIn from start to finish. In case you haven't already joined, I show you how you can sign up. If you're already a member, this book is also very useful because I show you how to build your identity and take advantage of Linked-In's functionality. This book is useful regardless of your skill level, whether you want to join or you've been on LinkedIn for years but feel stuck.

About This Book

This book covers all aspects of using the LinkedIn site: from signing up and building your profile, to growing your network of contacts, to taking advantage of some of the sophisticated options, and everything in between. I include a lot of advice and discussion of networking concepts, but you also find a lot of step-by-step instructions to get things done. In this fourth edition, I revisit some of the newer facets of LinkedIn, including its Groups, mobile apps, Pulse, and Companies sections, and have updated all the core processes, from creating your profile to looking for a job.

This book is organized as a guide; you can read each chapter one after the other, or you can go straight to the chapter on the topic you're interested in. After you start using LinkedIn, think of this book as a reference where you can find the knowledge nugget you need to know and then be on your merry way. Lots of details are cross-referenced, so if you need to look elsewhere in the book for more information, you can easily find it.

And Just Who Are You?

I assume that you know how to use your computer, at least for the basic operations, like checking e-mail, typing up a document, or surfing the great big World Wide Web. If you're worried that you need a Ph.D. in Computer Operations to handle LinkedIn, relax. If you can navigate your way around a website, you can use LinkedIn.

You may be utterly new to the idea of social networking, or the specific ins and outs of using a site like LinkedIn. LinkedIn allows you to do some really cool stuff and enhance your professional life. There's more to it, and this book is here to show you the ropes — and help you take full advantage of what LinkedIn has to offer.

This book assumes that you have a computer that can access the Internet; any PC or Macintosh line of computer is fine, as well as Linux or any other operating system with a web browser. All the main web browsers can access LinkedIn just fine. In some parts of the book, I discuss specific applications such as Microsoft Outlook; if you have Outlook, I assume you know how to use it for the purposes of importing and exporting names from your address book.

Icons Used in This Book

As you go through this book, you'll see the following icons in the margins.

TIP

The Tip icon notifies you about something cool, handy, or nifty that I highly recommend. For example, "Here's a quicker way to do the described task the next time you have to do it."

REMEMBER

Don't forget! When you see this icon, you can be sure that it points out something you should remember, possibly even something I said earlier that I'm repeating because it's very important. For example, "If you are only going to do one of my bullet point suggestions, do the last one because it's the most powerful."

WARNING

Danger! Ah-oo-gah! Ah-oo-gah! When you see the Warning icon, pay careful attention to the text. This icon flags something that's bad or that could cause trouble. For example, "Although you may be tempted to go into personal details in your profile, you should never post anything that could embarrass you in a future job interview."

Beyond the Book

In addition to what you're reading right now, this product comes with a free access-anywhere Cheat Sheet that gives you steps on building your LinkedIn network, tips for enhancing your LinkedIn profile, advice for getting the most out of LinkedIn, and tips for using LinkedIn to search for a job. To get this Cheat Sheet, simply go to www.dummies.com and search for "LinkedIn For Dummies Fourth Edition Cheat Sheet" in the Search box.

Where to Go from Here

You can read this book cover to cover, or just jump in and start reading anywhere. Open the Table of Contents and pick a spot that interests or concerns you or that has piqued your curiosity. Everything is explained in the text, and important details are cross-referenced so that you don't waste your time reading repeated information.

Good luck with LinkedIn. Happy networking!

1

LinkedIn Basics

IN THIS PART. . .

Explore all that LinkedIn has to offer.

Navigate the LinkedIn website.

Sign up with LinkedIn and create an account.

Build a LinkedIn profile that details your professional and educational experience.

Chapter 1

Looking into LinkedIn

When I hear the terms "social networking" and "business networking," I always go back to one of my favorite phrases: "It's not *what* you know; it's *who* you know." Now imagine a website where both concepts are true, where you can demonstrate *what* you know and see the power of *who* you know. That's just one way to describe LinkedIn, one of the top websites today where you can do professional networking and so much more. Social networking has gotten a lot of attention over the years, and the two sites that everyone talks about are Twitter and Facebook. Let me state right now, in the first paragraph of the first chapter, that LinkedIn is *not* one of those sites. You can find some elements of similarity, but LinkedIn isn't the place to tweet about what you had for lunch or show pictures of last Friday's beach bonfire.

LinkedIn is a place where Relationships Matter (the LinkedIn slogan). It was developed primarily for professional networking. When you look at its mission statement, LinkedIn's goal "is to help you be more effective in your daily work and open doors to opportunities using the professional relationships you already have." This is not a website that requires a lot of constant work to be effective. It's designed to work in the background and help you reach out to whomever you need while learning and growing yourself. The key is to set up your online identity, build your network, and steadily take advantage of the opportunities that most affect you or greatly interest you.

In this chapter, I introduce you to LinkedIn and the basic services it has to offer. I answer the questions "What is LinkedIn?" and, more importantly, "Why should I be using LinkedIn?" I talk about how LinkedIn fits in with the rest of your online activities, and then I move into the tangible benefits that LinkedIn can provide you, regardless of your profession or career situation. I discuss some of the premium account capabilities that you can pay to use, but rest assured, LinkedIn has a lot of features that are free. The last part of the chapter covers basic navigation of the LinkedIn site. I show you the different menus and navigation bars, which you use throughout this book.

Discovering Your New Contact Management and Networking Toolkit

When describing how people can be connected with each other, think of a tangible network. For example, roads connect cities. The Internet connects computers. A quilt is a series of connected pieces of fabric. But what about the intangible networks? You can describe the relationship among family members using a family tree metaphor. People now use the term "social network" to describe the intangible connections between them and other people, whether they're friends, co-workers, or acquaintances.

People used to rely on address books or contact organizers (PDAs) to keep track of their social networks. You could grow your social networks by attending networking events or by being introduced in person to new contacts, and then you would continue to communicate with these new contacts, and eventually the new contacts were considered a part of your social network.

As people began to rely more and more on technology, though, new tools were created to help manage social networks. Salespeople started using contact management systems like ACT! to keep track of communications. Phone calls replaced written letters, and cellular phones replaced landline phones. E-mail replaced phone calls and letters, and with the mass adoption of cell phones, text messaging increasingly handles short bursts of communication. Today, with the mass adoption of smartphones, laptops, and tablets, Internet browsing has dramatically increased. People manage their lives through web browsers, SMS communications, and apps on their smartphones.

Internet tools have advanced to the point where online communication within your network is much more automated and accessible. Sites such as LinkedIn have started to replace the older ways of accessing your social network. For example, instead of asking your friend Michael to call his friend Eric to see whether Eric's friend has a job available, you can use LinkedIn to see whether Eric's friend works for a company you want to contact, and you can then use LinkedIn to send a message through Michael to Eric (or in some cases, directly to Eric's friend) to accomplish the same task. (Of course, this assumes you, Michael, and Eric are all members of LinkedIn.)

In the past, you had no way of viewing other people's social networks (collections of friends and other contacts). Now, though, when folks put their social networks on LinkedIn, you can see your friends' networks as well as their friends' networks, and suddenly hidden opportunities start to become available to you.

This means you can spend more time doing research on potential opportunities (like finding a job or a new employee for your business) as well as receiving information from the larger network and not just your immediate friends. This makes the network more useful because you can literally see the map that connects you with other people.

However, just because this information is more readily available, that doesn't mean there's no work involved in networking. You still have to manage your connections and use the network to gain more connections or knowledge. Remember, too, that nothing can replace the power of meeting people in person. But because LinkedIn works in the background to guide the way in finding contacts and starting the process, you spend your time more productively instead of making blind requests and relying solely on other people to make something happen.

Keeping track of your contacts

You made a connection with someone — say, your roommate from college. It's graduation day; you give him your contact information, he gives you his information, and you tell him to keep in touch. As both of you move to different places, start new jobs, and live your lives, you eventually lose track of each other, and all your contact information grows out of date. How do you find this person again?

One of the benefits of LinkedIn is that after you connect with someone you know who also has an account on LinkedIn, you always have a live link to that person. Even when that person changes e-mail addresses, you'll be updated with his new e-mail address. In this sense, LinkedIn always keeps you connected with people in your network, regardless of how their lives change. LinkedIn shows you a list of your connections, as shown in Figure 1-1.

Sort by Recent Conversation ▾   Filter by All Contacts ▾   🔍 Search

☐ Select All

☐ **Lynn Northrup** 1st   8 days ago   in
   Editor at Northrup Editorial Services
   Charlotte, North Carolina Area

☐ **Cynthia (Cindy) Beale Campbell** 1st   19 days ago   in
   Entrepreneur at (Self-Employed)
   United States
   🎓 classmates

☐ **R Douglas Tondro** 1st   19 days ago   in
   General Manager at THE SPOT La Jolla
   San Diego, California

☐ **Kristie Spilios** 1st   21 days ago   in
   Quality Assurance & Financial Auditor at Bank of America
   Greater Los Angeles Area
   🎓 classmates

☐ **Michael Bellomo** 1st   24 days ago   in
   Graduate Student, Master of Public Policy Program at UC Irvine
   Greater Los Angeles Area

FIGURE 1-1:
See all your connections in one centralized list.

Understanding the different degrees of network connections

In the LinkedIn universe, the word *connection* means a person who is connected to you through the site. The number of connections you have simply means the number of people who are directly connected to you in your professional network.

Here are the different degrees of how you're connected with people on LinkedIn:

» **First-degree connections:** People you know personally; they have a direct relationship from their account to your account. These first-degree connections make up your immediate network and are usually your past colleagues, classmates, group members, friends, family, and close associates. Unlike Facebook, where everyone you connect to is a "friend," on LinkedIn, you can connect to friends who don't necessarily have a work, school, or group connection to you, but are people who you know personally outside those criteria. Similar to Facebook, though, you can see your first-degree connections' contact list and they can see yours — provided your settings (and those of your connections) are configured so any connection can see other people's connections list.

» **Second-degree network members:** People who know at least one member of your first-degree connections: in other words, the friends of your friends. You can reach any second-degree network member by asking your first-degree connection to pass along your profile as an introduction from you to his friend.

>> **Third-degree network members:** People who know at least one of your second-degree network members: in other words, friends of your friends of your friends. You can reach any third-degree network member by asking your friend to pass along a request to be introduced from you to her friend, who then passes it to her friend, who is the third-degree network member.

The result is a large chain of connections and network members, with a core of trusted friends who help you reach out and tap your friends' networks and extended networks. Take the concept of Six Degrees of Separation (which says that, on average, a chain of six people can connect you to anyone else on Earth), put everyone's network online, and you have LinkedIn.

So, how powerful can these connections be? Figure 1-2 shows a snapshot of how someone's network on LinkedIn used to look.

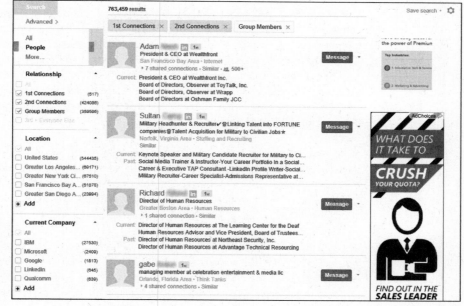

FIGURE 1-2:
Only three degrees of separation can give you a network of millions.

The account in Figure 1-2 had 517 first-degree connections. When you add all the network connections that each of these 517 people have, the user of this account could reach more than 424,000 different people on LinkedIn as second-degree network members. Add in over 359,000 LinkedIn users who are members of groups that this account belongs to, plus millions of third-degree network members, and the user could have access to millions of LinkedIn users, part of a vast professional network that stretches across the world into companies and industries of all sizes. Such a network can help you advance your career or professional goals — and in turn, you can help advance others' careers or goals. Of course, as of this writing, the LinkedIn community has more than 400 million members, and LinkedIn focuses on your first-degree connections instead of your second- and third-degree network members, but the concept is still valid. Your network can be vast, thanks to the power of LinkedIn.

THE DIFFERENCE BETWEEN A USER AND A LION

Given all this power and potential to reach people around the world, some people — LinkedIn open networkers (LIONs) — want to network with anyone and everyone who's eager to connect with them. Their goal is to network with as many people as possible, regardless of past interaction or communication with that person.

One of your most prominently displayed LinkedIn statistics is the number of first-degree connections you have. After you surpass 500 connections, LinkedIn doesn't display your current count of first-degree connections, but just the message 500+. (It's kind of like how McDonald's stopped displaying the running total of hamburgers sold on its signs. Or am I the only one who remembers that?) Part of the reason LinkedIn stops displaying updated counts past 500 is to discourage people from collecting connections. Many LIONs have thousands or even tens of thousands of first-degree connections, and the 500+ statistic is a badge of honor to them.

LIONs encourage open networking (that is, the ability to connect with someone you have never met or worked with in the past) by advertising their e-mail address as part of their professional headline (for example, John Doe; Manager >firstname@lastname. com<), so anyone can request this person be added to their network. You can find more information at sites such as www.opennetworker.com.

LinkedIn offers a formal program — Open Profile — for people interested in networking with the larger community. You can sign up for this premium service any time after you establish a premium account. When you enable the Open Profile feature, you can send and receive messages with any other Open Profile member. I discuss this in the upcoming section, "Understanding LinkedIn Costs and Benefits."

I've been asked many times whether it's okay to be a LION: if there is any meaning or benefit to having so many connections. My answer is that I don't endorse being a LION *at all!* Although some people feel that they can find some quality hidden in the quantity, LinkedIn is designed to cultivate the real quality connections that people have. Not only does LinkedIn heavily discourage a user being a LION to the point of almost banning them, but also the random connections make it next to impossible to tap the real power and potential of LinkedIn.

Learning About What You Can Do with LinkedIn

Time to find out what kinds of things you can do on LinkedIn. The following sections introduce you to the topics you need to know to get your foot in the LinkedIn door and really make the site start working for you.

Building your brand and profile

On LinkedIn, you can build your own brand. Your name, your identity, is a brand — just like Ford or Facebook — in terms of what people think of when they think of you. It's your professional reputation. Companies spend billions to ensure that you have a certain opinion of their products, and that opinion, that perception, is their brand image. You have your own brand image in your professional life, and it's up to you to own, define, and push your brand.

Most people today have different online representations of their personal brand. Some people have their own websites, others create and write blogs, and others create profile pages on sites like Facebook. LinkedIn allows you to define a profile and build your own brand based on your professional and educational background. I use my profile as an example in Figure 1-3.

FIGURE 1-3: Create a unified profile page to showcase your professional history.

Your LinkedIn profile can become a jumping-off point, where any visitor can get a rich and detailed idea of all the skills, experiences, and interests you bring to the table. Unlike a resume, where you have to worry about page length and formatting, you can provide substance and detail on your LinkedIn profile, including any part-time, contract, nonprofit, and consulting work in addition to traditional professional experience. You also have other options to consider; for example, you can

>> Write your own summary.

>> List any groups you belong to.

>> Describe any courses you have completed and test scores you have achieved.

>> Show any memberships or affiliations you have.

>> Cite honors and awards you have received.

>> Identify any patents or certifications you have earned.

>> Provide links to any publications you've written or published.

>> Give and receive endorsements of people's skills. (I discuss endorsements in Chapter 7.)

>> Give and receive recommendations from other people. (I discuss recommendations in Chapter 9.)

>> Indicate your professional interests or supported causes.

>> Upload presentations, graphic design projects, or portfolio examples for others to view.

>> Post website links to other parts of your professional identity, such as a blog, a website, or an e-commerce store you operate.

The best part is that *you* control and shape your professional identity. You decide what the content should be. You decide what to emphasize and what to omit. You decide how much information is visible to the world and how much is visible to your first-degree connections. (I talk more about the power of your profile in Chapters 2 and 3.)

Looking for a job now or later

At some point in your life, you'll probably have to look for a job. It might be today, it might be a year from now, or it may be ten years from now. The job search is, in itself, a full-time job, and studies show that 60 to 80 percent of all jobs are found not through a job board like Monster.com or a newspaper classified ad, but rather through a formal or informal network of contacts where the job isn't even posted yet. LinkedIn makes it easy to do some of the following tedious job search tasks:

>> **Finding the right person** at a target company, like a hiring manager in a certain department, to discuss immediate and future job openings

>> **Getting a reference** from a past boss or co-worker to use for a future job application

>> **Finding information** about a company and position before the interview

>> **Enabling the right employers to find you** and validate your experience and job potential before an interview

>> **Searching posted job listings** on a job board like the one on LinkedIn

The hidden power of LinkedIn is that it helps you find jobs you weren't looking for or applying to directly. This is when you're a *passive job seeker*, currently employed but interested in the right opportunity. As of this writing, hundreds of thousands of recruiters are members of LinkedIn, and they constantly use the search functions to go through the database and find skilled members who match their job search requirements. Instead of companies paying big money for resume books, they now have instant access to millions of qualified professionals, each of whom has a detailed profile with skills, experience, and recommendations already available.

This practice of finding passive job seekers is growing quickly on LinkedIn, mainly because of the following reasons:

>> **Companies can run detailed searches** to find the perfect candidate with all the right keywords and skills in his profile, and they then contact the person to see whether he is interested.

>> **LinkedIn users demonstrate their capabilities** by providing knowledge on the site, which gives companies insight into the passive job seeker's capabilities. Not only does LinkedIn give users the opportunity to share updates and knowledge, but it also hosts an extensive network of groups on the site. Each group runs its own "discussion board" of conversations, where LinkedIn users can pose a question or start a conversation, and other LinkedIn members can provide insight or link to relevant articles and continue the discussion.

>> **Companies can review a person's profile** to find and check references ahead of time and interview only people they feel would be a great match with their corporate culture.

>> **Employed individuals can quietly run their own searches** at any time to see what's available, and they can follow up online without taking off a day for an in-person or phone interview.

REMEMBER

LinkedIn research shows that "People with more than 20 connections are 34 times more likely to be approached with a job opportunity than people with fewer than 5 connections." Therefore, your connections definitely influence your active or passive job search.

Finding out all kinds of valuable information

Beyond getting information about your job search, you can use the immense LinkedIn database of professionals to find out what skills seem to be the most popular in a certain industry and job title. You can learn how many project managers live within 50 miles of you. You can even find current or past employees of a company and interview them about that job. LinkedIn now has hundreds of thousands of detailed Company pages that not only show company statistics but also recent hires, promotions, changes, and lists of employees closely connected with you. (Read more about Company pages in Chapter 15.)

Best of all, LinkedIn can help you find specific information on a variety of topics. You can do a search to find out the interests of your next sales prospect, the name of a former employee you can talk to about a company you like, or how you can join a start-up in your target industry by reaching out to the co-founder. You can sit back and skim the news, or you can dive in and hunt for the facts. It all depends on what method best fits your goals. (I discuss LinkedIn search techniques in depth in Chapter 4.)

Expanding your network

You have your network today, but what about the future? Whether you want to move up in your industry, look for a new job, start your own company, or achieve some other goal, one way to do it is to expand your network. LinkedIn provides a fertile ground to reach like-minded and well-connected professionals who share a common interest, experience, or group membership. The site also provides several online mechanisms to reduce the friction of communication, so you can spend more time building your network instead of searching for the right person.

First and foremost, LinkedIn helps you identify and contact members of other people's professional networks, and best of all, you don't have to contact them via a cold call, but with your friend's recommendation or introduction. (See Chapters 9 and 5, respectively, for more information.) In addition, you can find out more about your new contact before you send the first message, so you don't have to waste time figuring out whether this is someone who could be beneficial to have in your network.

You can also meet new people through various groups on LinkedIn, whether it's an alumni group from your old school, a group of past employees from the same company, or a group of people interested in improving their public speaking skills and contacts. LinkedIn Groups help you connect with other like-minded members, search for specific group members, and share information about the group with other members. (I cover LinkedIn Groups in Chapter 16.)

Understanding LinkedIn Costs and Benefits

Signing up for LinkedIn is free, and many functions are open to all account holders, so you can take advantage of most of the opportunities that LinkedIn offers. You don't have to pay a setup or registration fee, but you can pay a monthly fee for a premium account to get additional functions or communication options. Finally, tailored solutions are available for corporations that want to use LinkedIn as a source for hiring quality candidates.

Weighing free versus paid accounts

There's not much difference between a free account and paid account on LinkedIn. And the basic account is anything but basic in usage.

Your free account with LinkedIn allows you to use most of LinkedIn's most popular features, including

>> Building a network of connections with no limits on size or numbers.

>> Reconnecting with any member of the LinkedIn network, provided that he knows you and agrees to connect with you.

>> Creating a professional and detailed LinkedIn profile.

>> Giving and receiving an unlimited number of recommendations.

>> Joining or creating up to 100 different LinkedIn Groups.

>> Performing an unlimited number of searches for LinkedIn members in your extended network of first- and second-degree members plus group members.

If you want to step up to a paid account, some of the main features include

>> Sending a message to anyone in the LinkedIn community — regardless of whether she is in your extended network — through an InMail messaging service.

>> Viewing more LinkedIn profile information of people not in your LinkedIn network when you conduct advanced searches.

>> Seeing more LinkedIn network profile information when you conduct advanced searches.

>> Seeing who has viewed your profile (if they have not configured their settings to be anonymous when viewing profiles) and how they arrived at your profile.

>> Obtaining membership in the Open Profile program, which gives you unlimited Open Profile messages.

Comparing the paid accounts

LinkedIn offers a few levels of paid accounts, each with a specific level of benefits. For the most up-to-date packages that LinkedIn offers, check out the Free and Paid Accounts Help page at `http://bit.ly/LinkedInAccountTypes`, which should look like what you see in Figure 1-4. You can also click the Try Premium for Free link at the top right of your screen, below your Account & Settings button (the thumbnail of your photo), to see a comparison of the paid accounts.

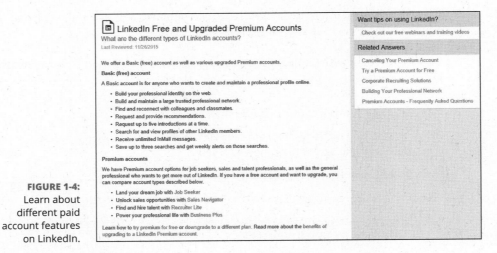

FIGURE 1-4:
Learn about different paid account features on LinkedIn.

Every premium account comes with certain benefits regardless of the level you choose. These benefits include

>> Open Profile network membership.

>> Unlimited Open Profile messages.

>> Ability to see who viewed your profile.

>> Access to premium content.

>> One-business-day customer service for your LinkedIn questions.

As of this writing, LinkedIn offers three premium packages targeted at individual users: Job Seeker (formerly Business), Business Plus, and Sales Navigator Professional. Each account level comes with specific benefits:

>> **Job Seeker:** $29.99 per month, billed monthly. This account includes

- Three InMail credits per month, which allow you to contact any LinkedIn member regardless of whether he is in your network, as long as the other member agreed to receive InMail messages.

- Expanded profile views and a total of 250 search results outside your network when you search. You will see who viewed your profile in the last 90 days and how they located you.

- Applicant Insights to see how you (and your skill set) compare to other candidates for a potential job.

- Featured Applicant status when a recruiter searches for applicants. You will be moved to the top section of a recruiter's search screen.

>> **Business Plus:** $59.99 per month, billed monthly, or $575.88 per year when you buy an annual subscription at a 20 percent savings. This account includes

- Fifteen InMail credits per month. (See Chapter 5 for more on InMail.)

- The ability to view unlimited profiles when you perform a LinkedIn search, including any third-degree network members. You can also see who viewed your profile in the last 90 days and how they located you.

- Additional search filters that you can use to run advanced searches.

>> **Sales Navigator Professional:** $79.99 per month, billed monthly, or $779.88 per year when you buy an annual subscription at a 20 percent savings. This account includes

- Fifteen InMails per month.

- Expanded profile views of anyone who has viewed your profile in the last 90 days and how they located you.

- Lead Builder and Recommendation tools to help you find the right people to close the deal in your sales life.

- Full name visibility when looking at your third-degree network members or group connections (other plans display only limited name information for these people).

Upgrading to a premium account

What's the value in getting a premium account? Besides the features listed in the previous section for each account level, premium accounts are designed to give you more attention in areas like job search. When an employer lists a job posting and collects applications through LinkedIn, premium account holders show up at the top of the applicant list (similar to the Sponsored result in a Google search) with a Featured Applicant status next to their name. LinkedIn provides special content in the form of e-mails, video tutorials, and articles that provide job search and professional development tips and advice from leaders in the industry. Finally, you get to see who has viewed your profile, which can be helpful when you're applying for jobs or trying to set up business deals. A premium account is not essential for everyone, so consider what you need from your LinkedIn experience and decide if upgrading is right for you.

TIP

As of this writing, LinkedIn gives you the option to try any premium plan for free during the first month, and it automatically charges your credit card each month afterward for the full amount, unless you bought a yearly plan, for which the charges renew every 12 months.

To upgrade to a premium account, I highly recommend starting by creating your free account and using the various functions on LinkedIn. If you find that after some usage, you need to reach the larger community and take advantage of some of the premium account features, you can always upgrade your account and keep all your profile and network information that you previously defined.

WARNING

If you're in charge of human resource functions at a small, medium, or large company and you are interested in using the Recruiter functions for your company, don't follow the steps in this section. Instead, visit `https://talent.linkedin.com` for more information on their Business Solutions.

To subscribe to a premium account, just follow these steps. (You must have created a LinkedIn account already; see Chapter 2 for details.)

1. **Go to the LinkedIn home page at** `https://www.linkedin.com`. **Hover your mouse over your photo or Account & Settings icon in the top-right corner of the home page, then click the Upgrade link next to Account: Basic.**

2. On the Premium Products page that appears, click the Select Plan button to bring up that premium account's specific options, as shown in Figure 1-5.

LinkedIn accepts Visa, MasterCard, American Express, or Discover to pay for your premium account. Make sure the billing address you provide matches the credit card billing address on file.

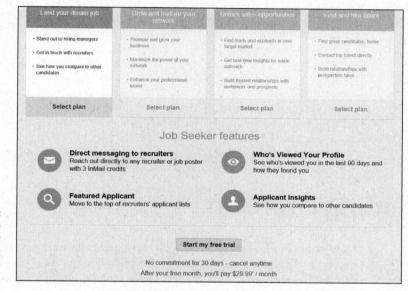

FIGURE 1-5:
Review the options for the premium account you are considering.

3. Click the yellow Start My Free Trial button for the premium level to which you want to upgrade.

4. Fill in the appropriate billing information, as shown in Figure 1-6, and then click the Review Order button.

5. Verify the information you've provided, then scroll down and select the check box to agree to automatic billing every month and LinkedIn's Terms and Conditions.

6. Click the yellow Place Order button.

That's it! Expect to get e-mails from LinkedIn to help explain and demonstrate the new features you can take advantage of on the website.

REMEMBER

If you decide to stop subscribing to a LinkedIn premium account, you must go to your settings page, click Account on the left side of the screen, and then click the Downgrade or Cancel Your Premium Account link so you won't get billed anymore. (See "Looking at the Account & Settings page" later in this chapter for information about how to reach and use this page.)

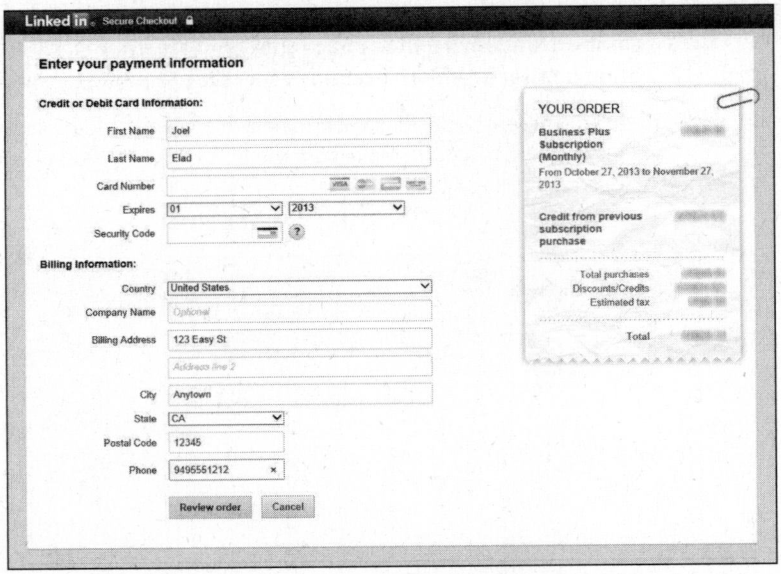

FIGURE 1-6:
Enter your billing information.

Navigating LinkedIn

When you're ready to get started, you can sign up for an account by checking out Chapter 2. Before you do, however, take a look at the following sections, which walk you through the different parts of the LinkedIn website so you know how to find all the cool features I discuss in this book.

After you log on to your LinkedIn account, you see your personal LinkedIn home page, as shown in Figure 1-7. There are two important areas on your LinkedIn home page that you'll use a lot, and I cover those areas in the following sections.

Touring the top navigation bar

Every page on LinkedIn contains certain links to the major parts of the site, and I call this top set of links the "top navigation bar" throughout this book. As of this writing, the major parts of the top navigation bar are

>> **Home:** Link to your personal LinkedIn home page.

>> **Profile:** Links to the profile part of LinkedIn.

>> **Connections:** Links to view your connections on LinkedIn or add/import new connections.

>> **Jobs:** Links to the different job searches and postings you can do on LinkedIn.

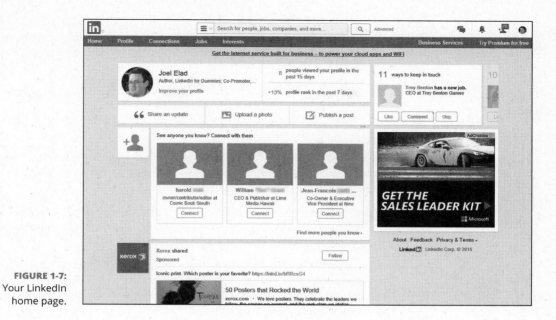

FIGURE 1-7:
Your LinkedIn home page.

>> **Interests:** Links to search LinkedIn Company pages or keep track of companies you can follow using LinkedIn, as well as links to LinkedIn Groups, news items grouped into the LinkedIn Pulse page, LinkedIn Education (which includes schools and students on LinkedIn), SlideShare, and Online Learning.

>> **Business Services:** Links to post a job on LinkedIn, use the Talent Solutions section of LinkedIn, create a LinkedIn ad to run on the site, or use the Sales Solutions section of LinkedIn.

When you hover your mouse next to any of these words, you can see the various options in each section, like the Profile options shown in Figure 1-8.

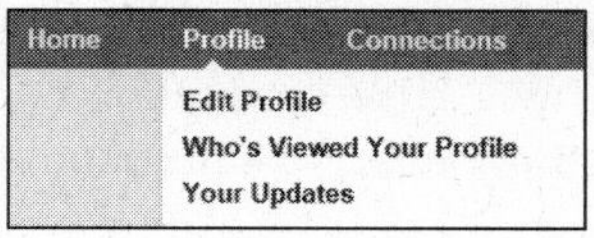

FIGURE 1-8:
Hover your mouse over each menu element to see options for each section.

Home	Profile	Connections
	Edit Profile	
	Who's Viewed Your Profile	
	Your Updates	

If you simply click the word, like "Profile" or "Jobs," you're taken to the main page for that section. You can also click the Advanced link to the right of the Search box, above the top navigation bar, to bring up an Advanced People search, or you can click the drop-down list before the Search box to search for Jobs, Companies, Groups, Universities, Posts, or Inbox from any page on the site. If you already changed the search criteria to another function, like Jobs, Companies, or Groups, clicking the Advanced link brings up the appropriate search page.

Finally, there are several icons along the top right of the screen:

>> **Inbox:** The picture of two word balloons opens up the LinkedIn Inbox, where you can see incoming messages.

>> **Notifications:** The flag icon indicates new actions you should be aware of when using LinkedIn, like when you are mentioned, receive an endorsement or recommendation, or have a new connection.

>> **Add Connections:** The picture of the + with a person is a quick link to show the invitations you have received and the People You May Know function to add more connections to your LinkedIn network.

>> **Account & Settings:** After you add a profile picture, this is a thumbnail of your profile photo, and clicking this button expands a list of options that allow you to check your settings, check your job posting or Company page (if applicable), and reach the LinkedIn Help Center.

TIP

As you scroll down any LinkedIn page, be aware that the top navigation bar will disappear from view. As you scroll back up the page, or if you move your cursor to the top of the page, the navigation bar will reappear.

Looking at the Account & Settings page

If you need to update any aspect of your LinkedIn account, go to the Account & Settings page, shown in Figure 1-9. You can always find a link to this page at the top right of any page within LinkedIn by hovering your mouse over the Account & Settings button, and then clicking the Manage link next to the Privacy & Settings header.

At the top of your Account & Settings page, you first see the settings for your particular account level, especially if you have a premium account. I cover this earlier in the chapter, in the section "Upgrading to a premium account."

Below the basic account information, you can see all the different settings you can update for your LinkedIn account.

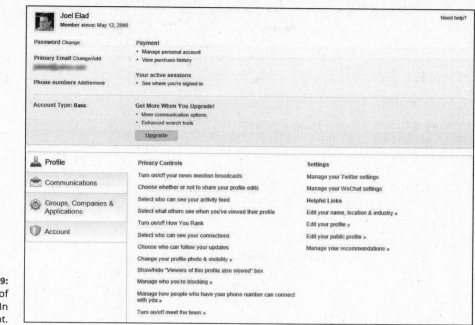

FIGURE 1-9:
See the details of
your LinkedIn
account.

Following are the settings you can access from this page:

>> **Profile:** Set how much of your profile is accessible by your contacts, and also how much information you want to make available to your network in terms of profile or status updates. Update any part of your profile, add a profile photo, change your status and public profile settings, and manage your recommendations.

>> **Communications:** Set the frequency of e-mails from LinkedIn, as well as who from LinkedIn's partners can reach you. Select how other LinkedIn members can communicate with you and who can send you invitations.

>> **Groups, Companies & Applications:** Update settings for your memberships with different LinkedIn Groups, view companies that you're following, and view or add applications that you're using with LinkedIn.

>> **Account:** Update privacy settings, e-mail addresses and password on file, language and security settings, and links to upgrade, downgrade, or cancel your LinkedIn account. You can also enable an RSS feed of your LinkedIn account from a link in this category.

Chapter 2

Sign Up and Create Your Profile

When LinkedIn first launched, it grew primarily through invitations — you joined only if someone who was already a member invited you and encouraged you to join. However, membership is now open to anyone 13 years or older (as long as the user hasn't previously been suspended or removed from LinkedIn, of course). You can have only one active account, but you can attach multiple e-mail addresses, past and present, to your account so that people can more easily find you.

You'll be presented with some configuration settings during the signup process that you might not know what to do with until you get more familiar with the system. Fortunately, you can customize all those settings later, but for now, I suggest some initial settings. In addition, based on your initial settings, LinkedIn recommends people to invite to your network. In Chapter 6, I discuss the ways you can grow your network more extensively, but this chapter touches on the initial recommendation process.

Joining LinkedIn

Many people join LinkedIn because a friend or colleague invited them. You can join just as easily without receiving an invitation, though. Everyone joins at the basic level, which is free. (You can opt for different levels of paid membership, as spelled out in Chapter 1.) Being able to start at the basic level makes the signup process quite straightforward. Most importantly, the basic level still gives users the ability to take advantage of the most powerful tools that LinkedIn offers.

Joining with an invitation

When a friend or colleague invites you to join, you receive an e-mail invitation. The e-mail clearly identifies the sender and usually has `Invitation to connect on LinkedIn` as its subject line. (There's a chance, though, that the sender came up with a custom header, but hopefully that message still has the word "LinkedIn" in the subject line.)

When you open the message, you see an invitation to join LinkedIn, like the message shown in Figure 2-1. There might be some extra text if the person inviting you personalized the message. You also see a button or link that takes you back to LinkedIn to create your account, such as the Confirm That You Know Joel button shown in Figure 2-1.

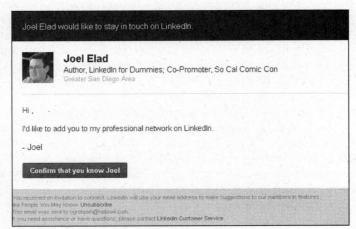

FIGURE 2-1:
An invitation to connect on LinkedIn.

When you're ready to join LinkedIn with an invitation, you'll start with these two steps:

1. **Click the button or link from your invitation e-mail.**

You should see a new window open that goes to the LinkedIn website, as shown in Figure 2-2, and asks you to input your name and verify your e-mail address, as well as enter a password for your new LinkedIn account.

TIP

If you want to be known on LinkedIn by another version of your name (say a nickname, maiden name, middle initial, or proper name), or if you want to use a different e-mail address from the one used for your invitation, you can change the details in those fields — First Name, Last Name, Email.

Linked**in**

You've been invited to the world's largest professional network

Joel Elad invited you to connect on LinkedIn

First name

Last name

Email

Password (6 or more characters)

By clicking Join Joel's network, you agree to LinkedIn's User Agreement, Privacy Policy, and Cookie Policy.

Join Joel's network

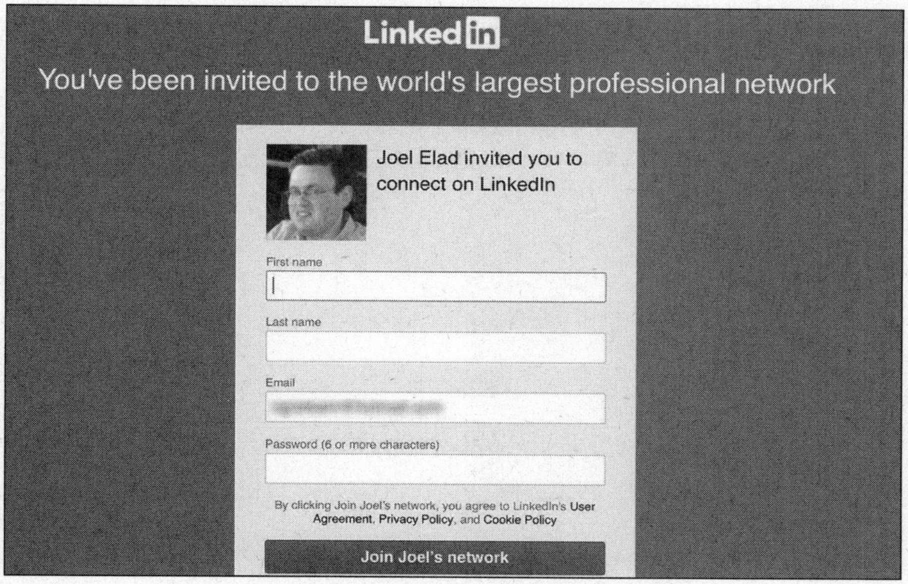

FIGURE 2-2:
Provide your name and create a password.

2. **Enter your correct first name and last name, and create a new password for your account. Then click the Join *Name's* Network button.**

Once you click the button, you will be taken to the next part of the sign-up process, where you provide some basic information that LinkedIn will use to create your account. I cover the remainder of the sign-up process in "Completing the sign-up process," later in this chapter.

TIP

Try to pick a password that no one else can guess. You should use a combination of letters and numbers, and avoid commonly used passwords like your name, the word "password," a string of letters or numbers that are next to each other on the keyboard (for example, "qwerty"), or a password that you use on many other sites.

Joining without an invitation

If you haven't gotten an invitation to join LinkedIn, don't let that turn you into a wallflower. You can join LinkedIn directly, without an invitation from an existing user. Open your web browser and go to https://www.linkedin.com. You see the initial LinkedIn home page, as shown in Figure 2-3. When you're ready to join LinkedIn, simply provide your first name, last name, and e-mail address, and enter a password in the boxes provided, as shown in the figure. Then click the Join Now button.

This takes you to the next part of the sign-up process, where LinkedIn collects some basic information to create your account.

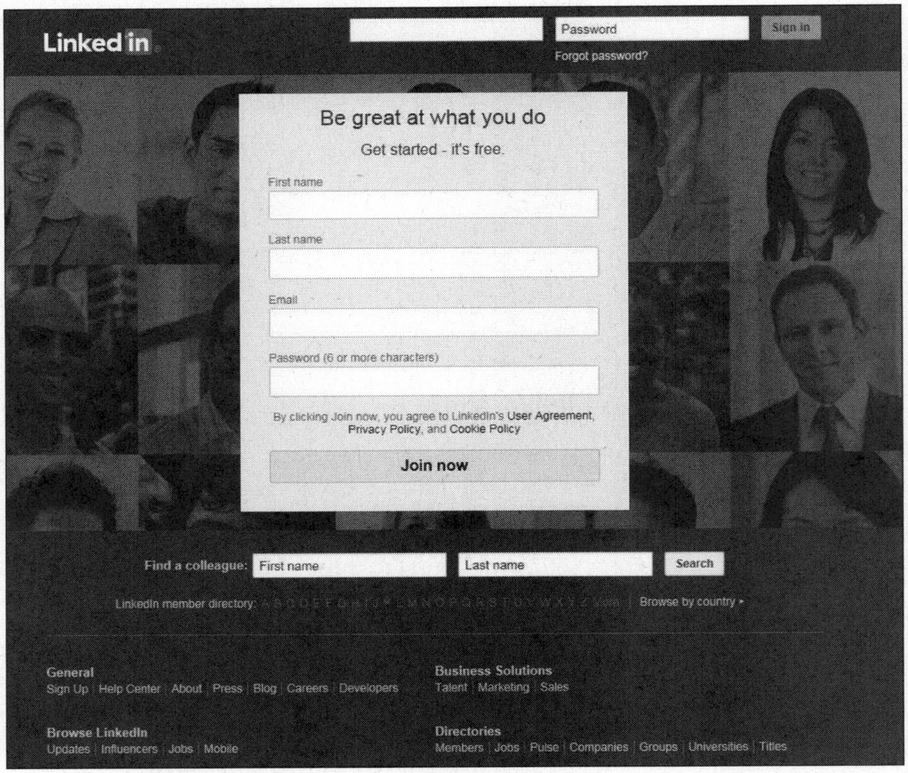

FIGURE 2-3: Join LinkedIn from its home page.

Completing the sign-up process

Whether you've been invited to join LinkedIn or created an account directly from its home page, LinkedIn requires some basic information beyond your name and e-mail address to finish creating the basic account. When you're ready to complete the sign-up process, follow these steps:

1. **In the Let's Start with Your Profile window, pick the country where you reside. LinkedIn then asks for more precise information, like a ZIP code or postal code, as shown in Figure 2-4.**

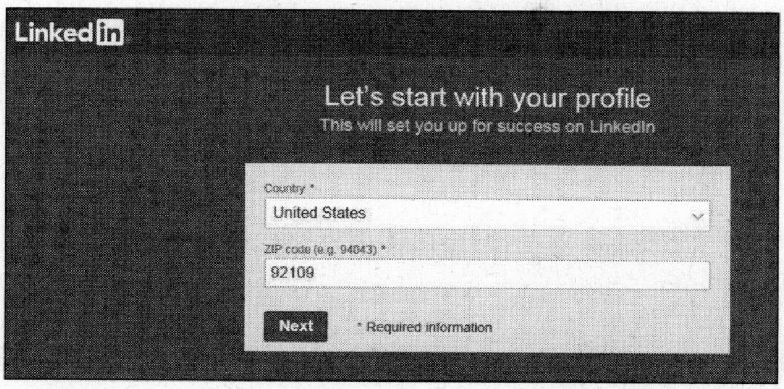

FIGURE 2-4:
Tell LinkedIn
where you are
located.

2. **Click the Next button.**

   You're taken to the next step, where LinkedIn starts to build your professional profile by asking about your current employment status and whether you are a student, as shown in Figure 2-5.

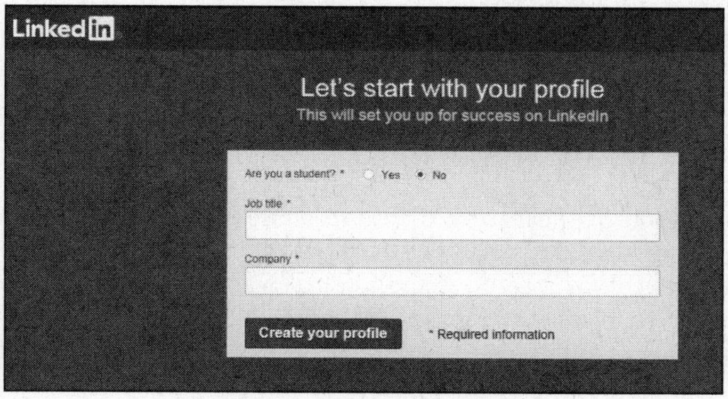

FIGURE 2-5:
Tell LinkedIn a
little about
yourself to create
your account.

3. **Complete the fields regarding your current employment and student status.**

   Specifically, you need to provide the following information:

   - **Are you a student?:** Select the appropriate radio button to indicate Yes or No.

   - **Job title:** If you are not a student, indicate your current job title, whether you're employed, unemployed (aka "a job seeker"), or self-employed.

   - **Company:** LinkedIn asks for a company name and prompts you by showing existing companies in its database as you type in the name of your company, as shown in Figure 2-6. Once you provide the company name, LinkedIn adds the Industry field. Use the drop-down list to identify which industry you feel you belong to, as shown in Figure 2-7.

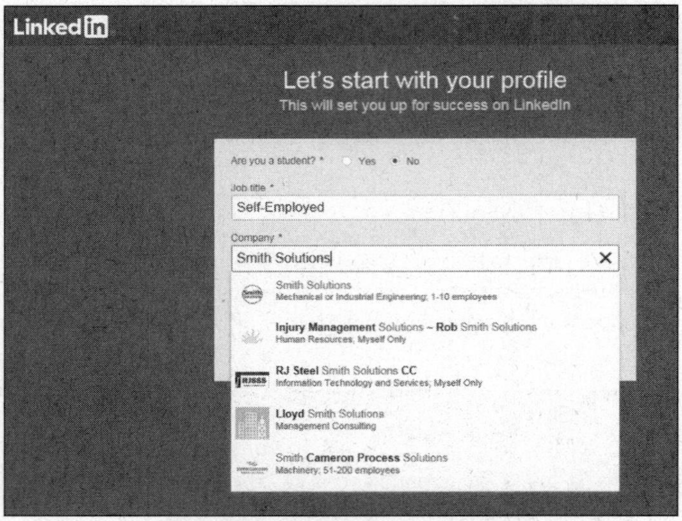

FIGURE 2-6: LinkedIn can help associate you with known companies in its database.

If you find it difficult to choose an industry that best describes your primary expertise, just choose one that's closest. You can always change the selection later. If you're employed but looking for another job, you should still pick the industry of your current profession.

TIP

4. **Click the blue Create Your Profile button to continue (refer to Figure 2-5).**

   LinkedIn then offers to import your contacts from your e-mail program, as shown in Figure 2-8. LinkedIn walks you through the steps of importing your address book and offers you the chance to connect with existing members of LinkedIn. You can also do this after you create your account by clicking the Skip link.

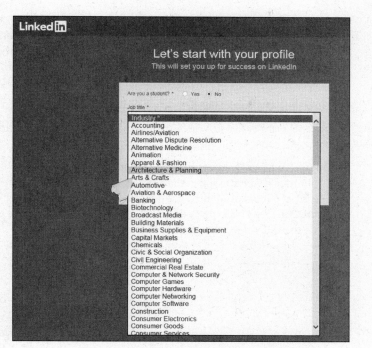

FIGURE 2-7:
Pick the industry that best matches your current job.

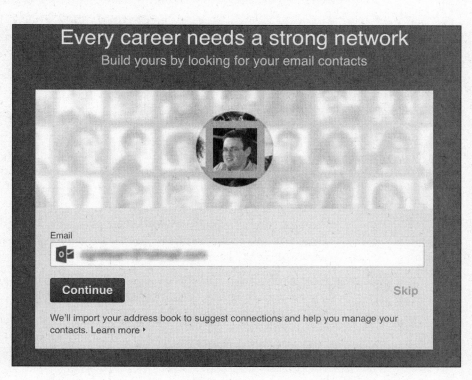

FIGURE 2-8:
LinkedIn can help you identify who to add to your network.

REMEMBER

It might be tempting to start inviting friends and colleagues to connect with you right away, but you might want to work on creating your complete and up-to-date profile first before flooding people's e-mail Inboxes with invitations. You can always invite people to connect with you at any time.

5. **LinkedIn asks you to confirm the e-mail address for your account.**

    LinkedIn will e-mail you a confirmation to help verify the e-mail account you are using, especially if you joined LinkedIn without an invitation.

    Open your e-mail program and look for an e-mail from LinkedIn Email Confirmation with the subject line *Please confirm your email address*. When you open that e-mail, you should see a request for confirmation, as shown in Figure 2-9. Either click the Confirm Your Email Address button or copy and paste the URL provided in the e-mail into your web browser.

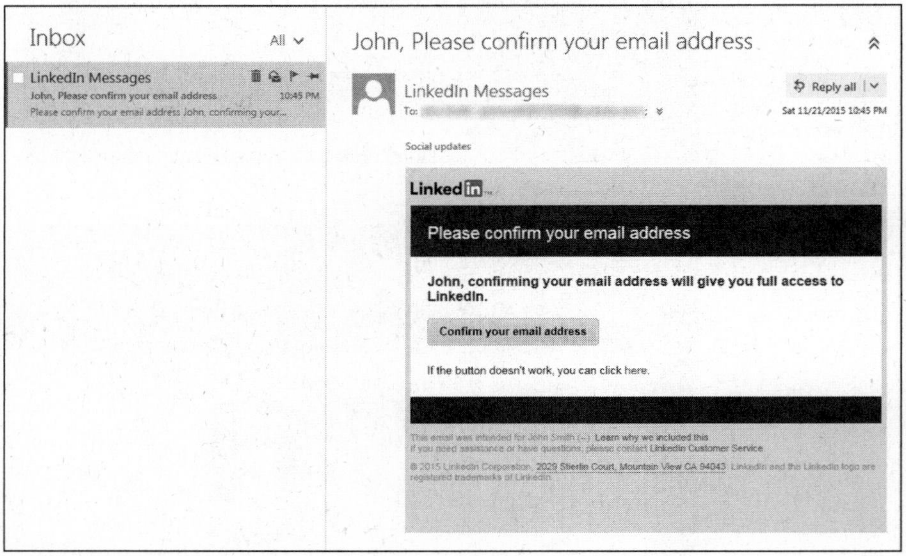

FIGURE 2-9:
Confirm your e-mail address with LinkedIn.

When you click the button, you're taken back to LinkedIn and it confirms your address. You may be asked to log in to your account, so simply provide your e-mail address and password when prompted.

WARNING

If you skip the step of confirming your e-mail with LinkedIn, you won't be able to invite any connections, apply for jobs on the LinkedIn job board, or take advantage of most other LinkedIn functions.

6. **Your account is created, and LinkedIn prompts you to build your profile based on your goals for using LinkedIn.**

   You are taken to a web page, as shown in Figure 2-10, where LinkedIn asks you what you are most interested in doing on the website. Based on the choice you make, LinkedIn prompts you for steps like reviewing other profiles or picking companies or influencers to follow.

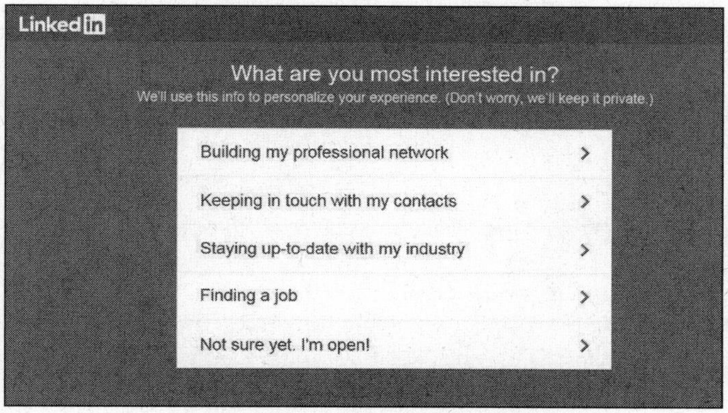

FIGURE 2-10: LinkedIn asks you to choose what you're most interested in doing.

7. **Go through the LinkedIn prompts to pick what channels (companies, interests, and influencers) you want to follow.**

   You'll be prompted with the most relevant channels based on the company title and industry you provided during the sign-up process, and they will be automatically checked, as shown in Figure 2-11. You can change the automated selections by clicking any plus sign to turn on that selection or clicking the check mark to turn off that selection. Once you've picked the channels you want to follow, click the Follow X Channels button at the bottom right of the screen, as shown in Figure 2-12.

8. **LinkedIn prompts you to receive a link to download its mobile app. Provide your mobile number in the text box provided to receive that link, and then click the Get the App button.**

   You can also click the Skip button and install the app later. (I discuss mobile applications in depth in Chapter 12.)

9. **You are taken to your LinkedIn home page. LinkedIn provides you with prompts to guide you through the rest of the creation process.**

   You will see pop-up windows, like the one shown in Figure 2-13, offering you more information on aspects of LinkedIn, such as the messaging center and sections you can add. Just click the Next button on each prompt to go through the options. When you see the Done button on a prompt, click it to complete the walkthrough.

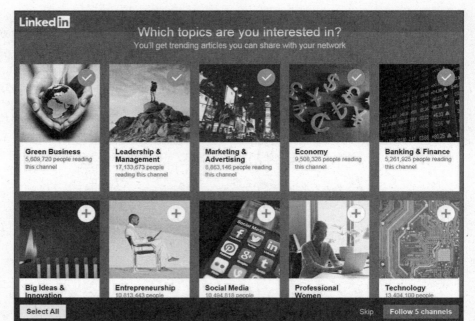

FIGURE 2-11:
LinkedIn offers
you suggestions
on what to follow.

FIGURE 2-12:
Pick the
channels you
want to follow.

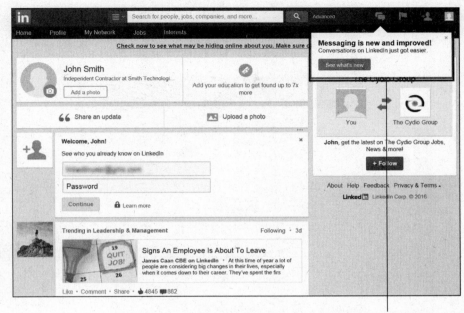

FIGURE 2-13:
Follow the
LinkedIn prompts
for more
information.

10. **LinkedIn provides you with a long series of prompts to help you build your profile.**

You will see a blue prompt box at the top of your LinkedIn profile page (as shown in Figure 2-14) asking you for information to help complete your profile. You will see prompts for areas such as your skills, educational background, past employers, and current job details.

Fill in information for each prompt and click the Save button to advance in the process. You can always click Skip to move along the process and save those tasks for later.

Once you've gone through the series of prompts, you will see your profile page, as shown in Figure 2-15. From here, you can decide what to update next. I go into more detail in Chapter 3 about the main sections you can update on your profile.

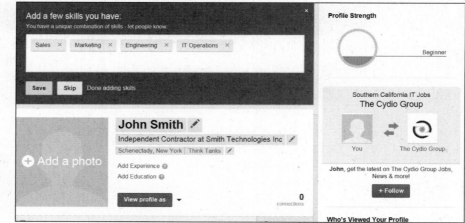

FIGURE 2-14:
LinkedIn prompts
you to complete
your profile.

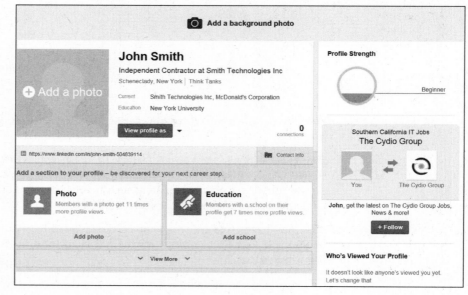

FIGURE 2-15:
Continue to work
on your profile.

If you want to take a break to check your e-mail, you'll find a nice Welcome to LinkedIn! message there, as shown in Figure 2-16, assuring you that you're now a registered LinkedIn user once you created your account. The e-mail encourages you to take advantage of the world's largest professional network by offering links that help you "Stay connected, be discovered, and get inspired" on the website.

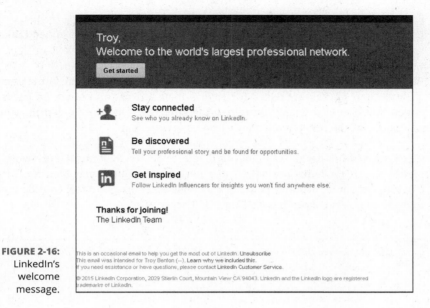

FIGURE 2-16:
LinkedIn's
welcome
message.

Starting to Build Your Network

You're ready to look at how to build your network, with tools and forms provided by LinkedIn. Your first step is to decide who you want to invite to connect with you on LinkedIn.

Be sure to completely fill out your profile before you start inviting people to connect. Having a complete profile makes it easier to find former colleagues and classmates. After all, if you invite someone to connect who you haven't spoken to recently, he'll probably take a quick look at your profile before responding. If he doesn't see a part of your professional history where he knows you, he will most likely ignore your invitation.

Your best bet now is to start using LinkedIn with some thought and planning. Here are some common pitfalls after signing up:

>> You feel compelled to start inviting friends and colleagues to connect with you right away, before working on your profile.

>> You get nervous and decide not to invite anybody beyond one or two close friends or family members.

>> You wonder about the value of LinkedIn (or get busy with your career and daily activities) and leave your account alone for a long period of time with no activity.

I've seen all three scenarios occur with various people who have joined LinkedIn, so don't feel bad if one of these is your natural reaction.

When you want to start using LinkedIn, begin by navigating to the home page and clicking Sign In. You are asked for your e-mail address and LinkedIn password, which you provided when you joined the site. After you are logged in, you can access any of the functions from the top navigation bar.

Next, start thinking about who you'd like to invite to join your network (see Figure 2-17). LinkedIn provides some neat tools to help you identify, in your existing networks, people you know and trust well enough to feel confident about inviting them and expecting that they will accept.

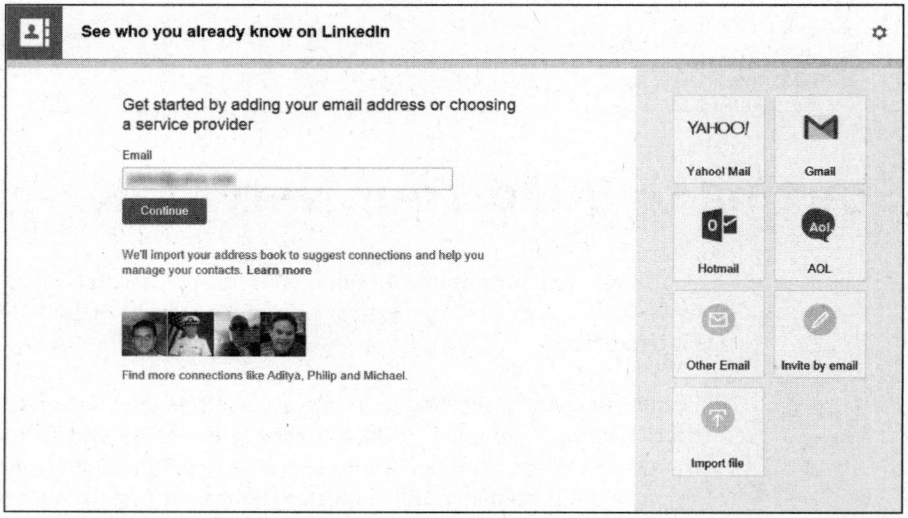

FIGURE 2-17: Add connections to your network.

The Add Connections section of LinkedIn is always available by clicking the Network link from the top of any LinkedIn page, and then clicking the Add Connections link from the drop-down list that appears. The Add Connections section incorporates some basic options to identify and grow your network:

>> Check the address book for your web-based e-mail system, like Yahoo! Mail, Gmail, Hotmail, and AOL.

>> Check your address book for contacts to invite with options for systems like Microsoft Outlook and Apple's Mail app by importing your desktop e-mail contacts with the link provided.

>> Upload contact files from other applications.

>> Invite people to connect by their e-mail address. (By specifying people's individual e-mail addresses, you can decide who you want to invite without sending a blind invitation to everyone in your address book.)

I cover these techniques in greater detail in Chapter 6. I recommend that you first spend a little time thinking about who you want to invite. Then focus on setting up your profile, and then invite people to connect.

PRIVACY CONFIDENTIAL

When you give LinkedIn access to your existing contact lists (such as on Gmail or Yahoo! Mail), rest assured that LinkedIn respects your privacy. LinkedIn is a licensee of the TRUSTe Privacy Program. In its Privacy Policy, LinkedIn declares its adherence to the following key privacy principles:

- LinkedIn will never rent or sell your personally identifiable information to third parties for marketing purposes.

- LinkedIn will never share your contact information with another user without your consent.

- Any sensitive information that you provide will be secured with all industry standard protocols and technology.

Chapter 3

Completing Your Profile

After you register with LinkedIn and work to build your network by looking outward, it's time to look inward by focusing on your profile. Think of your LinkedIn profile as your personal home page to the professional world: This profile exists to give anyone a complete picture of your background, qualifications, and skills as well as paint a picture of who you are beyond the numbers and bullet points.

In this chapter, I walk you through all the different sections of your profile and explain how to update them and put the right information in a concise and appealing manner. I take you through adding information at each stage so you can update your profile now or down the road (say, when you finish that amazing project or get that spiffy promotion you've been working toward).

REMEMBER

At any time, you can go to `https://www.linkedin.com` and click the Profile link in the top navigation bar to access your LinkedIn profile to view or make changes.

Adding Your Summary and Basic Information to LinkedIn

Your LinkedIn profile Summary section, which appears in the top third of your profile, should give any reader a quick idea of who you are, what you've accomplished, and most importantly, what you're looking for on LinkedIn. Some people think of their summary as their "elevator pitch," or their 30-second introduction of themselves that they tell to any new contact. Other people think of their summary as simply their resume summary, which gives a high-level overview of their experience and job goals. Each summary is as individual as the person writing it, but there are right ways and wrong ways to prepare and update your summary. You should always keep in mind what your professional or career goals are, and what kind of image, or brand, you are trying to portray in support of those goals, because those goals should give you direction on how to write your summary.

In order to keep your Summary easy to read so it can be digested quickly, you could divide the Summary section into two distinct parts:

>> **Your professional experience and goals:** This is typically a one-paragraph summary of your current and past accomplishments and future goals. See the next section, "Writing your summary first," for more on how to construct the right paragraph for this part.

>> **Your specialties in your industry of expertise:** This is a list of your specific skills and talents. It is separate from your professional experience in that this section allows you to list specific job skills (for example, contract negotiation or writing HTML software code) as opposed to the daily responsibilities or accomplishments from your job that you would list in the professional experience and goals paragraph. This not only gives readers a precise understanding of your skill set, but it also gives search engines a keyword-rich list to associate with you, and it's at the top of your profile.

Other core elements of your LinkedIn profile are stored in the Basic Information section. Be sure to polish these elements so they reflect well on you:

>> **Your name:** Believe it or not, defining your name properly can positively or negatively affect your LinkedIn activity. Because people are searching for you to connect to you, it's important that LinkedIn knows any sort of variations, nicknames, maiden names, or former names that you may have held, so be sure you correctly fill in your First, Last, and Former/Maiden name fields. Also, LinkedIn allows you to choose a display name of your first name and last initial, in case you want to keep your name private from the larger LinkedIn community outside of your connections.

You can also include your middle name in the First Name field, which is highly recommended if you have a common name (for example, John Smith) so people can find the "right you" when searching.

>> **Your professional headline:** Think of this as your job title. It is limited to 120 characters and displayed below your name on LinkedIn, in search results, in connections lists, and on your profile. Therefore, you want a headline that grabs people's attention. Some people put their job titles; other people add some colorful adjectives and include two or three different professions. For example, I use "Author, LinkedIn for Dummies; Co-Promoter, So Cal Comic Con" indicating two of my main professions. Your headline changes only when you update the headline field, so if you add a new position to your profile, your headline doesn't update to show that addition. You have to decide what changes are worth reflecting in your headline.

Don't overload your headline with too many titles, keywords, or unrelated job skills. Although the headline does not have to be a complete sentence, it should read well and make sense. You're not scoring points with a Google search here — that's what your entire profile is for.

>> **Your primary location and industry of experience:** As location becomes a more important element when networking online, LinkedIn wants to know your main location (in other words, where you hang your hat . . . if you wear a hat) so it can help identify connections close to you. Then, LinkedIn provides a list of industries you can choose from to indicate your main industry affiliation.

Writing your summary first

Before you update your summary on LinkedIn, I advise writing it out, using a program like Microsoft Word so that you can easily copy and paste it. This allows you to organize your thoughts, decide the right order of your statements, and pick and choose the most important statements to put in your summary.

Of course, the goals of your summary should be the same as your goals for using LinkedIn. After all, your summary is the starting point for most people when they read your profile. As you write your summary, keep these points in mind:

>> **Be concise.** Remember, this is a summary, not a 300-page memoir of your life. Most summaries are one paragraph long, with a separate paragraph to list your skills and/or specialties. Give the highlights of what you've done and are planning to do. Save the detailed information for when you add your individual employment positions to your profile.

>> **Pick three to five of your most important accomplishments.** Your profile can have lots of detail regarding your jobs, skill sets, education, and honors, but your summary needs to reflect the three to five items throughout your career that you most want people to know. Think of it this way: If someone were introducing you to another person, what would you want this new person to know about you right away?

Depending on your goals for LinkedIn, the accomplishments you put in your summary might not be your biggest accomplishments overall. For example, if you're trying to use LinkedIn to get a new job, your summary should include accomplishments that matter most to an employer in your desired field.

>> **Organize your summary in a "who, what, goals" format.** Typically, the first sentence of your summary should be a statement of *who* you are currently, meaning your current profession or status; for example, "Software project manager with extensive experience in Fortune 500 firms." The next few sentences should focus on *what* you've done so far in your career, and the end of your summary should focus on your *goals.*

>> **Use the right keywords in your summary.** Keywords are especially important if you're looking for a new job or hoping to pick up some consulting work. Although you should use a few keywords in your professional experience paragraph, you should really use all the appropriate keywords for skills you've acquired when you write the Specialties section of your summary. Potential employers scan that section looking for the right qualifications first, before making any contact. If you're unsure what keywords are the most important, scan the profiles of people in your industry, see what articles they are posting, or look at job opportunity postings in your field to see what employers want when they hire personnel with your title.

>> **Be honest with your specialties, but don't be shy.** Your Specialties section is your opportunity to list any skill or trade you feel you've learned and demonstrated with some ability. Some people stuff their Summary section with the buzzworthy skills for their industry (even if the person doesn't know those skills at all) in hopes of catching a potential employer's eye. Typically, a prospective employer can detect this resume skill padding during the interview phase, which wastes everybody's time. Conversely, however, some people don't list a skill here unless they feel they're an expert at it. You should list any skill or specialty that you believe puts you above the level of a novice or pure beginner.

If you need help coming up with your various summary sections, click the Show Examples link below each section header to see examples provided by LinkedIn, or you can view profiles of other people in similar industries. Reach out to your LinkedIn network or find people in your industry or field for help.

Updating your LinkedIn profile's Summary and Basic Information sections

When you have an idea of what you want to put in your profile's Summary and Basic Information sections, it's time to go into LinkedIn and plug that data into the correct fields. When you're ready, follow these steps:

1. **Go to LinkedIn and log in:**

```
www.linkedin.com/secure/login
```

2. **Hover your mouse over the Profile link in the top navigation bar, and then click Edit Profile from the drop-down list that appears.**

You're taken to the profile page, as shown in Figure 3-1. When you hover your mouse over the sections of the profile page, you will see little pencil icons (such as the ones in Figure 3-1) that, when clicked, allow you to edit that section.

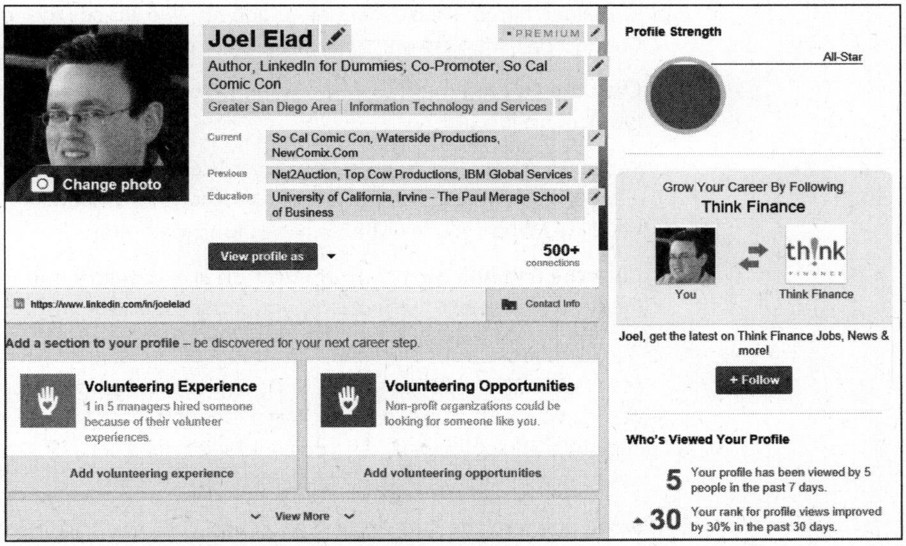

FIGURE 3-1: Bring up your LinkedIn profile page.

3. **Click the Edit link (that looks like a pencil) next to your name to update your name.**

You now see the Edit Your Profile Name box, as shown in Figure 3-2.

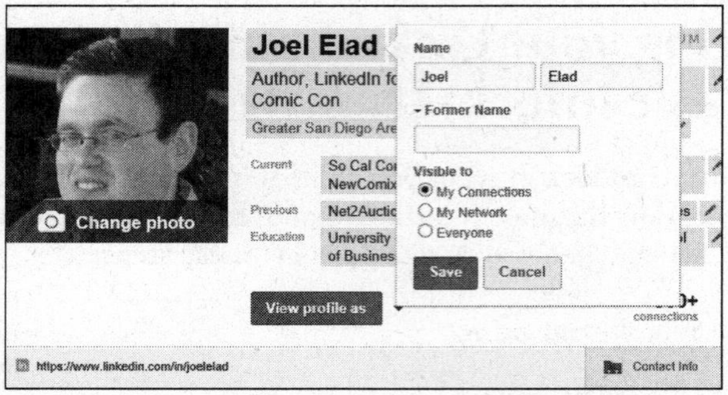

FIGURE 3-2:
Define your name
on LinkedIn.

4. **In the Edit Your Profile Name box, double-check your name and add any maiden or former name in the text box provided. Decide whether you want your former/maiden names visible to just your connections, your extended network, or everyone on LinkedIn. When you're done, click the blue Save button.**

   You can click the down arrow next to the Former Name box and enter a former or maiden name. Then choose an option for who will see this former name: My Connections, My Network, or Everyone.

5. **Click the Edit link next to your headline to enter your professional headline (your main job title).**

   You can put any job title here, but make sure it conveys your main role as you want others to see it. (See the previous sections for what to include in your headline.) When you're done, click the blue Save button.

6. **Click the Edit link next to your Location and Industry line to update your location and select the industry you most associate with your career.**

   You can choose from more than 140 designations, so take a few moments to scan the list. Note that some of the industries listed are more specific than others. You want to pick the best match possible. For example, if you create custom graphics for websites, you could select Internet as your industry, but an even better choice would be Online Media.

7. **Scroll down to the Summary section and click the Add Summary link below the Summary section header.**

   You see the Summary page, as shown in Figure 3-3.

8. **In the Summary text box, enter a paragraph or two that sums you up professionally (as discussed in the previous section).**

   You're limited to 2,000 characters, but keep your text concise and focused.

9. **In the same box, enter your skills and/or specialties as a separate list, as shown in Figure 3-3.**

   Separate each item with a comma and don't put any punctuation after the last item in your list. You don't need to press Enter/Return between skills.

10. **Click the blue Save button to save your summary.**

   You're taken back to your profile page. Next, you need to update the Contact Info and Additional Information sections of your LinkedIn profile.

You've now covered the core of your LinkedIn profile. In the next sections, you find out about the other essential elements to include in your profile, namely your contact and additional information, plus your current/past experience and education.

THE $5,000 PROFILE UPDATE

I have a great example of why you should update your profile. Jefre Outlaw's LinkedIn profile says that he's a "portfolio entrepreneur." His profile doesn't mention, however, that he spent more than 25 years as a real estate investor and developer, nor that he obtained his own real estate license and joined his cousin Blake's agency, Outlaw Realty. He realized a golden opportunity was available to him through LinkedIn.

Outlaw was interviewed for the Linked Intelligence blog (www.linkedintelligence. com/the-5000-profile-update). "At first I completely forgot about updating my LinkedIn profile," he said. "But I got a request to forward an introduction, and it reminded me that I should probably go update my profile to include my new gig as a Realtor."

This turned out to be a valuable update for Outlaw.

(continued)

(continued)

Several weeks later, someone from his extended network was using LinkedIn to search for Realtors and saw Outlaw's profile. This person contacted Outlaw about listing a home for sale. Well, the potential client signed up with Outlaw's agency, which was able to sell the house quickly for $170,000. When you do the math, $170,000 home × 3% commission = about $5,000 to the brokerage.

As Outlaw relayed his experience to Linked Intelligence, he wanted his story to be clear. "Let's not overstate what happened," said Outlaw. "Being on LinkedIn didn't get me the business. We [Outlaw's real estate agency] were one of several Realtors the client talked to, and I brought in my cousin, who's a great closer and more experienced than I, to meet with the client. But the fact that I was on [LinkedIn], that my profile was up to date, that I have over 20 really good recommendations on my profile — all that put us on the short list."

The moral of the story is simple. Keep your profile up to date on everything you're doing. If your profile isn't up to date, plan to update it right away — you may never know what opportunities you're missing by ignoring your profile.

Completing the Contact Info and Additional Information for Your Profile

Whenever you meet someone, the most common questions you ask are, "So, what do you do?" and "Where did you go to school?" However, there's more to you than your jobs and education, and LinkedIn has two sections, Contact Info and Additional Information, to tie your LinkedIn profile to your other Internet and real-life identities. (Some of these sections, like Interests, Groups, and Associations, are farther down the page, so you will need to scroll down to see them.)

These sections allow you to provide lots of information in these areas:

>> **Twitter:** You can link your Twitter and LinkedIn accounts so that your Twitter updates show up on your LinkedIn profile, and your LinkedIn network activity can be tweeted to your Twitter followers automatically.

>> **WeChat:** As LinkedIn increases its global membership, it's added integration with WeChat, the world's fastest-growing "social app" that has a platform integrating various messaging, gaming, and social features. When you link your WeChat account with LinkedIn, you will be able to see which of your LinkedIn connections are currently on WeChat.

>> **Websites:** LinkedIn allows you to add up to three different website links, which point from your LinkedIn profile to whatever website(s) you designate, such as your personal website, your company website, a blog, an RSS feed, or any other promotional mechanisms you use online.

Adding a link from your LinkedIn profile to your other websites helps boost search engine rankings for those pages. Those rankings are partially determined by the quantity and quality of web pages that link to them, and LinkedIn is a high-quality site as far as the search engines are concerned.

TIP

You must make your profile public to receive these benefits. You can find out more about your public setting later in the chapter, in the section "Setting your profile URL and public view."

>> **Interests:** Highlight your extracurricular activities to allow potential contacts to see what they have in common with you (for example, favorite hobbies or sports) and give potential employers a glimpse into what else interests you outside of a job.

>> **Organizations:** Illustrate what organizations you belong to and what formal activities you do in your spare time. Many people use this section to highlight charity work, networking groups they belong to, or affiliations with religious or political groups.

REMEMBER

Although completing these sections is optional, a strong, well-rounded profile usually helps you in your career or networking goals because it gives you more opportunities to connect with someone ("Hey, Joel's a big travel fan. So am I!") or allows people to identify with your situation.

When you're ready to update the rest of the information on your profile, follow these steps:

1. **Go to LinkedIn and log in. Hover your mouse over the Profile link in the top navigation bar, then click Edit Profile from the drop-down list that appears.**

2. **On your profile page, click the Contact Info link at the bottom right of the section containing your profile picture, name, and headline, in order to expand that section.**

   You see an Expanded contact information section, as shown in Figure 3-4, where you can update your contact information, including e-mail, phone, IM, and physical address. Click the Edit link (the pencil icon) to add the appropriate information.

   If you want to update your Twitter setting, click the Edit link next to the Twitter header to bring up the Twitter Settings page, as shown in Figure 3-5, to add or edit your Twitter account that's connected with LinkedIn.

FIGURE 3-4:
Update your
contact informa-
tion here.

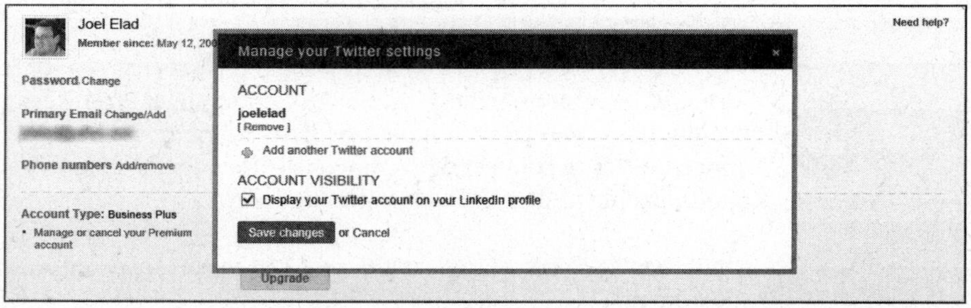

FIGURE 3-5:
This page is
where you define
your Twitter
account to be
referenced.

TIP

Updating your Twitter setting will take you to your Account & Settings page, so
when you're done, you'll need to press the back button on your web browser
or repeat Steps 1 and 2 to go back to editing your Contact Info section.

3. **Under Websites, in the drop-down lists on the left, select short descriptions
for the sites you intend to display.**

You can pick from the predefined list of descriptions (My Company, My
Website, and so on). Or, you can pick Other, as shown in Figure 3-6; in the
blank text box that appears, type in a brief custom description for your website
link (such as My E-Commerce Site or the name of your activity).

This description appears as a link on your profile — the reader doesn't see the site's URL.

TIP

Search engines look at the text used in these links when calculating rankings. So if there are certain keywords you want to include that will rank your site higher, include them in the link text. For example, you might want to say "Springfield Toastmasters" rather than "My Toastmasters Club."

4. **Still in the Websites section, in the text boxes to the right, enter the URLs of the websites you want to list on your profile, corresponding to the correct descriptions on the left. Click the blue Save button when you are done.**

You can add up to three URLs to your LinkedIn profile, so use them wisely.

WARNING

This might seem obvious, but, well, people are going to be able to click those links and check out your websites. Sure, that's the point, but do you remember that hilarious yet embarrassing picture of yourself you added to your personal site, or that tirade you posted in your blog about a co-worker or a tough project? Before you link to a site from your LinkedIn profile, scour it to make sure you won't end up scaring off or offending your contacts.

5. **Scroll down your profile until you get to the Additional Info section, as shown in Figure 3-7. Click the Edit link to complete the Interests text box. When you're done, click the Save button.**

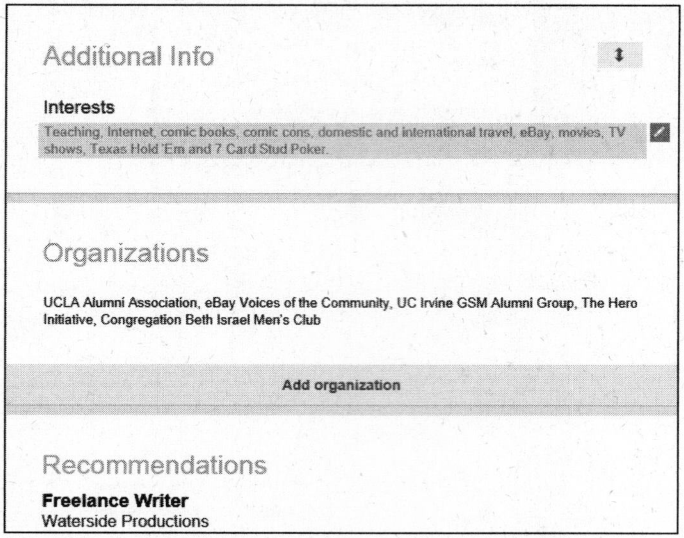

Additional Info

Interests

Teaching, Internet, comic books, comic cons, domestic and international travel, eBay, movies, TV shows, Texas Hold 'Em and 7 Card Stud Poker.

Organizations

UCLA Alumni Association, eBay Voices of the Community, UC Irvine GSM Alumni Group, The Hero Initiative, Congregation Beth Israel Men's Club

Add organization

Recommendations

Freelance Writer
Waterside Productions

FIGURE 3-7:
Edit your interests and additional organizations here.

Use this section to tell the world a little more about you besides your jobs and education. Make sure to separate each interest with a comma.

WARNING

You probably want to omit any interests that a potential employer wouldn't like to see. For example, if you work in the entertainment industry, talking about how you love to download pirated movies will not make any hiring manager happy. Talk instead about how you love to watch licensed content from approved sources like Netflix or Hulu!

6. **Scroll down and click the Edit link next to Organizations to fill in your other groups and associations. (These are non-LinkedIn groups.)**

   Here you can list your groups not listed under any school, such as any charity groups, religious organizations, alumni associations, and rotary clubs.

7. **Click the Save button.**

   This step updates your Additional Info section in your profile.

TIP

LinkedIn is continuing to add lots of exciting sections for you to use to highlight all of your achievements and skills. If you edit your profile, you see a list of recommended sections you can add to your profile, as shown in Figure 3-8. Simply click each section and fill in the appropriate information.

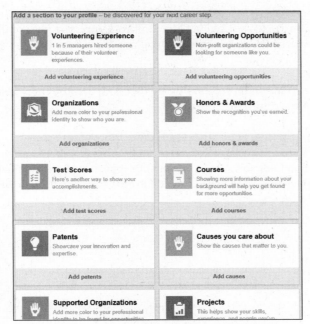

FIGURE 3-8:
See what other
sections of
information you
can add to your
LinkedIn profile.

Adding a Position to Your LinkedIn Profile

One of the most important aspects of your LinkedIn profile is the list of positions you've held over the years, including your current job. This list is especially important if you're using LinkedIn to find a new or different career or to reconnect with past colleagues. Hiring managers want to see your complete history to know what skills you offer, and past colleagues can't find you as easily through LinkedIn if the job they knew you from isn't on your profile. Therefore, it's critical to make sure you have all the positions posted on your profile with the correct information, as long as that fits with the brand or image you want to portray to the professional world.

For a company in LinkedIn's directory, you need to fill in the following fields:

>> Company name (and display name, if your company goes by more than one name)

>> Your job title while working for the company

>> The time period you worked for the company

>> Description of your job duties

If your company is *not* listed in LinkedIn's directory, you need to fill in the industry and website for the company when you're adding your position to your LinkedIn profile.

TIP

Use your resume when completing this section, because most resumes include all or most of the information required.

To add a position to your LinkedIn profile, follow these steps:

1. **Go to LinkedIn and log in. Hover your mouse over the Profile link in the top navigation bar, then click Edit Profile from the drop-down list that appears.**

   This step takes you to your profile page. Scroll down your profile until you see the Experience header, shown in Figure 3-9.

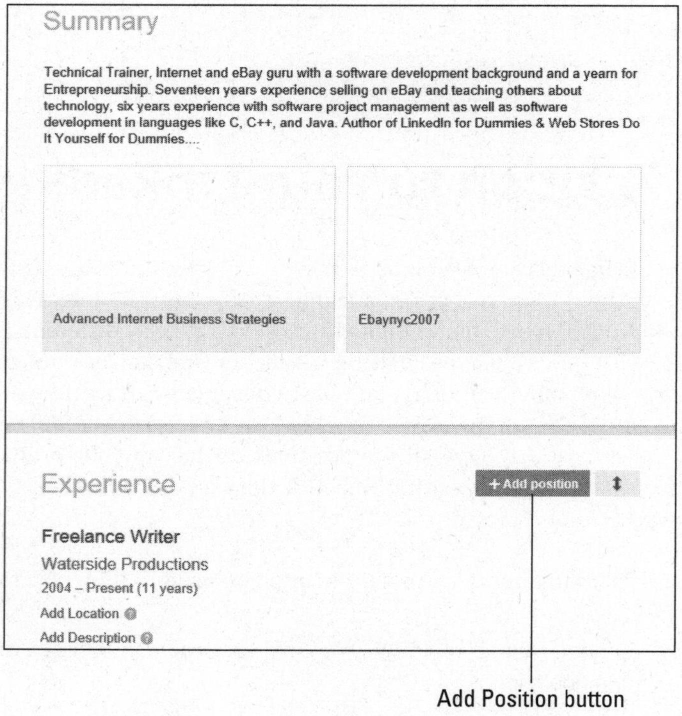

Summary

Technical Trainer, Internet and eBay guru with a software development background and a yearn for Entrepreneurship. Seventeen years experience selling on eBay and teaching others about technology, six years experience with software project management as well as software development in languages like C, C++, and Java. Author of LinkedIn for Dummies & Web Stores Do It Yourself for Dummies....

Advanced Internet Business Strategies

Ebaynyc2007

Experience   + Add position   ↕

Freelance Writer
Waterside Productions
2004 – Present (11 years)
Add Location ⊕
Add Description ⊕

FIGURE 3-9:
Start at your Experience section within your profile.

Add Position button

2. **Click the Add Position button to the right of the Experience header. (Depending on your web browser, the button may not be visible until you hover your mouse over the Experience header.)**

You see an expanded Experience section with all the necessary text boxes, as shown in Figure 3-10.

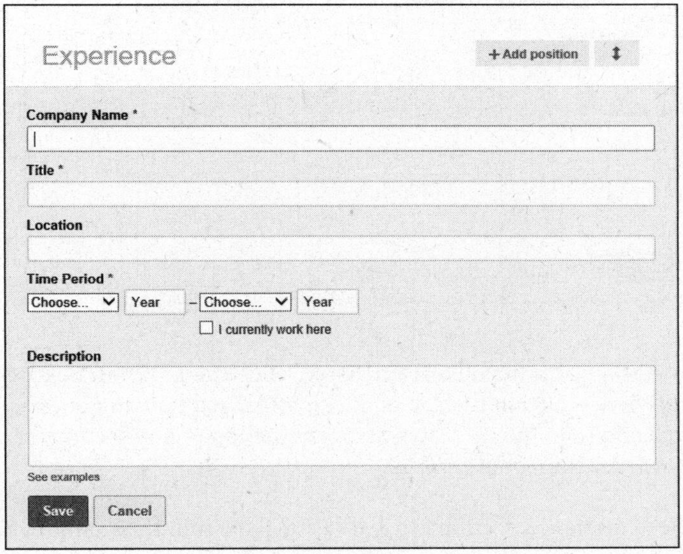

Experience   + Add position   ↕

Company Name *
[   ]
Title *
[   ]
Location
[   ]
Time Period *
[Choose... ▾] [Year] – [Choose... ▾] [Year]
                        ☐ I currently work here
Description
[   ]
[   ]
[   ]

See examples
[Save] [Cancel]

FIGURE 3-10:
Enter your job information here.

3. **In the text boxes provided, enter the information about your position, including company, title, location, time period, and job description.**

TIP

When you type in your company name, LinkedIn checks that name against its Company pages of thousands of companies from its records, and you see suggested company names while you type. (An example is shown in Figure 3-11.) If you see your company name in that list, click the name, and LinkedIn automatically fills in all the company detail information for you.

After entering the company name, enter your title, job location, the time period when you worked there, and a description of your position.

4. **Click the Save button.**

This adds the newly entered position into your profile, and you're taken back to your profile page.

5. **Repeat Steps 2–4 for any additional position you want to enter.**

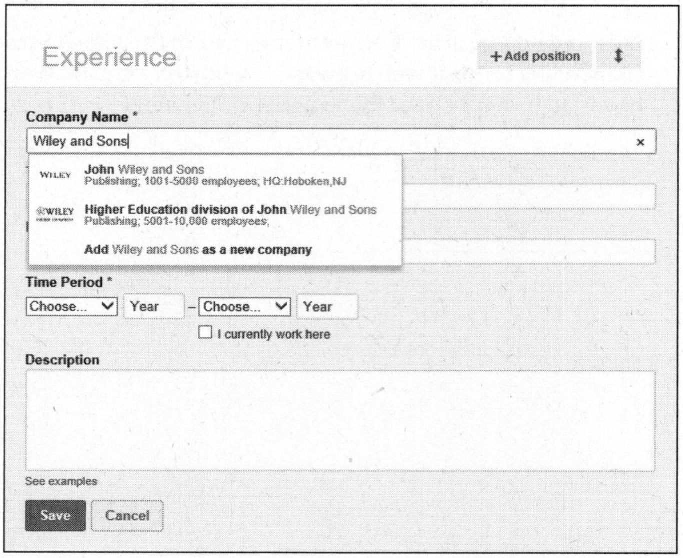

Experience

+ Add position ‡

Company Name *

Wiley and Sons ×

WILEY **John** Wiley and Sons
Publishing; 1001-5000 employees; HQ:Hoboken,NJ

WILEY **Higher Education division of John** Wiley and Sons
HIGHER EDUCATION Publishing; 5001-10,000 employees;

Add Wiley and Sons **as a new company**

Time Period *

Choose... ▾ Year – Choose... ▾ Year

☐ I currently work here

Description

See examples

Save Cancel

FIGURE 3-11:
LinkedIn checks
its Company
pages for your
company listing.

To edit a position you already listed, click the Edit link next to that record in the Experience section instead of clicking the Add Position button. In addition, if you click and hold the Up/Down arrow at the top of any section, you can rearrange its position within your profile.

REMEMBER

The Experience section isn't just for paid full-time employment. You can add position information for any contract work, nonprofit volunteer assignments, board of director membership, or other valid work experience that added to your skill set. If you've written a book, maintain a blog, or have a regular magazine column, you might want to list that as a separate position.

If you have most of the information that LinkedIn asks for a given position but you're missing a few details in the description, go ahead and add what you have. (You must provide a job title, company, and time period to save the position in your profile.) You can fill in any missing information later. In addition, if you make your profile public (as discussed later in "Setting your profile URL and public view"), make sure any position information you enter is something you don't mind the whole world — including past employers — seeing on your profile.

Reporting Your Education on Your Profile

After you document your past and current jobs, it's time to move on to the next part of your profile: education. After all, besides at your jobs, where else are you going to meet and stay in touch with so many people? At school, of course! Your

Education section says a lot about you, especially to potential employers and to former schoolmates who are looking to reconnect with you.

When you signed up with LinkedIn, you might have been asked to provide your basic education information. Maybe you have more than one school to list, or perhaps you didn't create a full listing for the schools you put down upon registration. In either case, you can go back to make sure that your profile is up to date and lists all your education.

Some people ask how much education to list on their profiles. Although you could theoretically go all the way back to preschool or kindergarten, most people start with high school or undergraduate college. This is up to you, but keep in mind that the more items you list, the greater the opportunity that your past schoolmates can locate and contact you.

REMEMBER

This section isn't limited to high school, undergraduate, and post-graduate education. You should also list any vocational education, certification courses, and any other stint at an educational institution that matters to your career or personal direction.

When you're ready to update or add your education information, follow these steps:

1. **Go to LinkedIn and log in. Hover your mouse over the Profile link in the top navigation bar, then click Edit Profile from the drop-down list that appears.**

2. **Scroll down your profile until you see the Education header. Click the Add Education link.**

   You see an expanded Education section with all the necessary text boxes, as shown in Figure 3-12.

3. **In the School text box, start entering the school name you wish to add to your profile.**

   As you're typing, LinkedIn displays a drop-down list of schools, as shown in Figure 3-13.

4. **Look through the alphabetized list to find your school and select it. If your school name doesn't appear, just finish typing the name of your school in the text box.**

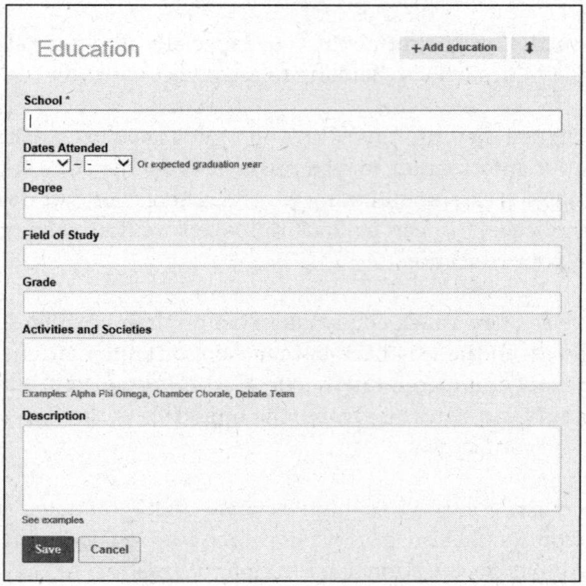

FIGURE 3-12:
Enter your school information into the Education section of your profile.

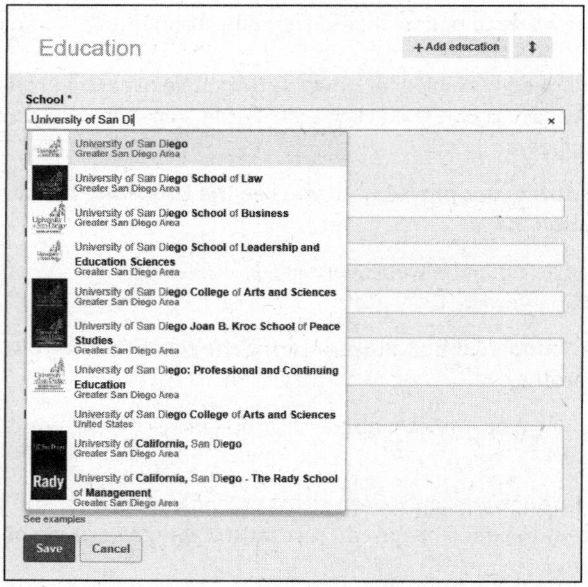

FIGURE 3-13:
Pick your school from the list provided, or continue typing the name of your school.

5. **Complete the degree information about your education.**

This includes filling in your degree type, fields of study (if applicable), grade you received (optional), and the years you attended this institution. For your degree type, you can either provide an abbreviation (BS, BA, and so on) or write the entire degree name (Masters of Science, Doctorate, and so on). The Field of Study text box is optional, but if you had a specific major or emphasis, this is where to put that information. Finally, for dates attended, if you're still attending this institution, simply fill in your expected graduation date. If you are an older worker and concerned about age discrimination, you can leave the dates of attendance blank; this is optional information.

6. **Scroll down to the Activities and Societies text box and fill it in.**

   Enter any extracurricular activities you participated in while attending this school. Also list any clubs or organizations you belonged to (including any officer positions you held in those clubs) and any societies you joined or were given membership to, such as honor societies, fraternities, or sororities. Be sure to separate each activity with a comma.

TIP

   Decide if listing these activities will support or enhance your overall professional goals and brand image. Make sure to list any activities, like current alumni organization activities, that apply to your situation today.

7. **Scroll down to the Description text box and enter any additional information about your education experience.**

   Enter any awards or honors received from this school, as well as any special events or experiences that didn't fit in the Activities and Societies box, such as studying abroad, events you organized, or committees that you served on at this school.

   You can separate each item with a period if you want.

8. **When you're done entering information, scroll down and click the Save button.**

   This step adds the newly entered education listing into your profile, and you're taken back to your profile page.

9. **Repeat Steps 2–8 for any additional education listings you want to enter.**

REMEMBER

To edit an existing education record, click the Edit link next to that record in the Education section, instead of the Add Education link.

Reviewing Your LinkedIn Profile

After you go through the various sections of your LinkedIn profile and add the critical information, review your profile to make sure it appears exactly the way you want other people to see it, as well as decide how much information is visible to the public and what others on LinkedIn can contact you about.

Viewing your profile as others see it

While you're updating your LinkedIn profile, take a minute to view your profile to see how it is displayed on the computer screen when anyone clicks to view it. The easiest way is to click the Profile link from the top navigation bar to see your profile, and then click the View Profile As button underneath your photo. It'll bring up your profile page as your Connections see it, as shown in Figure 3-14. You can click the arrows next to Connections, at the end of the sentence "This is what your profile looks like to Connections" near the top of the screen, to see how the public will view your profile as well. When you're done, click the Return to Your Profile button at the top right of the screen.

Setting your profile URL and public view

After you fully update your LinkedIn profile, your next goal is probably to share it with the entire world, not just your LinkedIn network. The best way to accomplish this is to set up your profile so that your full profile is available for public viewing.

Click the arrows to change your
view to what the public sees.

FIGURE 3-14:
View your
LinkedIn profile
as others see it.

Setting your profile to full public view gives you several advantages:

>> Anyone looking for you has a better chance of finding you because of the increased information tied to your name.

>> When you make your profile public, it gets indexed in both the Google and Yahoo! search databases. This makes your online identity accessible and controlled by your access to LinkedIn.

>> You give increased exposure to any companies, projects, or initiatives that you're working on by having that credit published on your LinkedIn profile.

When you're ready to set your profile to Public, follow these steps:

1. **Go to LinkedIn and log in. Hover your mouse over the Profile link in the top navigation bar and click Edit Profile.**

   You arrive at your profile page. Below your photo, headline, and name, look for your LinkedIn URL, as shown in Figure 3-15. (It's the web address ending in a string of characters and numbers.)

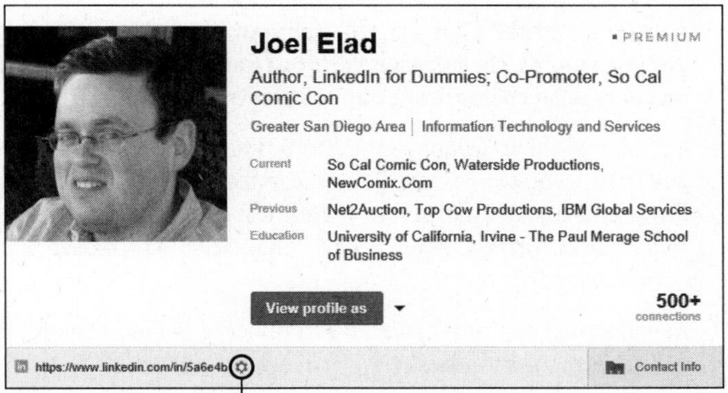

FIGURE 3-15: Edit your LinkedIn profile settings.

Click the cog to change your public profile URL.

2. **Hover your mouse over the LinkedIn URL and click the cog next to your LinkedIn URL to change your public profile URL.**

   This step takes you to the Public Profile settings page, as shown in Figure 3-16.

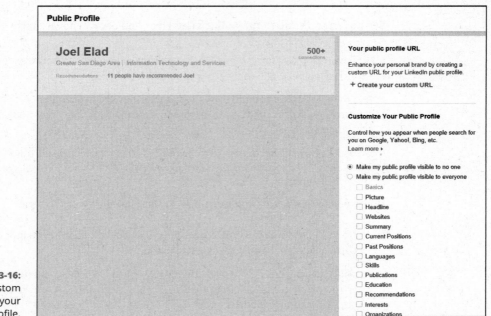

Public Profile

Joel Elad   500+
Greater San Diego Area | Information Technology and Services   connections
Recommendations   11 people have recommended Joel

Your public profile URL

Enhance your personal brand by creating a
custom URL for your LinkedIn public profile.

＋ Create your custom URL

Customize Your Public Profile

Control how you appear when people search for
you on Google, Yahoo, Bing, etc.
Learn more ▸

◉ Make my public profile visible to no one
○ Make my public profile visible to everyone

☐ Basics
☐ Picture
☐ Headline
☐ Websites
☐ Summary
☐ Current Positions
☐ Past Positions
☐ Languages
☐ Skills
☐ Publications
☐ Education
☐ Recommendations
☐ Interests
☐ Organizations

FIGURE 3-16:
Create a custom
URL for your
LinkedIn profile.

3. **(Optional) To set a custom URL for your LinkedIn profile (`www.linkedin.com/in/yourtext`), click Create Your Custom URL link and fill in the text box that appears with the part of your custom URL that I refer to as *yourtext*.**

For example, if you want your custom URL to be `www.linkedin.com/in/joelelad`, you would enter **joelelad** in the text box. You can type anywhere between 5 and 30 numbers or letters, but don't include any spaces, symbols, or special characters. When you're done, click the blue Save button to save your changes.

Keep in mind it's much easier to point people to `www.linkedin.com/in/joelelad/` than to `www.linkedin.com/in/5a6e4b/`.

TIP

WARNING

Keep your URL changes to a minimum (preferably, just set it once and leave it) so that everyone knows how to get to your profile, especially search engines. (If you change your custom URL later, the previous custom URL is no longer valid.) Otherwise, you'll have different versions of your profile with different URLs in different places on the Internet.

4. **Scroll down the Customize Your Public Profile section on the page and determine what parts of your LinkedIn profile you want available for public viewing.**

   Pick which sections of your LinkedIn profile are public. To reveal a section on your public profile, simply select the check box next to that section, as shown in Figure 3-17. Your basic information is already selected for you by default, but you can decide whether to add your education, positions, groups, or any other indicated section. As you add sections, the preview of your profile page on the left side of the page is updated.

5. **Scroll down and click the blue Save button to save your changes.**

   After clicking the Save button, you will still be on the Public Profile page. Therefore, when you are done making your changes, click any of the links in the top navigation bar to go about your business.

TIP

If you want to promote your LinkedIn profile on other websites, like a blog, social network, or personal website, you can create a special clickable LinkedIn icon (called a public profile badge) that can be added to a website to direct people to your public LinkedIn profile. Just click the Create a Public Profile Badge link underneath the Your Public Profile Badge section along the right side of the screen.

Public Profile

Joel Elad
Author, LinkedIn for Dummies; Co-Promoter, So Cal Comic Con

500+ connections

Greater San Diego Area | Information Technology and Services

Current	So Cal Comic Con, Waterside Productions, NewComix.Com
Previous	Net2Auction, Top Cow Productions, IBM Global Services
Education	University of California, Irvine - The Paul Merage School of Business
Recommendations	11 people have recommended Joel
Websites	JoelElad.Com So Cal Comic Con HotComics Comic Book Sales

Your public profile URL

Enhance your personal brand by creating a custom URL for your LinkedIn public profile.

www.linkedin.com/in/joelelad ✏

Customize Your Public Profile

Control how you appear when people search for you on Google, Yahoo!, Bing, etc.
Learn more ›

○ Make my public profile visible to no one
◉ Make my public profile visible to everyone

☐ Basics
☑ Picture
☑ Headline
☑ Websites
☑ Summary
☑ Current Positions
  ☑ Details
☑ Past Positions
  ☑ Details
☐ Languages
☑ Skills
☑ Publications
☑ Education
  ☑ Details

Summary

Technical Trainer, Internet and eBay guru with a software development background and a yearn for Entrepreneurship. Close to 20 years experience selling on eBay and teaching others about technology, six years experience with software project management as well as software development in languages like C, C++, and Java. Author of LinkedIn for Dummies & Web Stores Do It Yourself for Dummies. Co-author of 5 books, including Starting an Online Business All-in-One Desk Reference for Dummies, Facebook Advertising for Dummies, & Starting an iPhone Application Business for Dummies. Excellent public speaker and an Educational Specialist Trained by eBay. Former Lead instructor of eBay classes at the Learning Annex in NYC, Los Angeles, and San Diego. Consultant to small businesses and entrepreneurs on matters of eBay and e-commerce.

Specialties: Selling on eBay, technical training, technical writing, building websites, Selling on

FIGURE 3-17:
Decide what to add to your public LinkedIn profile, and the preview shows the changes instantly.

2

Finding Others and Getting Connected

Chapter 4

Searching LinkedIn

After you sign up for LinkedIn and build your profile (see Chapters 2 and 3, respectively, for more on those topics), it's time to go forth and find connections! As you start searching your own immediate network of your first-degree connections, plus second- and third-degree network members, you can see just how valuable LinkedIn can be to you. LinkedIn is the embodiment of the Six Degrees of Separation concept because in most cases, you can connect to any other person in the network regardless of whether you already know that person.

In this chapter, I demonstrate the different ways you can search the LinkedIn network. By that I mean your ever-growing personal network and the greater LinkedIn member network. I talk about viewing your own network, searching within the second and third degrees of your network, and performing searches on LinkedIn using different types of criteria or search terms.

Searching Your First-Degree Connections

I recall an old saying: "You have to know where you have come from to know where you are going." This holds true even for LinkedIn. Before you start searching throughout the network, it's helpful to understand the reach of your own immediate network and how your first-degree connections' networks add up to keep you connected with a lot of people. The first thing you should do is get familiar with your own LinkedIn network.

To view and search through your LinkedIn network, just follow these steps:

1. **Log in to LinkedIn. From the top navigation bar, click the Connections link.**

   This brings up a list of your current connections on the Contacts page, as shown in Figure 4-1. You can scroll through the list or hover your mouse over the Sort By link and then click the Last Name option (located below the tiled bar of potential contacts) to sort the list of connections in an alphabetical order.

2. **Use the search box and down arrow next to the Filter By link in the middle of the screen to filter your list of connections.**

   Click the word "Search" and a search box appears in its place. This search box in the middle of the screen is designed to help you search for a particular name. As you start typing a first or last name into the search box, LinkedIn will

FIGURE 4-1:
Sort your connections by last name.

Filter By link   Click the Search box.

automatically show you all the connections that match the name you are typing. You can press Enter after typing in a name to bring up a filtered list of connections. You can also use one of the predefined filters (Tags, Companies, Locations, Titles, and Source) to display connections who, say, live in a greater metropolitan area of a certain city or work in a particular industry. You can also click the Advanced link at the top of the page to bring up all the filtering options.

REMEMBER

The drop-down lists contain options only for your first-degree connections.

When you want to search for more than just someone's name, you can use the Advanced LinkedIn search feature along the top of the screen. Suppose you're looking for Internet professionals. After clicking the Advanced link at the top of the page and clicking the check box next to 1st Connections, you simply expand the Industry filter by clicking the name Industry, clicking the Internet check box, and then clicking Search (see Figure 4-2). LinkedIn can show you who in your network matches that request! If you're looking for an option in any of these filter lists (like Austin, TX, as a location) that doesn't appear on the filter list, none of your first-degree connections have that option defined in their profiles. (In this case, it would mean that none of your first-degree connections reside in Austin.)

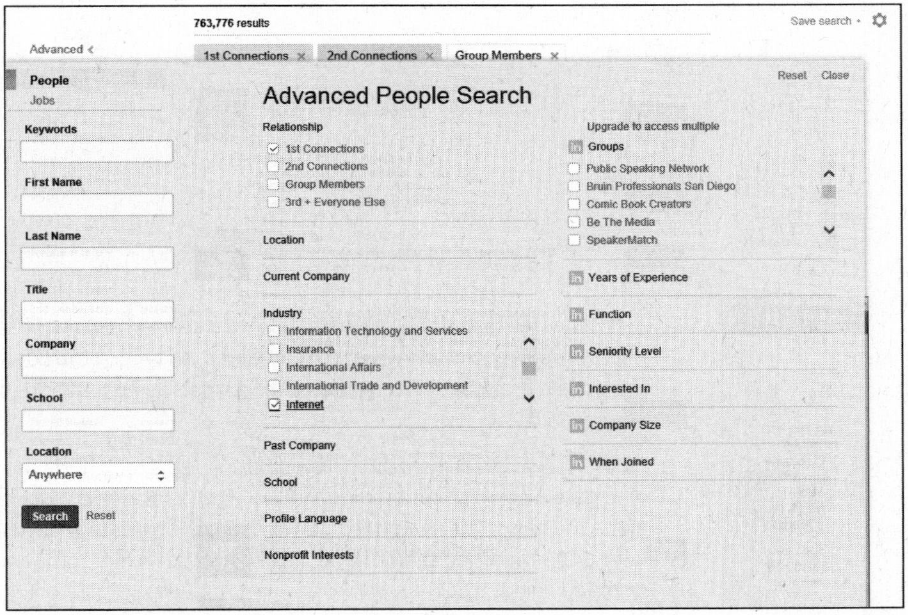

FIGURE 4-2: Generate a targeted list of your connections based on a filter.

763,776 results	Save search · ⚙

Advanced < | 1st Connections ✕ 2nd Connections ✕ Group Members ✕

Advanced People Search   Reset   Close

People
Jobs

Keywords

First Name

Last Name

Title

Company

School

Location
Anywhere ⬍

[Search] Reset

Relationship
☑ 1st Connections
☐ 2nd Connections
☐ Group Members
☐ 3rd + Everyone Else

Location

Current Company

Industry
☐ Information Technology and Services
☐ Insurance
☐ International Affairs
☐ International Trade and Development
☑ Internet

Past Company

School

Profile Language

Nonprofit Interests

Upgrade to access multiple
🔒 Groups
   ☐ Public Speaking Network
   ☐ Bruin Professionals San Diego
   ☐ Comic Book Creators
   ☐ Be The Media
   ☐ SpeakerMatch
🔒 Years of Experience
🔒 Function
🔒 Seniority Level
🔒 Interested In
🔒 Company Size
🔒 When Joined

3. **Use the other filters, such as Location (as shown in Figure 4-3), to see a more targeted set of connections.**

LinkedIn catalogs a wealth of information about you and your connections, allowing you to run specific searches on your network. Let's say you are looking for connections who have Disney as a current or past employer and who live in either Orange County or San Diego, California. You simply update the Company and Location filters (refer to Figure 4-3) and then click Search to see the connections in your network that match this query.

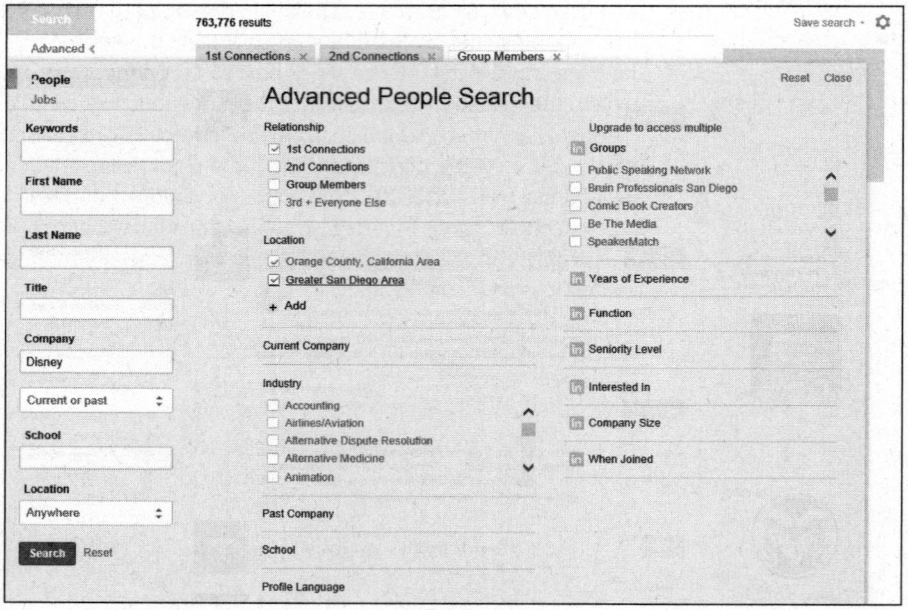

FIGURE 4-3:
See a detailed search query of your network.

In most cases, you simply type words into a search box, but for the Location filter, you have to click the word "Add" and then type in the Location and select the closest area that LinkedIn has defined in its system to add that Location to your search.

Once you have run the search, if your result list is too short, you can eliminate a search filter by clicking the X next to a criteria (such as Location) along the top of the search results, or change/eliminate a word along the left-hand side of the search window, like the name of a company in the Company field.

Searching the LinkedIn Network

When you're ready to find a specific person, use the LinkedIn search engine, with which you can scan the hundreds of millions of LinkedIn members, based on keywords. The two main ways to search the network are a basic search and an Advanced Search.

At the top of every page on LinkedIn is a simple search box, with which you can run a keyword search via the LinkedIn database. This is your go-to tool if you're searching for a specific name, employees of a particular company, or people with a specific job title. In fact, you'll get a lot of results with the basic search because you're searching each LinkedIn member's entire profile for your keywords, not just one field. For example, if you type **Mike Jones** in the basic search box (as opposed to searching by the name Mike Jones; see "Searching by name" later in this chapter), you get a larger set of results because you see every profile where the words "Mike" and "Jones" were anywhere in the profile. (When you search by name, LinkedIn searches only everyone's Name field.) Keep this in mind when you do your search, and pick the method you want based on your goals.

In some situations, though, a simple search just doesn't cut it because you want to specify whether you're searching for someone's name, title, employer, industry, skills, location, or some combination thereof. In those cases, use the Advanced Search function:

>> From almost any page on LinkedIn, click the Advanced link at the top of the page to bring up the search page. If you're using LinkedIn Jobs or LinkedIn Groups, clicking this link brings up the Job Search or Groups Search page, respectively. In addition, on the Job Search page, for example, there is an Advanced Search link below the job search text box that expands and shows filters for searching jobs.

>> Click the down arrow next to the search box at the top of any LinkedIn page to bring up links to the searches for People, Jobs, Companies, Groups, Universities, or your messages Inbox, as shown in Figure 4-4.

>> If you download the LinkedIn mobile app (as discussed in Chapter 12), you can perform a search from the search box in that program.

REMEMBER

The examples in the rest of this chapter assume that you're clicking the Advanced link. Of course, feel free to pick the method of search you're most comfortable with.

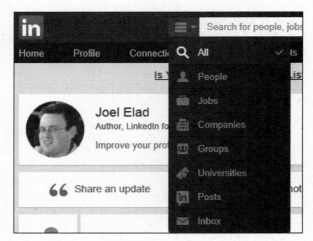

FIGURE 4-4:
Access the
LinkedIn search
page from one of
several links.

Searching by keyword

Quick, do you know someone who can write software code in PHP? Who do you know that enjoys mountain climbing or hiking? Do you know anybody who gives presentations on a regular basis? Well, with LinkedIn's search capabilities, you can find out when you search by keyword.

When you search by keyword, LinkedIn analyzes everyone else's profiles to find that matching word. You can put any sort of skill, buzzword, interest, or other keyword that would be present in someone's profile to see who in your network is a match. To search by keyword, follow these steps:

1. **While logged in to LinkedIn, click the Advanced link at the top of the page.**

   You're taken to the Advanced People Search page.

2. **Enter the keyword(s) in the Keywords text box.**

   In Figure 4-5, I'm searching for "Six Sigma." If you enter multiple keywords like I did, LinkedIn looks for members who have all the keywords in their profile.

TIP

   I recommend tacking on additional search criteria, such as picking one or more industries, location information (country and ZIP/postal code), or perhaps a job title to get a more meaningful search result. Otherwise, your result list will be long and unhelpful.

WARNING

   If you're searching for a specific keyword phrase, put those words in quotation marks so LinkedIn searches for the exact phrase; for example, "Six Sigma." Otherwise, LinkedIn searches each individual word, and you might get a result like mine in Figure 4-6, where I have the words "six" and "Sigma" in different places in my profile. (Although it's not visible in the figure, I have the word

"Sigma" as a keyword in my profile because I'm a member of Beta Gamma Sigma.) Because LinkedIn found both words in my profile, even though those words didn't appear together in one phrase, I came up on the search results page.

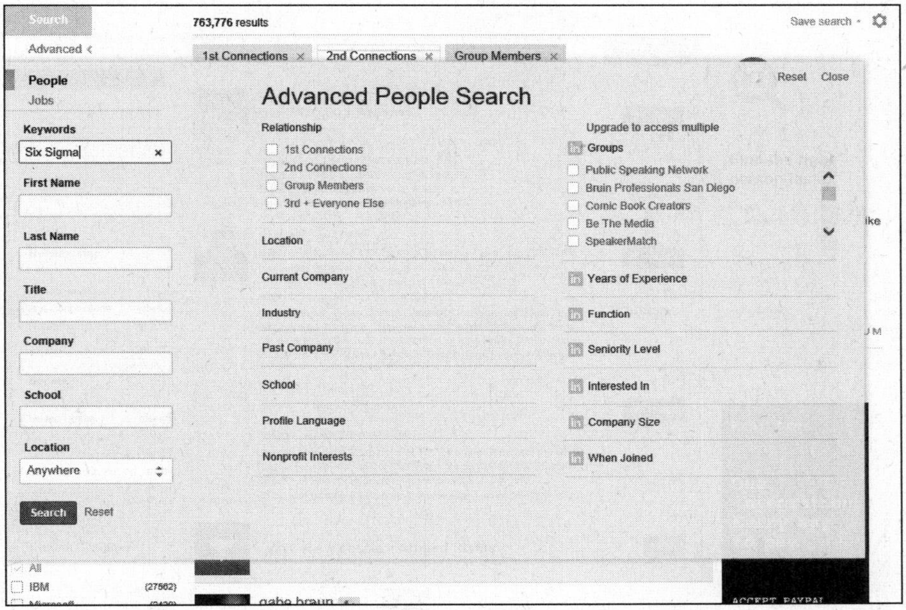

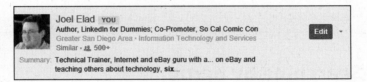

FIGURE 4-5:
Search for people by the keywords in their profile.

FIGURE 4-6:
Incorrect search results appear when you don't use quotes.

3. **Click the blue Search button.**

   You see the people in your extended network with those keywords in their profile.

4. **(Optional) Fine-tune your results with the filtering options.**

   You can expand the various filters along the left side of the Search Results screen and use them to refine your results by entering more information, such as keywords, job titles, user types, and location information, by selecting the check boxes provided. (See Figure 4-7.) As of this writing, you can filter by

Relationship (degree of connection), Location, Current Company (of the people you're searching), Industry, Past Company, School, Profile Language, and Nonprofit Interests. LinkedIn Premium members can also search by LinkedIn Group membership, Years of Experience, Function, Seniority Level, Interests, Company Size, and when someone joined LinkedIn.

FIGURE 4-7:
Add more information to get a more targeted list of matching people.

Searching by name

When you want to find a specific person on LinkedIn, you can search by name. By default, LinkedIn's search box at the top of any page is set to People Search. When you start to type a name, let's say John Doe, into the search box, LinkedIn dynamically searches its entire database and shows you a specific list of people based on what you typed, as shown in Figure 4-8. If someone is a second- or third-degree connection to you, that shows up next to his name.

You can click any name from that list to go directly to that person's profile, or you can keep typing to update the list you see. Let's say you are looking for John Doe who works at IBM. By adding IBM as an extra search term, you will see a new list of John Does who work at IBM, as shown in Figure 4-9.

FIGURE 4-8:
Search LinkedIn
by someone's
name.

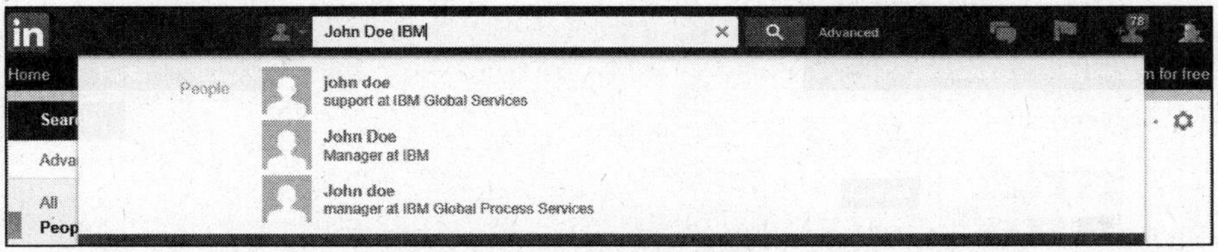

FIGURE 4-9:
Search LinkedIn
by someone's
name and
company.

LinkedIn has numerous ways to search for someone using different filters. If you want to do a detailed Name search and you have several details about the person to help refine your search, I recommend doing an Advanced People search based on that person's name.

REMEMBER

When you search by name, you are required to enter the last name; entering the first name is optional.

When you're ready to perform a detailed search by name, follow these steps:

1. **While logged in to LinkedIn, click the Advanced link at the top of the page.**

   You're taken to the Advanced People Search page.

2. **Enter the last name (and first name, if you know it) into the Last Name and First Name text boxes.**

3. **Input additional information to help find the person you're looking for.**

   For example, if you know a company where the person used to work or is currently employed, you can input a company name into the Company text box. Choose the Current or Past option beneath that box to indicate LinkedIn can search current or past experience in someone's profile.

4. **(Optional) If you know the approximate location of this person, use the Location drop-down list to select the Located In or Near option. Then use the Country drop-down list and fill in the Postal Code text box.**

TIP

Only after you select Located In or Near can you pick a country from the Country drop-down list, input Postal Code in the box indicated, and pick a Within search radius, as shown in Figure 4-10.

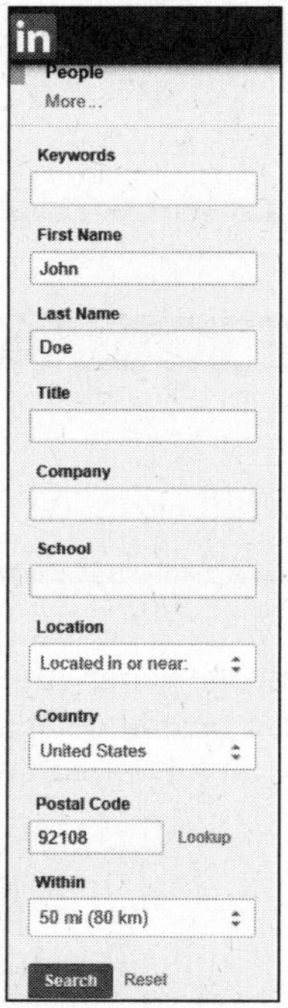

FIGURE 4-10:
Give LinkedIn location information to find your person.

5. **Click the Search button.**

You see a results list of people, sorted by the relevance of your name search and then by the degrees of connection in your overall LinkedIn network. (For example, people who are second-degree network members appear above people who are third-degree network members.)

6. **(Optional) For better results, use additional or different filters in your search.**

If you haven't already done so, you can add more keywords, a company name, or location information into the boxes provided on the left side of the Search Results screen. Then click the Search button. Also, you can scroll down and pick specific filters to refine your search results.

Searching for someone by company or job title

You might need to search for someone by his company (employer). Or maybe you're thinking of applying to a company, and you want to see who you know (or, rather, who is in your extended network) who works for that company so you can approach them to ask some questions or get a referral. Perhaps you're looking for a decision maker at a company who can help you with a deal, or you're curious how active a particular company's employees are on LinkedIn. You can also look for key thought leaders whom you might want to approach for an informational interview.

Whatever the reason, LinkedIn is an excellent place for searching detailed corporate profiles of specific companies. When you're ready to search by company, follow these steps:

1. **While logged in to LinkedIn, click the Advanced link at the top of the page.**

   You're taken to the Advanced People Search page.

2. **Enter the name of the company in the Company text box (as shown in Figure 4-11).**

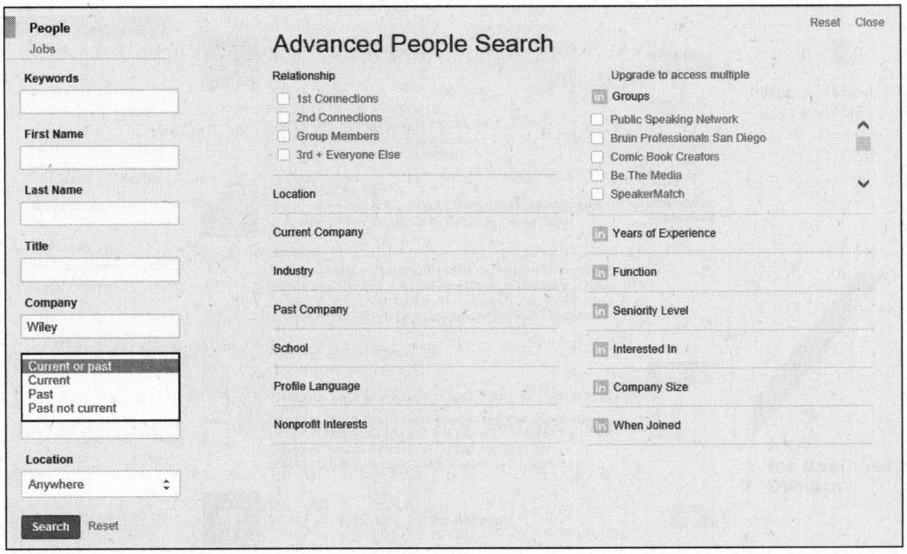

FIGURE 4-11: Search for people by the company where they work(ed).

If you want to search for only current employees of the company, change the drop-down list choice from the Current or Past option to just Current. If you don't change the default option, your search results will include all the people who ever worked for that company and included that job on their LinkedIn profiles.

3. **Click the Search button.**

You see as many as 100 results that match your company and exist somewhere in your extended network. (If you've paid for a premium account, you see more results, depending on the level of your account.)

4. **(Optional) For better results, modify your search.**

You can enter more information, such as job titles, user types, or location information, into the boxes provided on the left side of the Search Results screen. Then click the Search button. Also, you can scroll down and pick specific filters to refine your search results.

Sometimes you might need to look for someone in a specific position rather than for a specific person. After all, who knows what you go through better than other people with the same job, right? Who better to give advice on a topic like search engine optimization (SEO) than someone whose job relates to SEO?

Therefore, LinkedIn gives you the ability to search by job title instead of person. When you're ready to search by job title, follow these steps:

1. **While logged in to LinkedIn, click the Advanced link at the top of the page.**

You're taken to the Advanced People Search page.

2. **Enter the job title in the Title box provided; Figure 4-12 shows Project Manager entered.**

To search for only those people who currently have that title, change the drop-down list choice to Current. If you leave the default choice of Current or Past, your search results will include all the people who have ever defined that job title in one of the positions on their LinkedIn profiles.

3. **(Optional) Select at least one industry from the list provided so your search results are relevant to the job title search.**

Although this step is optional, I highly recommend doing it. After all, a Project Manager in Construction is completely different from a Project Manager in Computer Software. Click the word "Industry" in the center of the screen to bring up the list of industries you can select from.

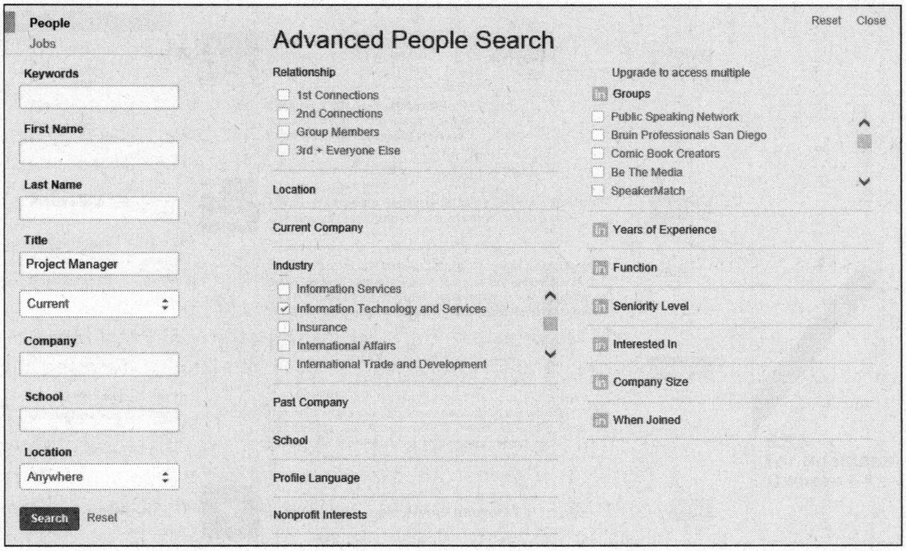
People
Jobs
Advanced People Search
Reset Close
Keywords
First Name
Last Name
Title
Project Manager
Current
Company
School
Location
Anywhere
Search
Reset
Relationship
1st Connections
2nd Connections
Group Members
3rd + Everyone Else
Location
Current Company
Industry
Information Services
Information Technology and Services
Insurance
International Affairs
International Trade and Development
Past Company
School
Profile Language
Nonprofit Interests
Upgrade to access multiple
Groups
Public Speaking Network
Bruin Professionals San Diego
Comic Book Creators
Be The Media
SpeakerMatch
Years of Experience
Function
Seniority Level
Interested In
Company Size
When Joined

FIGURE 4-12: Search for people by their current or previous job titles.

TIP

You can select multiple industries from the list. Simply scroll through the list and select the check box next to each industry you want to select.

4. **Click the Search button to see your results.**

   You see a set of results that match your job title request. You can use the filtering options on the left side of the Search Results screen and the middle of the screen, as shown in Figure 4-12, to add more information and get a more targeted list.

Performing advanced searches

LinkedIn's search screens allow you to perform detailed searches by using check boxes and drop-down lists, so you don't need to know any programming or sophisticated languages to dig deep into the LinkedIn network. However, there are built-in options available to you if you want to add specific words, called *boolean operators*, into your search. Here are some of your options:

- **OR.** When you are doing a search that could call for one or more options, but the search *must* contain at least one of those terms, the OR command becomes incredibly useful. For example, if you are looking for someone who knows how to program in either Java or JavaScript, you can type the words **Java OR JavaScript** to get the desired result. Even if you're looking for something that could be typed as one word or two, like "Help desk" or "helpdesk," you can search by putting OR between the two terms: "Help desk OR helpdesk."

>> **AND.** When your search requires multiple criteria, the AND operator becomes essential. Let's say you need a Certified Public Accountant (or CPA) who knows QuickBooks and lives in California. You can search for "CPA AND QuickBooks AND California." Thankfully, the way LinkedIn is designed today, when you type in multiple keywords without the word AND in between each keyword, LinkedIn will still look for every keyword, assuming that the word AND is there.

>> **NOT.** When your search requires you to exclude a particular term, you can use the word NOT (or a minus sign) in front of the term you want to exclude. For example, if you type **Director NOT President**, you are looking for people who work as a Director, but NOT the President of the company.

>> **" " (Quotation marks).** When your search requires exact phrases instead of a string of keywords (like my example earlier in this chapter with "Six Sigma"), you need to add quotation marks around each phrase. That way, when you look for "Executive Assistant," you will get results for an executive assistant, but not for an executive who has a job duty of Assistant to the President, for example.

>> **( ) (Parenthetical searches).** You can take the above operators and combine them and use parentheses to build complex searches. For example, if you need a software developer or engineer who knows either Java or JavaScript, but who isn't a manager, you can search this by typing:

```
(Java OR JavaScript) AND ("software developer" OR "software
    engineer") AND NOT Manager
```

Saving your searches for future use

LinkedIn enables you to save your searches so you can run them in the future. Let's say you are a recruiter who wants to check her network every week for someone who can fill a specific job opening, or a job seeker who wants to see if the right person pops up in one of the companies she is targeting.

To save your searches to use later, follow these steps:

1. **Log in to LinkedIn and click the word "Advanced" at the top of the LinkedIn home page next to the search box.**

You're taken to the Advanced People Search page.

2. **Perform the search you wish to save by entering the appropriate keywords in the boxes and selecting the check boxes next to each filter, and then click Search.**

   Your Search Results page should appear, as shown in Figure 4-13.

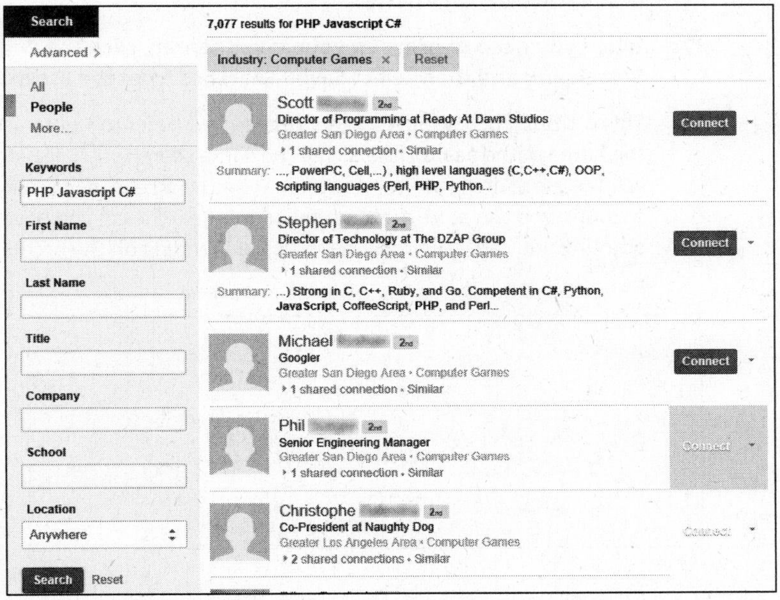

FIGURE 4-13: Perform a search on LinkedIn that you want to save for future usage.

3. **Click the Save Search link in the top right corner of the search page.**

   LinkedIn pops up a Saved Searches window (see Figure 4-14). You can create a title for your search, so pick a memorable name that will remind you of the search parameters you have saved. In addition, you can set LinkedIn to e-mail you Never, Weekly, or Monthly with search results for this saved search.

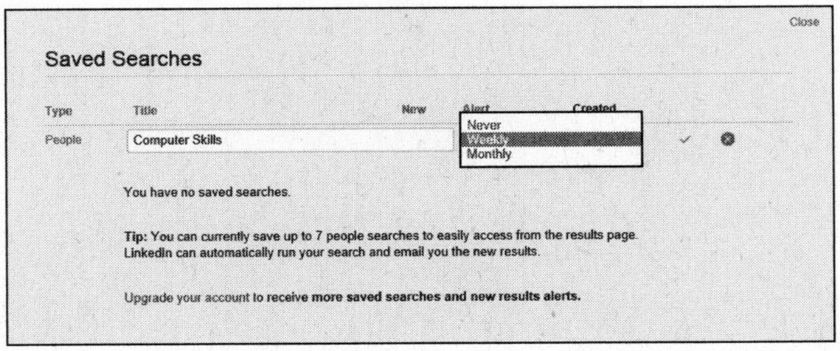

FIGURE 4-14: Set the parameters to save your search.

4. **Set the parameters for your search, and then click the green check mark to save your search.**

   After you've given your search a title and e-mail frequency, and clicked the check mark, you should see the title of the saved search in the window, as shown in Figure 4-15. Click Close to exit this process and go back to your normal LinkedIn activities.

5. **When you need to bring up your saved search, click the Cog next to the Save Search link and then select Saved Searches from the list that appears.**

   This will bring up the Saved Searches window (refer to Figure 4-15). Simply click the name of the search to execute the same search you did before, and you will see the search results page appear on the screen. If you have a basic account, you can store three saved people searches. If you have a premium account, you can store more searches, depending on the account level.

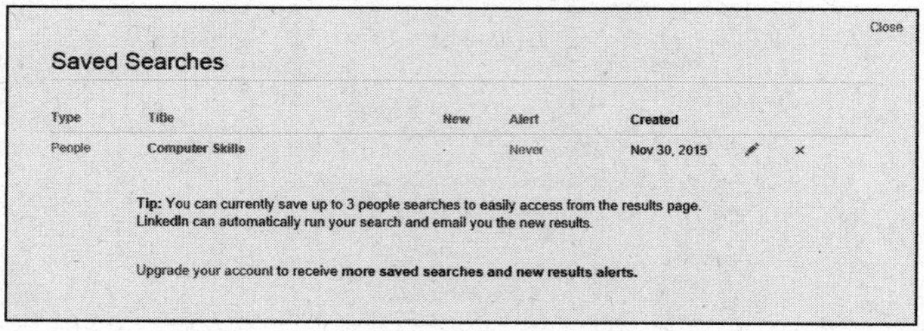

Close

Saved Searches

Type	Title	New	Alert	Created		
People	Computer Skills		Never	Nov 30, 2015	✎	✕

Tip: You can currently save up to 3 people searches to easily access from the results page. LinkedIn can automatically run your search and email you the new results.

Upgrade your account to receive more **saved searches and new results alerts.**

FIGURE 4-15:
See your saved searches in a list.

Chapter 5

Managing Introductions and InMail

One of the goals of using LinkedIn is to expand your personal network of friends and colleagues by seeing who is connected to you at each degree level. When you can see the second and third degrees of your network, your next goal is to start interacting with these people and see how they might fit into your network, goals, or ambitions. However, the whole system of contacting people requires some order and decorum (otherwise, nobody would feel comfortable signing up for the site in the first place). Therefore, LinkedIn offers methods for meeting and connecting with people outside your immediate network: using your network for introductions and InMail. Not so coincidentally, I cover those concepts in this very chapter.

Introductions are simply where you use LinkedIn messages to contact a friend and ask to be introduced to a friend of that friend, and your friend can decide whether to "pass along your introduction" and connect with your intended target. InMail allows you to directly communicate with anyone in the LinkedIn network through a private LinkedIn message. I also cover what to do when you get a request from a connection on LinkedIn.

Using InMail Versus Asking for Introductions

Your first question is most likely, "What's the difference between asking for an introduction and using InMail?" (Figure 5-1 shows an InMail example at the top and an introduction request message at the bottom.) The answer depends on how involved your common friend or colleague is in connecting you with this new contact.

WARNING

Every LinkedIn user decides on his own contact level, and a user can decline to allow any message or InMail to reach him, regardless of sender. If you don't want to receive any messages or InMail, simply deselect all the Contact Settings options. (See Chapter 3 for the section on checking your contact settings.)

TIP

If you don't mind your network sending you messages but really don't want to have to deal with any InMail, just deselect the InMail option in the Contact Settings section and leave the Introductions option alone. Otherwise, leave the InMail option selected, since it is a valuable tool for sending and receiving communication with people who might become a valuable part of your network or help you with one of your professional goals.

Understanding introductions

Say you're at a party with your friend Michael, and you say to him, "You know, I'd really like to meet someone who can help me with some software tasks for my company." Michael looks around, sees his friend James, and introduces you to James by saying, "Hello, James. This is my entrepreneur friend from business school, [Your Name Here]. [Your Name Here], this is my old buddy James. He and I studied computer science together in college." After that, Michael might give some more background information about each person to the other.

On LinkedIn, an *introduction* is very similar to my real-world example. You send a message to someone in your immediate first-degree network (Michael) and ask that person to introduce you to someone in his network (James). In some cases, if you're trying to reach someone in your third-degree network (maybe James has a programming buddy you should talk to), your message would have to go to two different parties before reaching the intended recipient.

Here are some benefits of using introductions:

>> **You're represented by someone close.** Instead of sending a random, unexpected e-mail to a stranger, you're introduced by somebody who knows the intended party, even though that introduction is done with a LinkedIn message. That gives your message a much higher chance of being read and getting a response.

>> **You get your network involved.** When you ask people in your network to get involved, they learn more about you and your intentions, and sometimes you might find what you're looking for is closer than you think. In addition, when you ask them to pass along your introduction request, you can offer to facilitate an introduction on their behalf, which helps both parties.

>> **You leverage the power of your network.** By using LinkedIn, you not only expand your network by using your first-degree connections to help you meet new people, but you can also decide who would make the introduction for you. I recommend that you read up on your friend's profile and your intended party's profile to see what they have in common.

Getting to know InMail

Because everyone on LinkedIn has a profile and a secure message Inbox, communicating with other people online is easy. LinkedIn allows you to send InMail directly to an intended party, regardless of whether he is directly or indirectly connected with you. The e-mail gets immediately delivered to the recipient's Web-based Inbox on the LinkedIn site (and, if the recipient has configured his settings to get e-mails of all his InMail, in the Inbox at his e-mail address); the sender never learns the recipient's address, so each party has some privacy. The recipient can then read your profile and decide whether to respond.

The cost of using InMail depends on whether you subscribe to a premium account. If you have a Business Plus or Job Seeker account, you can purchase additional InMail credits (one credit allows you to send one message) at a cost of $10 per InMail message. Premium accounts, such as the Job Seeker account for $29.99/month, come with a set number of InMail credits per month that roll over to the next month if unused. The Job Seeker account gets 3 credits per month, the Business Plus or Sales Navigator Professional account gets 15 credits per month, and the Recruiter Lite account gets 30 credits per month.

Here are some benefits of using InMail:

>> **Delivery is instant.** With InMail, you simply write your message or request and send it directly to the intended party. There's no delay as a request gets passed from person to person and waits for approval or forwarding.

>> **You owe no favors.** Sometimes, you just want to reach somebody without asking your friends to vouch for you. InMail allows you to send a request to someone new without involving anyone else.

>> **It's sure to be delivered.** With introductions, the party(ies) involved in the middle could choose to deny your request and not pass along the message. With InMail, you know that the intended party will get a copy of your message in his e-mail account and LinkedIn Inbox.

Setting Up an Introduction

When you want to bring two (or more) parties together, you usually need to apply some thought to the process, whether it's figuring out what both parties have in common, thinking up the words you'll use to introduce party A to party B, or coming up with the timing of exactly when and where you plan to make the introduction. On LinkedIn, you should do your best to make sure the introduction process goes smoothly — but don't worry, there's not nearly as much social pressure. The following sections give you tips and pointers for setting up an introduction.

Planning your approach to each party in the introduction

When you want to send an introduction request, spend some time planning your request before you log on to LinkedIn to generate and send it. Preparing a quality and proper introduction goes a long way toward keeping your network in a helpful and enthusiastic mood, and it increases your chances of making a new and valuable connection.

You need to prepare two messages: one for your intended recipient and one for your connection/friend. Each message needs to perform a specific objective. Start with the message to your friend, and keep the following tips in mind when you're writing it:

>> **Be honest and upfront.** Say exactly what you hope to achieve so there are no surprises. If you tell your friend that you're hoping her contact will be a new bowling buddy for you, but when you reach that contact, you ask for funding for your new business plan, you're in trouble. Your friend will probably never forward another request again, and the contact, who expected one type of interaction and got another, will see you as untrustworthy and be unlikely and/or unwilling to help on this request or any in the future. Even if your eventual goal is something big, such as asking someone for a job, start with an initial goal that is reasonable, such as asking for information or advice. Let the other person know that you would like to keep talking to see what possibilities might occur in the future.

>> **Be polite and courteous.** Remember, you're asking your friend to vouch for you or back you up when your request goes to the intended party. So be polite when making your request and show your gratitude regardless of the outcome.

>> **Be ready to give in order to get.** One of the best ways to go far with your network is to offer some sort of reciprocal favor when you want someone to do a favor for you. Perhaps you can introduce your friend to one of your other contacts in exchange for your friend accepting your introduction request.

>> **Be patient.** Although you might be eager and under a deadline, your friends probably operate on different schedules driven by different levels of urgency. Some people are online all the time, other people log in to LinkedIn infrequently, and most people are completely disconnected at times, like when they're on vacation or behind on a project. Asking your friend every day whether she forwarded your request is an almost surefire way of getting that request bounced back to you.

When writing your message to your intended recipient, keep these tips in mind:

>> **Be honest and upfront.** Just like with your friend, when you have a specific goal or request in mind, make it known in the message. The recipient is most likely busy and doesn't know you, so if he spends the time to talk to you and finds out that you have an ulterior motive, he feels like his time was wasted and that he was deceived, which are *not* good feelings to create when trying to get help from someone.

>> **Be succinct.** You're asking someone for his time, resources, or advice, so don't beat around the bush. Introduce yourself in your first sentence or two. Then explain why you're contacting the recipient and how you hope he can help you.

>> **Be original.** If you stick to the sample text that LinkedIn gives you, your message has an air of "Hey, I want to talk to you, but I don't want to spend a few seconds of effort to really tell you what I'm after." When you customize your message, you have a greater chance of capturing the other person's attention. If your intended recipient gets a lot of requests, you'll stand out if you show some effort to rise above the daily noise this person encounters.

>> **Be ready to give in order to get.** You're asking for help of some sort, so again, be ready to give something, whether it's gratitude, a reciprocal favor, or something more tangible. Most people are eager to help, especially when they understand the situation, but having something to offer in exchange rarely hurts. Explain to your recipient how you might provide something useful in return.

Sending an introduction request message

When you've prepared your messages (one to your contact and one to the recipient) and you're all ready to send an introduction request message, just follow these steps:

1. **While logged in to LinkedIn, search for the person you'd like to meet.**

   You can use the Search box at the top of any LinkedIn page, or you can click your Connections and search your friend's networks. (See Chapter 4 for the lowdown on searching LinkedIn.)

2. **From the list of search results, click the name of the person you want to contact. (If you didn't find the person you're looking for, try another search.)**

   This step takes you to the recipient's profile page, where, as you scroll down the page, you should see two things: a chart along the right side of the page showing how you're connected to this person and a link entitled Ask X about Y. (If you don't have anyone in your network yet, you won't see the chart or the link.)

   Suppose I'm hoping to be introduced to Sarah Lundy, Payroll Supervisor at a charitable foundation. When I get to Sarah's profile page, I see that I have a connection to her (see Figure 5-2) in the form of a business contact and friend who went to the same university as me, Kristie Spilios. If you notice from the figure, LinkedIn will provide a window to explain how I'm connected to the first-degree connection that I need to make the introduction to the second-degree network member.

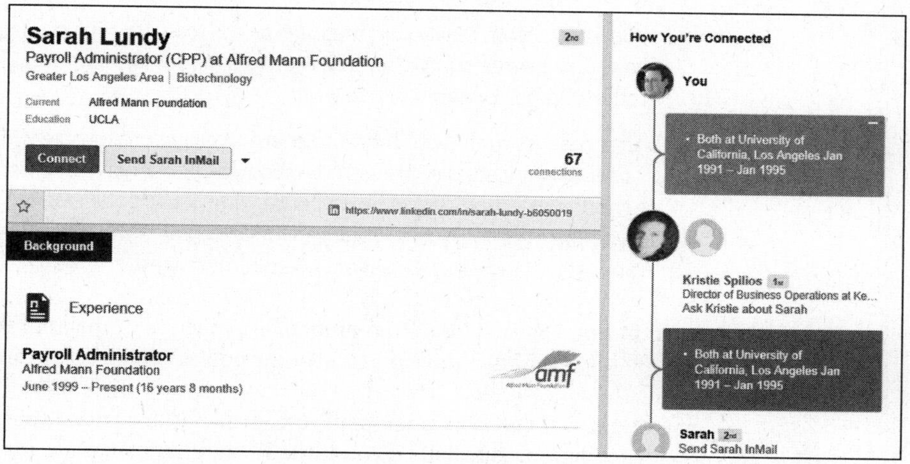

FIGURE 5-2:
See how you're connected to your intended recipient via LinkedIn.

3. **On the person's profile page, click the Ask X about Y link to start a LinkedIn message.**

   You will be taken to the LinkedIn messaging system, and hopefully a new message has been created to your first-degree connection. If the window doesn't open, click the New Message icon and type in your first-degree connection, and send her a message that starts the introduction process, as shown in Figure 5-3. Mention the second-degree network member who you'd like to meet, and what your first-degree connection should say to that person on your behalf.

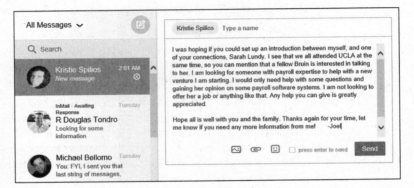

FIGURE 5-3: Message the person you are requesting to make your introduction.

4. **Click the Send button.**

   You will see your newly sent message as the top entry on your Inbox screen, and your first-degree connection will receive this message with your introduction request in her LinkedIn Inbox.

   After that, it's up to your friend to share that person's profile with you so you can communicate directly with the second-degree network member. In order to add this second-degree member to your network, one of you will have to Invite the other person to your network. You can always view your introduction request message in your list of LinkedIn messages.

Keep in mind some LinkedIn members are inactive or may not respond, so try not to take it personally. Move on to another potentially helpful contact.

TIP

You might want to send an e-mail to your facilitator friend first before requesting the introduction, especially if you think she might not want to forward your request, you want to make sure the facilitator has kept in contact with the intended recipient well enough to make the introduction, or the intended recipient might be too busy to receive an introduction request message. This also gives the facilitator a chance to let you know first that she is not interested or able in making the introduction.

Sending InMail

If you're looking to connect with someone right away and you don't have an immediate or secondary connection with someone, you can use the InMail feature to send a message directly to another LinkedIn member without anyone else getting involved.

REMEMBER

This feature is currently available to premium members of LinkedIn with available InMail credits. If you're using a free account, you have to upgrade your account, earn InMail credits through posting a job offer, or contact someone with an Open Profile. Consult the LinkedIn Help Center for more information (`https://help.linkedin.com`).

InMail is basically a private e-mail message that enables you to reach other members, but it protects those members' privacy and e-mail address information. If your message is accepted, you'll receive a message in your LinkedIn Inbox with the other party's name and link to her profile, and you can communicate further. In some cases, you see only the other person's professional headline first, and then you see the person's name after she accepts the InMail message.

When you're ready to send someone an InMail, follow these steps:

1. **While logged in to LinkedIn, search for the person you'd like to meet.**

   You can use the Search box at the top of any LinkedIn page, or you can click your Contacts and search your friend's networks. (Chapter 4 has all sorts of details for you about searching LinkedIn.)

2. **From the list of search results, click the name of the person you want to contact. (If you didn't find the person you're looking for, try another search.)**

   You're taken to the person's profile page.

3. **Click the Send InMail link.**

   For example, suppose that I want to connect with Lynn Dralle, the Queen of Auctions, who can not only teach you how to sell on eBay, but who sells more than $100,000 a year in antiques and collectibles herself. When I look at her profile (see Figure 5-4), I see the Send InMail button, which means she is open to receiving InMail. I would click the Send InMail button to send her a message.

   After you click that button, you can start filling out the Compose Your Message form, as shown in Figure 5-5.

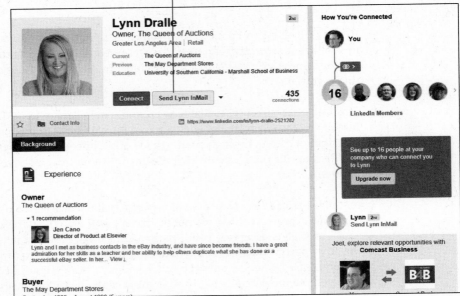

Send InMail button

FIGURE 5-4:
See if the person you want to contact is open to receiving InMail.

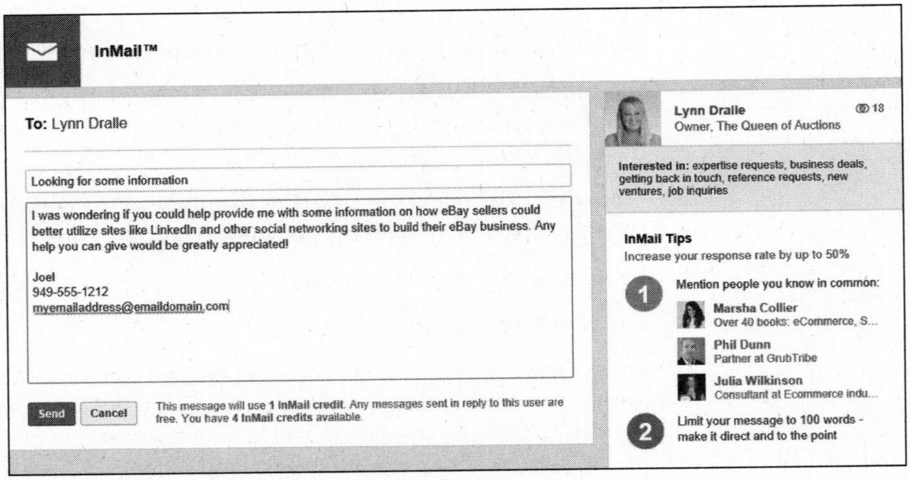

FIGURE 5-5:
Compose your InMail message.

4. **Type in a subject, and then type a message in the text box.**

As with an introduction, keep your message focused on why you would like to talk with this person, and/or what information you are hoping to exchange. ("Planning your approach to each party in the introduction" earlier in this chapter has advice about writing to an intended recipient that applies to InMail messages as well.) At the bottom of Figure 5-5, you can see how many InMail credits you have; remember that you need at least one credit to send this message.

TIP

Be sure to proofread your message before sending it out. If you send a message with typos, it won't help your case at all.

5. **Click the Send button to send off your InMail.**

   Your recipient receives this InMail in her LinkedIn Inbox and can decide whether to accept it. (If she has configured LinkedIn to get immediate e-mails of her InMail messages, she will receive the InMail in her e-mail account Inbox as well.) If your message is accepted, it's up to the recipient to contact you in return. Be patient. While you're waiting, I recommend a game of Connect Four or Internet Chess.

Managing Introduction Requests

What if someone in your network is looking for your help to meet someone in your network? You can facilitate the introduction between your LinkedIn first–degree connections. Now that your reputation is on the line, too, you should spend some time thinking about and responding to any and all introduction requests that come your way.

You really have only two options for handling an introduction request:

>> Accept it by sending a message to both the person requesting the introduction and the party it's intended for, so they can communicate directly with each other.

>> Decline it (politely!).

I cover these two options in more detail in the following sections. However you decide to handle the request, keep these tips in mind:

>> **Act or reply quickly.** The reason why LinkedIn works so well is that people are active with their networks and build upon their profile by answering questions, meeting new people, or joining groups. When you get a message requesting an introduction, you should either act on it or respond to the person with the reason why you won't act on it. Ignoring it isn't a productive use of the LinkedIn system and makes you look very unprofessional.

>> **Don't be afraid to ask for clarification.** Sometimes you might need some-one to remind you exactly how you're connected with her. Hopefully, in the note you get from this person, she includes some reminder or thought that helps you place her, or you can see the information that LinkedIn keeps on both of you. If there's no information, don't be afraid to shoot back a message and ask for clarification or a gentle reminder.

>> **Read your friend's request before forwarding.** Chances are good that the person to whom you forward this request might come back to you and ask, "Hey, why did I get this?" or "What do you really think about this person?" If you don't know the details of your friend's request, the intended party might think you're a quick rubber-stamper who sends off stuff without offering to screen anything, and that lowers this person's impression of you. Knowing what your friend is requesting can help you decide how to promote and encourage the connection, perhaps by giving you an idea of how best to approach the intended party.

Accepting requests and forwarding the introduction

When you're ready to accept your friend's request and make the introduction, follow these steps:

1. **Click the Messages button in the top navigation bar. Bring up the message asking for the introduction.**

   This brings up your Inbox of messages, as shown in Figure 5-6. Look for the message where the person asks for the introduction, and click that message from the left-hand side to bring up the full message in the middle of the screen. In this example, I got a request from Troy Benton to be introduced to one of my contacts, Doug Tondro.

   Read the full text before acting on the request. Don't just skim it — you might miss an important detail.

REMEMBER

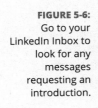

FIGURE 5-6:
Go to your
LinkedIn Inbox to
look for any
messages
requesting an
introduction.

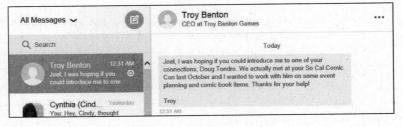

2. **If you decide to accept the request, use LinkedIn to search for the person he wants to meet. Bring up his profile, click the down arrow next to the Send a Message button, and then select Share Profile from the list provided to start the introduction.**

This brings up a newly created message, as shown in Figure 5-7. Here you can see boilerplate text indicating that I am sharing Doug Tondro's profile and offering to make an introduction.

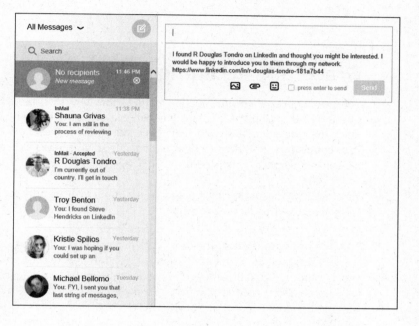

FIGURE 5-7:
Share someone's profile to make the introduction.

3. **In the subject line of the message you just created, type the name of the person requesting the introduction and the name of the person whom you're introducing.**

In this example, since Troy asked to meet Doug Tondro, and I'm sharing Doug's profile, I enter Troy's and Doug's names into the subject line so they each receive a copy of this message. I then click inside the message box to edit the request so the person receiving the introduction request (Doug) understands why I'm sending this message, as shown in Figure 5-8.

4. **Click the Send button to send the request.**

In this case, both Troy Benton and Doug Tondro will receive a LinkedIn message from me with the ability for them to see each other's profile. Troy will not be able to send Doug a direct e-mail, and Doug can decide whether to reach out to Troy and form a connection by sending Troy an invitation.

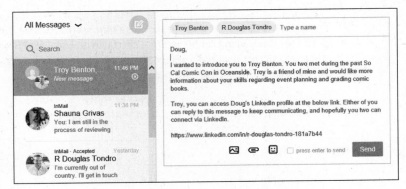

FIGURE 5-8:
Read the
introduction
request from
your contact.

Gracefully declining requests

You might receive an introduction request that you just don't feel comfortable sending to the recipient. Perhaps you don't know enough about your contact who made the request, or you're unclear about that person's true motivations. Or maybe your connection with the recipient isn't at the stage where you feel you can introduce other people to this person.

Whatever the reason, the best response is simply to gracefully decline the request. Here are some tips on how to respond:

>> **It's not you, it's me.** The most common way to decline is to simply inform the initial contact that you're not that deeply connected with the intended recipient, and you really don't feel comfortable passing on a request to someone who isn't a strong contact. Often, you might have first-degree connections in your network who are "weak links" or people with whom you're acquainted but aren't particularly close to or tight with.

>> **The recipient doesn't respond well to this approach.** You can respond that you know the intended recipient, and you know what she's going to say, either from past requests or other experiences with that person. Because you know or feel that the intended recipient wouldn't be interested, you would rather not waste anyone's time in sending the request.

>> **I just don't feel comfortable passing along the request.** Be honest and simply state that you don't feel right passing on the request you've received. After all, if the original contact doesn't understand your hesitation, he'll probably keep asking, and LinkedIn will want you to follow up on any unresolved introduction. Just as in life, honesty is usually the best policy.

>> **I think your request needs work.** Because you're vouching for this person, you don't want to pass along a shoddy or questionable request that could reflect badly on you. In this case, simply respond that you think the request needs to be reworded or clarified, and offer concrete suggestions on what should be said as well as what requests you feel comfortable forwarding.

When you're ready to decline the request, simply click Reply on the LinkedIn message and let the person requesting the introduction know your reasons for not acting on his request. The person asking for the introduction will see your response in his LinkedIn Inbox, and depending on his preferences, his e-mail account as well, and he can decide how to proceed once you've notified him.

Chapter 6

Growing Your Network

Maybe by now, you've signed on to LinkedIn, created your profile, searched through the network, and started inviting people to connect to you — and you're wondering, what's next? You certainly shouldn't be sitting around on your hands, waiting for responses to your invitations. LinkedIn is designed to open doors to opportunities using the professional relationships you already have (and, with luck, by creating new ones). The best use of it, therefore, is to capture as much of your professional network as possible in the form of first-degree connections to your LinkedIn network so that you can discover those inside leads as well as those friends of friends who can help you.

In this chapter, I discuss how you can grow your LinkedIn network and offer some guidelines to keep in mind when growing your network. I also cover various search tools for you to use to stay on top of LinkedIn's growing membership and how others may relate to you.

Of course, to expand your network, you need to know how to send invitations as well as how to attract LinkedIn members and your contacts who haven't yet taken the plunge into LinkedIn membership. I cover all that here, too. And finally, this chapter helps you deal with the etiquette of accepting or declining invitations that you receive, and shows you how to remove connections that you no longer want to keep in your network.

REMEMBER

An *invitation* is when you invite a colleague or friend of yours to join LinkedIn and stay connected to you as part of your network. An *introduction* is when you ask a first-degree connection to introduce you to one of her connections so you can get to know that person better. I cover the concept of introductions through messaging in more depth in Chapter 5, while invitations are covered right here.

Building a Meaningful Network

When you build a house, you start with a set of blueprints. When you start an organization, you usually have some sort of mission statement or guiding principles. Likewise, when you start to grow your LinkedIn network, you should keep in mind some of the keys to having and growing your own professional network. These guiding principles help decide who to invite to your network, who to search for and introduce yourself to, and how much time to spend on LinkedIn.

Undoubtedly, you've heard of the highly popular social networking sites Facebook and Twitter. LinkedIn is different from these sites because it focuses on business networking in a professional manner rather than encouraging users to post pictures of their latest beach party or tweet their latest status update. The best use of LinkedIn involves maintaining a professional network of connections, not sending someone an Event invitation or game request.

That said, you'll find variety in the types of networks that people maintain on LinkedIn, and much of that has to do with each person's definition of a meaningful network:

>> **Quality versus quantity:** As I mention in Chapter 1, some people use LinkedIn with the goal of gaining the highest number of connections possible, thereby emphasizing quantity over the quality of their LinkedIn connections. Those people are typically referred to as LinkedIn open networkers (LIONs). At the other end of the spectrum are people who use LinkedIn only to keep their closest, most tightly knit connections together without striving to enlarge their network. Most people fall somewhere in between these two aims, and the question of whether you're after quality or quantity is something to keep in

mind every time you look to invite someone to join your network. LinkedIn strongly recommends connecting only with people you know, so its advice is to stick to quality connections. Here are some questions to ask yourself to help you figure out your purpose. Are you looking to

- Manage a network of *only* people you personally know?

- Manage a network of people you know or who might help you find new opportunities in a specific industry?

- Promote your business or expand your professional opportunities?

- Maximize your chances of being able to reach someone with a new opportunity or job offering, regardless of personal interaction?

» **Depth versus breadth:** Some people want to focus on building a network of only the most relevant or new connections — people from their current job or industry who could play a role in one's professional development in that particular industry. Other people like to include a wide diversity of connections that include anyone they have ever professionally interacted with, whether through work, education, or any kind of group or association, in hopes that anyone who knows them at all can potentially lead to future opportunities. For these LinkedIn users, it doesn't matter that most of the people in their network don't know 99 percent of their other connections. Most people fall somewhere in between these two poles but lean toward including more people in their network. Here are some questions to keep in mind regarding this question. Do you want to

- Build or maintain a specific in-depth network of thought leaders regarding one topic, job, or industry?

- Build a broad network of connections that can help you with different aspects of your career or professional life?

- Add only people to your network who may offer an immediate benefit to some aspect of your professional life?

- Add a professional contact now and figure out later how that person might fit with your long-term goals?

» **Strong versus weak link:** I'm not referring to the game show *The Weakest Link*, but rather to the strength of your connection with someone. Beyond the issue of quality versus quantity, you'll want to keep differing levels of quality in mind. Some people invite someone after meeting him once at a cocktail party, hoping to strengthen the link as time goes on. Others work to create strong links first and then invite those people to connect on LinkedIn afterward. This issue comes down to how much you want LinkedIn itself to play a role in your business network's development. Do you see your LinkedIn network as a work in progress or as a virtual room in which to gather only your closest allies? Here are some questions to keep in mind:

- What level of interaction needs to have occurred for you to feel comfortable asking someone to connect with you on LinkedIn? A face-to-face meeting? Phone conversations only? A stream of e-mails?

- What length of time do you need to know someone before you feel that you can connect with that person? Or, does time matter less if you have had a high-quality interaction just once?

- Does membership in a specific group or association count as a good enough reference for you to add someone to your network? (For example, say you met someone briefly only once, but he is a school alum: Does that tie serve as a sufficient reference?)

>> **Specific versus general goals:** Some people like to maintain a strong network of people mainly to talk about work and job-related issues. Other people like to discuss all matters relating to their network, whether it's professional, personal, or social. Most people fall somewhere in between, and herein lies what I mean by the "purpose" of your network. Do you want to simply catalog your entire network, regardless of industry, because LinkedIn will act as your complete contact management system and because you can use LinkedIn to reach different parts of your network at varying times? Or do you want to focus your LinkedIn network on a specific goal, using your profile to attract and retain the "right kind" of contact that furthers that goal? Here are some more questions to ask yourself:

- Do you have any requirements in mind for someone before you add him to your network? That is, are you looking to invite only people with certain qualities or experience?

- Does the way you know or met someone influence your decision to connect to that person on LinkedIn?

- What information do you need to know about someone before you want to add him to your network?

TIP

By the way, this isn't a quiz — there is no one right answer to any of these questions. You decide what you want to accomplish through your LinkedIn network, and how you want to go from there. Also keep in mind that although you might start LinkedIn with one goal in mind, as with most other things in life, your usage and experience might shift you to a different way of using the site. If that happens, just go with it, as long as it fits with your current goals.

After you establish why you want to link to other people, you can start looking for and reaching out to those people. In the next section, I point you to a number of linking strategies that can help you reach your goals for your network. When you start on LinkedIn, completing your profile (see Chapter 3) helps you get your first round of connections, and you're prompted to enter whatever names you can remember to offer an invitation for them to connect with you. Now you're ready to generate your next round of connections, and to get into the habit of making this a continual process as you use the site.

Checking for LinkedIn Members

When you fill out your LinkedIn profile, you create an opportunity to check for colleagues and classmates as well as import any potential contact and invite that person to connect with you and stay in touch using LinkedIn. However, that search happens only after you define your profile (and when you update or add to your profile). After that, it's up to you to routinely check the LinkedIn network to look for new members on the site who might want to connect with you or with whom you might want to connect. Fortunately, LinkedIn provides a few tools that help you quickly scan the system to see whether a recently joined member is a past colleague or classmate of yours. In addition, it never hurts to use your friends to check for new members, as I discuss in a little bit.

Finding newly added colleagues

If you've worked at least one job in a medium-size or large company, you're probably familiar with the concept of the farewell lunch. The staff goes out to lunch, reminiscences about the good old days, and wishes the departing employee well as that person gives out her e-mail address and phone number, and pledges to keep in touch. But as time goes on, jobs change, people move around, and it's easy to lose touch with that co-worker. Thankfully, LinkedIn allows you to stay connected regardless of moves.

REMEMBER

Sometimes people you've fallen out of contact with have joined LinkedIn since the last time you checked, so do an occasional search to see whether you know any newly added colleagues.

When you want to search for colleagues (and add them to your network, if you choose), follow these steps:

1. **While logged in to your LinkedIn account, go to** www.linkedin.com/people/reconnect?posID=0.

2. **Pick an employer (current or past) from the list.**

   If there are no new connections, you see the message, "Sorry, we couldn't find any colleagues at Company X for you." Otherwise, you see potential new connections, as shown in Figure 6-1.

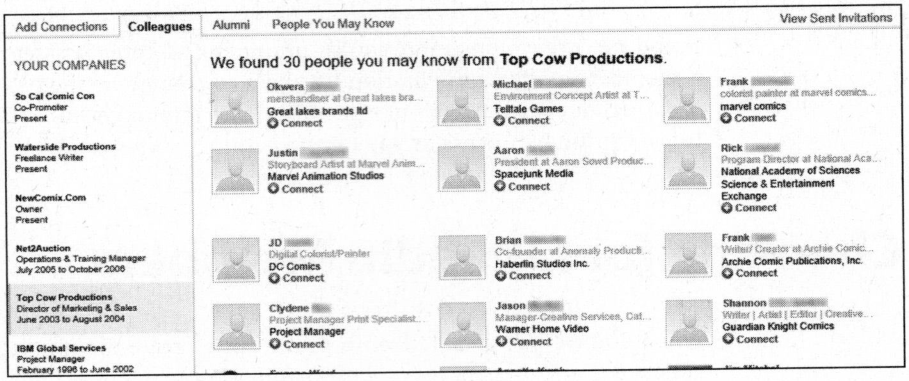

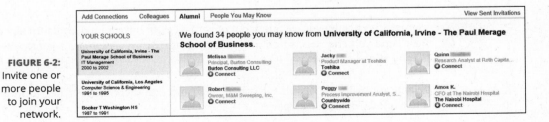

FIGURE 6-1:
The Colleagues window shows whether former colleagues are on LinkedIn.

3. **Go through the list of names to see names you recognize or wish to connect with via LinkedIn.**

   Click a name to see the person's profile for more information. If you want to invite someone to your network, you could click the Connect link below the name to have LinkedIn send that person an automatic invitation. The screen will update and you'll see that name disappear from the list.

TIP

   I encourage you to click the person's name, go to his profile, and then click the Connect button, so you can add a personal note with your invitation to help the contact remember who you are.

4. **Check other employers to see if there are any new colleagues available.**

   You can repeat the process by clicking each employer from the list provided. You can also click the Alumni tab and review the list of schools you attended to see any newly added classmates, as shown in Figure 6-2. The next section talks about another alumni function to find classmates.

FIGURE 6-2:
Invite one or more people to join your network.

Finding classmates

No matter how much time goes by since I graduated from college, I still remember my school years well. I met a lot of cool and interesting people, folks I wanted to stay in contact with because of common goals, interests, or experiences. As time progressed and people moved on to new lives after graduation, it was all too easy to lose touch and not be able to reconnect.

Through LinkedIn, though, you can reconnect with former classmates and maintain that tie through your network, no matter where anyone moves on to. For you to find them to begin with, of course, your former classmates have to properly list their dates of receiving education. And, just as with the search for former colleagues, it's important to do an occasional search to see what classmates joined LinkedIn.

To search for classmates — and to add them to your network, if you want —follow these steps:

1. **While logged in to your LinkedIn account, hover your mouse over the Connections link from the top navigation bar, then click the Find Alumni link from the drop-down list that appears.**

2. **In the screen that appears, filter the results for a better list.**

   The Students & Alumni window (for your most recent Education entry) appears, as shown in Figure 6-3, if you've prefilled in at least one educational institution. You can click any of the classifications, like "Where they live" or "Where they work" to add extra filters and get a more precise list. You can also change the years of attendance in the boxes provided to see a different set of candidates, or search by a specific graduation date. If the screen is blank, you haven't yet added any education entries to your profile. (I discuss how to add education information to your profile in Chapter 3.)

FIGURE 6-3: The schools you identified in your profile appear in the Students & Alumni window.

3. **Look over the list of potential classmates and connect with any people you recognize.**

   You can always click the name of the classmate to see her profile first, or just click the Connect link below the name to send an invitation to connect. If there are any shared connections, you can hover your mouse over the connection symbol and number next to their picture to see what connections you have in common.

TIP

   Before you invite people, click their name to read their profiles and see what they've been doing. Why ask them what they've been doing when you can read it for yourself? By doing your homework first, your invitation will sound more natural and be more likely to be accepted.

4. **Repeat the process for other schools by clicking the Change University button, as shown in Figure 6-4, and selecting another school from your educational history.**

   When you select a new school, you see the same screen as shown in Figure 6-3, but for the newly selected school. You can filter those results and invite whomever you recognize.

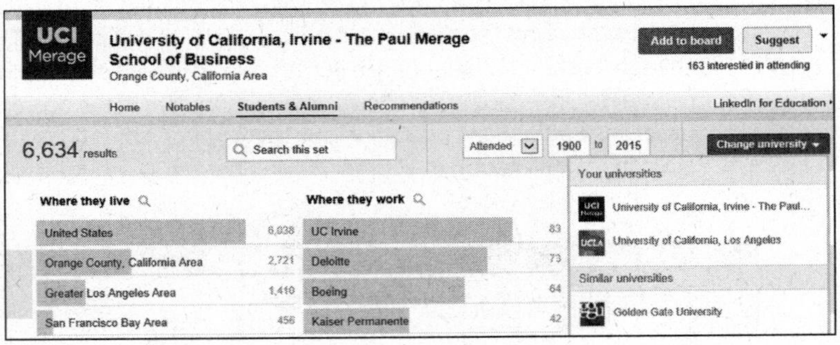

FIGURE 6-4:
Check for classmates from other schools you attended.

TIP

I cover more about sending invitations in "Sending Connection Requests," later in this chapter.

Using the People You May Know feature

One of the most common ways for you to increase your network is by using LinkedIn's functionality and suggestion system that it calls "People You May Know." Given all the data that LinkedIn imports and the global network it maintains, LinkedIn can use people's profile data, e-mail imports, common experience or education, and LinkedIn activity or other commonalities to help predict who may be in the same network with you.

The People You May Know feature exists in several places. A section of your LinkedIn home page news feed is dedicated to it, as well as the top section of your LinkedIn Connections page (as shown in Figure 6-5). As you click Connect for one person on your Connections page, LinkedIn will update that spot with a new potential connection for you to consider.

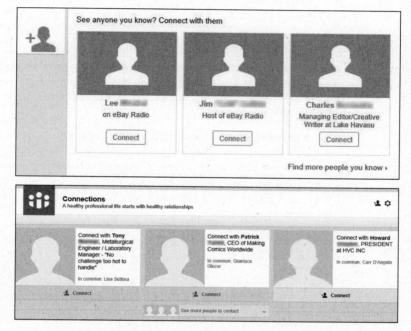

The most useful page for using this feature is the dedicated People You May Know page, which you can get to from the links in the previously described sections, or by hovering your mouse over My Network from the top navigational bar, then clicking on People You May Know. As you scroll down the page (as shown in Figure 6-6), LinkedIn will automatically update the page by adding rows of people you can send connection requests to via its system.

Here are some things to keep in mind as you review this section:

>> **Study the connections you have in common.** A little symbol and a number at the bottom right corner of someone's picture indicates that you and this person have shared first-degree connections. You can hover your mouse over that number to see a pop-up window of those connections. LinkedIn will

automatically sort people with more shared connections to the top of the page, assuming that if you have a lot of shared connections, perhaps that person belongs in your network.

>> **Some people have an Add to Network button.** If you see an e-mail address and the Add to Network button instead of the Connect button, that means this person is a contact that you imported to your LinkedIn account who isn't currently on LinkedIn. If you click the Add to Network button, LinkedIn will send that person an invitation to join LinkedIn, similar to the invitation you sent as an example in Chapter 2.

>> **You can spend a minute, an hour, or any time in between reviewing your connections.** This is not something you should dedicate large chunks of time to, but every once in a while, visit this page to see who you may want to connect with on LinkedIn.

>> **Visit a person's profile first and then click Connect.** I can't stress this enough. When you click Connect from the People You May Know page, LinkedIn sends that person a generic invitation. If you click her name and then click the Connect button, you will see a screen where you can write a customized message. (I cover this in detail in "Sending Connection Requests," later in this chapter.)

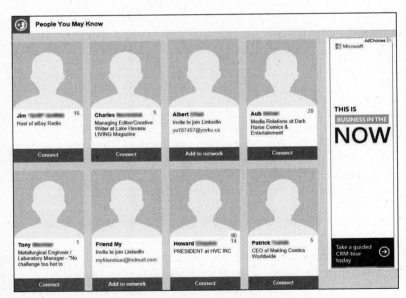

FIGURE 6-6:
Review the People You May Know page on LinkedIn.

Browsing your connections' networks

Although it's helpful for LinkedIn to help you search the network, sometimes nothing gives as good results as some good old-fashioned investigation. From time to time, I like to browse the network of one of my first-degree connections to see whether he has a contact that should be a part of my network. I don't recommend spending a lot of your time this way, but doing a "spot check" by picking a few friends at random can yield some nice results.

Why is this type of research effective? Lots of reasons, including these:

>> **You travel in the same circles.** If someone is a part of your network, you know that person from a past experience, whether you worked together, learned together, spoke at a conference together, or lived next door to each other. Whatever that experience was, you and this contact spent time with other people, so chances are you have shared connections — or, better yet, you will find people in that person's network who need to be a part of your network.

>> **You might find someone newly connected.** Say that you've already spent some time searching all your undergraduate alumni contacts and adding as many people as you could find. As time passes, someone new may connect to one of your friends.

One effective way to keep updated about who your connections have recently added is to review your Notifications. LinkedIn creates sections of the news feed to show you this information (see Figure 6-7).

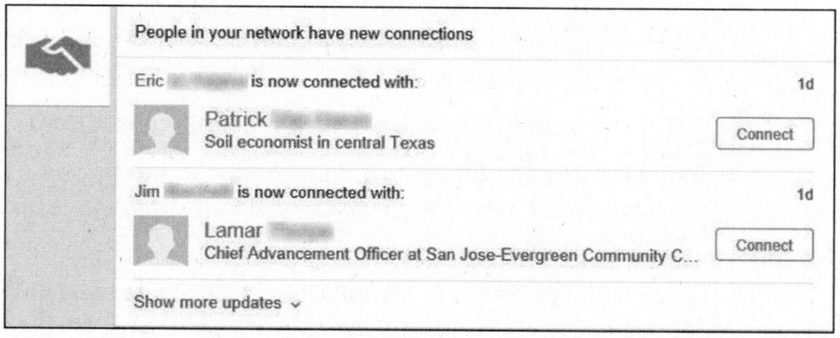

TIP

People in your network have new connections

Eric ▓▓▓▓▓ is now connected with: 1d

Patrick ▓▓▓▓▓
Soil economist in central Texas   [Connect]

Jim ▓▓▓▓▓ is now connected with: 1d

Lamar ▓▓▓▓▓
Chief Advancement Officer at San Jose-Evergreen Community C...   [Connect]

Show more updates ⌄

FIGURE 6-7:
See who your connections added to their network.

>> **You might recognize someone whose name you didn't fully remember.** Many of us have that contact who we feel we know well, have fun talking to, and consider more than just an acquaintance, but for some reason, we can't remember that person's last name. Then, when you search a common

contact's network and see the temporarily forgotten name and job title, you suddenly remember. Now you can invite that person to join your network. Another common experience is seeing the name and job title of a contact whose last name changed after marriage.

>> **You might see someone you've wanted to get to know better.** Have you ever watched a friend talking to someone who you wanted to add to your network? Maybe your friend already introduced you, so the other person knows your name, but you consider this person a casual acquaintance at best. When you see that person's name listed in your friend's LinkedIn network, you can take the opportunity to deepen that connection. Having a friend in common who can recommend you can help smooth the way.

WARNING

Looking through your friend's contacts list can be a cumbersome process if he has hundreds of contacts, so allow some time if you choose this technique.

To browse the network of one of your connections, follow these steps:

1. **Click the Connections link from the top navigation bar to bring up your network.**

2. **Click the name of a first-degree connection.**

   Alternatively, search for the name via the search box on the home page. Then, on the search results page, click the name you want.

   When perusing the person's profile, look for a link on a number above the word Connections, which should be next to the name and below the professional headline: something like "174 connections." If you see the number of connections but that word isn't hyperlinked, you can't proceed with this process because that person has chosen to make her connection list private. If that's the case, you need to select a different first-degree connection.

3. **Click the Connections link of the first-degree connection.**

   For the example in these steps, I picked a friend and associate, Michael Wellman, of the Comic Bug in Redondo Beach, California. His connection list is shown in Figure 6-8.

4. **Look through the list to see whether you'd like to send an invitation to anyone. If so, click the person's name to pull up his profile.**

   When I scan through Mike's list, I notice that his business partner, Jun Goeku, is in his network. I spoke with him several times about suggestions and projects I initiated with his store, so I clicked his name to bring up his profile, which is shown in Figure 6-9.

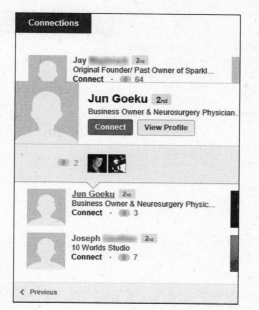

FIGURE 6-8:
You can look through your friend's network.

5. **Click the blue Connect button, which appears in the middle of the page.**

   The Invitation page appears, as shown in Figure 6-10.

6. **Select the option that best describes your connection to this person or provide the person's e-mail address.**

   In some cases, you might have to input the person's e-mail address to help prove that you actually know the person. In other cases, like in Figure 6-10, you simply have to indicate whether you're a colleague, classmate, business partner, or friend, or have another association with this person. It's a good idea to enter some text in the Include a Personal Note field. This text customizes your invitation, and you can use it to remind the person who you are and why you'd like to connect.

7. **Click the blue Send Invitation button.**

Presto! You're all done.

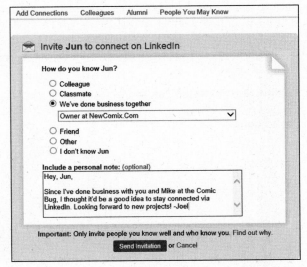

Jun Goeku `2nd`

Business Owner & Neurosurgery Physician Assistant

Torrance, California | Hospital & Health Care

Current   Self-employed, Los Angeles County Department of Human Resources
Education   Charles R. Drew University of Medicine and Science

Connect   **Send Jun InMail** ▾

133
connections

☆   in https://www.linkedin.com/in/jun-goeku-71272089

Background

Experience

Business Owner- The Comic Bug
Self-employed
May 2004 – Present (11 years 8 months) | Manhattan Beach, CA

Physician Assistant
Los Angeles County Department of Human Resources
April 1999 – Present (16 years 9 months)

D H R
Department of Human Resources

Education

Charles R. Drew University of Medicine and Science
Bachelor of Science (BSc), Allied Health Diagnostic, Intervention, and Treatment Professions
1997 – 1999

FIGURE 6-9:
Pull up the
person's profile
to add her to
your network.

Add Connections   Colleagues   Alumni   People You May Know

✉ Invite **Jun** to connect on LinkedIn

How do you know Jun?

○ Colleague
○ Classmate
◉ We've done business together
   | Owner at NewComix.Com   ▾ |

○ Friend
○ Other
○ I don't know Jun

Include a personal note: (optional)

Hey, Jun,

Since I've done business with you and Mike at the Comic
Bug, I thought it'd be a good idea to stay connected via
LinkedIn. Looking forward to new projects! -Joel

Important: Only invite people you know well and who know you. Find out why.

Send Invitation or Cancel

FIGURE 6-10:
Send a custom
invitation to your
new contact.

Sending Connection Requests

You can check out previous sections of this chapter to find out how to use LinkedIn to search the entire user network and find people you want to invite to join your personal network. In the following sections, I focus on sending out the invitation, including how to go about inviting people who haven't yet decided to join LinkedIn.

Sending requests to existing members

When you're on a LinkedIn page and spot the name of a member who you want to invite to your network, you can follow these steps to send that person a connection request:

1. **Click the person's name to go to his profile page.**

   You might find people to invite using one of the methods described in "Checking for LinkedIn Members," earlier in this chapter. You might also find them while doing an advanced people search, which I cover in Chapter 4. Figure 6-11 shows the profile page of a LinkedIn member.

2. **Click the blue Connect button to start the connection request.**

   The Invitation page appears, as shown in Figure 6-12.

3. **From the list of connection reasons, choose the option that best describes your relationship to this person.**

   You might have to input the person's e-mail address to help prove that you actually know the person. If you select the I Don't Know *Person's Name* option, LinkedIn denies the request, so keep that in mind. If you pick a category such as Colleague or Classmate, LinkedIn displays a drop-down list of options based on your profile. For example, if you pick Colleague, LinkedIn displays a drop-down list of your positions. You need to pick the position you held when you knew this person.

4. **Enter your invitation text in the Include a Personal Note field.**

   I highly recommend that you compose a custom invitation rather than use the standard text, "I'd like to add you to my professional network on LinkedIn." In my example in Figure 6-12, I remind the person how we recently met, acknowledge one of his achievements, and ask him to connect.

5. **Click the blue Send Invitation button.**

   You'll be notified by e-mail when the other party accepts your connection request.

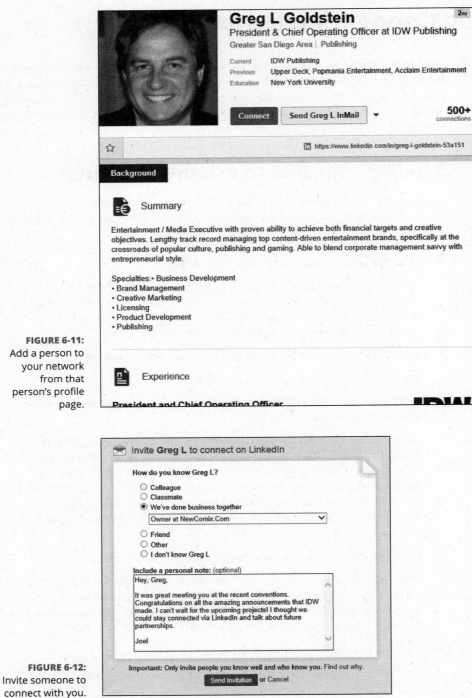

FIGURE 6-11:
Add a person to your network from that person's profile page.

FIGURE 6-12:
Invite someone to connect with you.

Why you shouldn't use canned invitations

You might be tempted to look at the "canned" invitation that LinkedIn displays when you go to the Invitation Request page, especially if you're having a rough or busy day, and just send off the invitation without adding to or replacing the canned invitation with some custom text. We all have things to do and goals to accomplish, so stopping to write a note for each invitation can grow tedious. However, it's becoming increasingly important, for the following reasons, to replace that text with something that speaks to the recipient:

>> **The other person might not remember you.** Quite simply, your recipient can take one look at your name, see no additional information in the note that accompanied it, and think, "Who is that guy (or gal)?" A few might click your name to read your profile and try to figure it out, but most people are busy and won't take the time to investigate. They are likely to ignore your request. Not good.

>> **The other person could report you as someone he doesn't know.** Having someone ignore your request isn't the worst possibility, though. Nope, the worst is being declined as unknown. Recipients of your invitation see an I Don't Know This Person button. If several people click this button from an invitation you sent, LinkedIn will consider you a spammer and will suspend you — and possibly even remove your profile and account from the site!

>> **You offer no motivation for a mutually beneficial relationship.** When people get an invitation request, they understand pretty clearly that you want something from them, whether it's access to them or to their network. If you've sent a canned invitation, they can't answer the question, "What is in it for me?" A canned invitation gives no motivation for or potential benefit of being connected to you. A custom note explaining that you'd love to swap resources or introduce that person to others is usually enough to encourage an acceptance.

>> **A canned invitation implies you don't care.** Some people will look at your canned invitation request and think, "This person doesn't have 30 to 60 seconds to write a quick note introducing herself? She must not think much of me." Worse, they may think, "This person just wants to increase her number of contacts to look more popular or to exploit my network." Either impression will quickly kill your chances of getting more connections.

Sending requests to nonmembers

Only members of LinkedIn can be part of anyone's network. Therefore, if you want to send a connection request to someone who hasn't yet joined LinkedIn, you must invite that person to create a LinkedIn account first. To do so, you can either send your invitee an e-mail directly, asking him to join, or you can use a LinkedIn function that generates the e-mail invitation that includes a link to join LinkedIn.

Either way, you need to have the nonmember's e-mail address, and you'll probably have to provide your invitee with some incentive by offering reasons to take advantage of LinkedIn and create an account. (I give you some tips for doing that in the next section.)

When you're ready to send your request using LinkedIn, follow these steps:

1. **Hover your mouse over the Connections link in the top navigation bar, and then click the Add Connections link from the drop-down list that appears.**

The Add Connections window appears.

2. **Click the Invite by Email button along the bottom right of the page.**

This brings up a text box, as shown in Figure 6-13. Fill in the e-mail addresses of the people you want to invite to LinkedIn in the box provided.

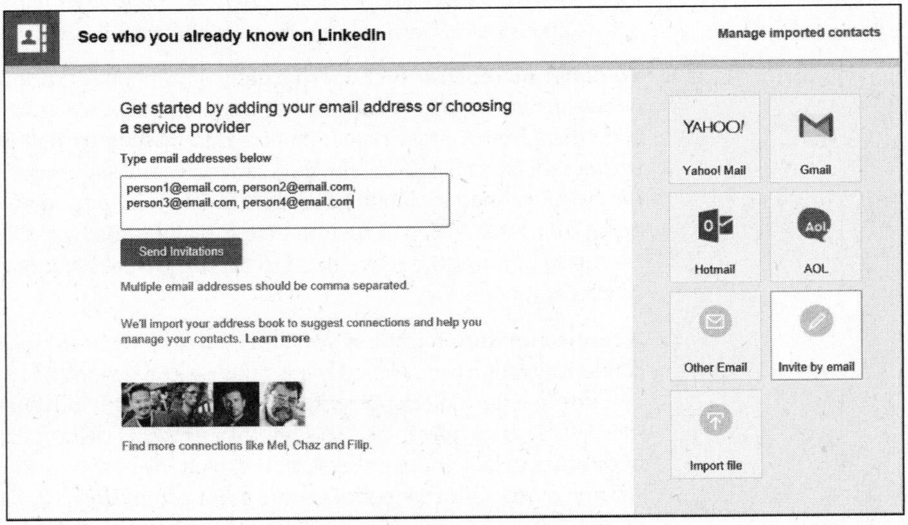

See who you already know on LinkedIn · Manage imported contacts

Get started by adding your email address or choosing a service provider

Type email addresses below

> person1@email.com, person2@email.com, person3@email.com, person4@email.com

Send Invitations

Multiple email addresses should be comma separated.

We'll import your address book to suggest connections and help you manage your contacts. Learn more

Find more connections like Mel, Chaz and Filip.

YAHOO! Yahoo! Mail · M Gmail · Hotmail · AOL · Other Email · Invite by email · Import file

FIGURE 6-13: Fill in the e-mail addresses of anyone you want to invite to join LinkedIn.

TIP

Because you can't personalize the invitation request to nonmembers, you may want to contact those people via e-mail or phone first to let them know this request is coming and encourage them to consider joining LinkedIn.

3. **Click the blue Send Invitations button.**

   You're returned to the Add Connections page, where you see a confirmation message. You can repeat the process at any time to invite additional people to join LinkedIn and be added to your network.

Communicating the value of joining LinkedIn

So you want to add some people to your LinkedIn network, but they haven't yet taken the plunge of signing up for the site. If you want them to accept your request by setting up their account, you might need to tout the value of LinkedIn to your contacts. After all, recommendations are one of the most powerful sales tools, which is why all types of businesses — from e-commerce stores and retail businesses to service directories and social networking websites — use recommendations so often. Offering to help them build their profile or use LinkedIn effectively wouldn't hurt either.

REMEMBER

As of this writing, LinkedIn does not allow you to personalize your invitation to nonmembers, so you will need to make this pitch either via e-mail or directly with the person you are recruiting.

So, how do you make the "sale"? (I use that term figuratively, of course. And as you know, a basic LinkedIn account is free — a feature that you should definitely not neglect to mention to your invitees!) If you send a super-long thesis on the merits of LinkedIn, it'll most likely be ignored. Sending a simple "C'mon! You know you wanna …" request may or may not work. (You know your friends better than me.) You could buy them a copy of this book, but that could get expensive. (But I would be thrilled! C'mon! You know you wanna …) The simplest way is to mention some of the benefits they could enjoy from joining the site:

>> **LinkedIn members always stay in touch with their connections.** If people you know move, change their e-mail addresses, or change jobs, you still have a live link to them via LinkedIn. You'll always be able to see their new e-mail addresses if you're connected (assuming that they provide it, of course).

>> **LinkedIn members can tap into their friends' networks for jobs or opportunities, now or later.** Although someone might not need a job now, she may eventually need help, so why not access thousands or even millions of potential leads? LinkedIn has hundreds of millions of members in all sorts of industries, and people have obtained consulting leads, contract jobs, new careers, and even startup venture capital or funding for a new film. After all, it's all about "who you know."

>> **LinkedIn can help you build your own brand.** LinkedIn members get a free profile page to build their online presence, and can link to up to three of their own websites, such as a blog, personal website, social media page, or e-commerce store. The search engines love LinkedIn pages, which have high page rankings — and this can only boost your online identity.

>> **LinkedIn can help you do all sorts of research.** You might need to know more about a company before an interview, or you're looking for a certain person to help your business, or you're curious what people's opinions would be regarding an idea you have. LinkedIn is a great resource in all these situations. You can use LinkedIn to get free advice and information, all from the comfort of your own computer.

>> **Employers are using LinkedIn every day.** Many employers now use LinkedIn to do due diligence on a job seeker by reviewing her LinkedIn profile before an interview. If you are not on LinkedIn, an employer may see this as a red flag and it could affect your chances of getting the job.

>> **A basic LinkedIn account is free, and joining LinkedIn is easy.** There are a lot of misconceptions that users have to pay a monthly fee or spend a lot of time updating their LinkedIn profiles. Simply remind people that joining is free, and after they set up their profiles, LinkedIn is designed to take up very little of their time to keep an active profile and to benefit from having an account.

Removing people from your network

The day might come when you feel you need to remove someone from your network. Perhaps you added the person in haste, or he repeatedly asks you for favors or introduction requests, or sends messages that you don't want to respond to. Not to worry — you're not doomed to suffer forever; simply remove the connection. When you do so, that person can no longer view your network or send you messages, unless he pays to send you an InMail message.

To remove a connection from your network, just follow these steps:

1. **While logged in to your LinkedIn account, click the Connections link from the top navigation bar to bring up your list of connections.**

2. **Scroll through the list to find the connection you wish to remove. When you hover your mouse over the connection's name, you see the Tag, Message, and More links appear below the person's name and headline, as shown in Figure 6-14.**

These links only appear when you hover your
mouse over someone's name.

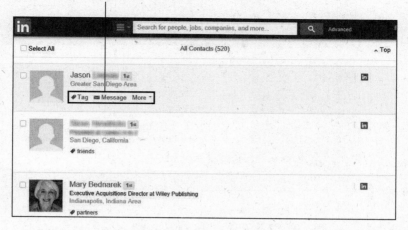

FIGURE 6-14:
Find the
connection you
wish to remove.

3. **Click the down arrow next to the More link, and then select Remove
Connection from the drop-down list that appears, as shown in Figure 6-15.**

   A pop-up box appears, warning you of what abilities you'll lose with this
   removal and asking you to confirm you want to remove the connection, as
   shown in Figure 6-16.

Click the Remove Connection link.

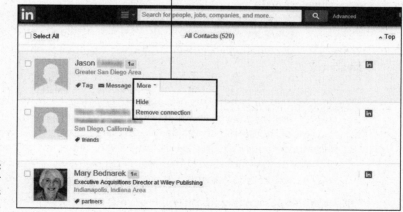

FIGURE 6-15:
Remove your
connection to this
person.

4. **Click the Remove button to remove this person from your network.**

   Your removed connection won't be notified of the removal.

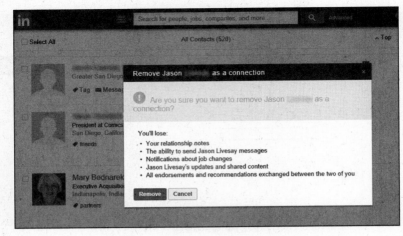

FIGURE 6-16:
Make sure you understand what you'll lose by removing this connection.

Accepting (or Gracefully Declining) Invitations

In this chapter, I talk a lot about how and why you might send invitations and add people to your network, and even cover what to do when you need to remove someone from your network. But what about the flip side of that coin — that is, being the invitee? In this section, I offer some guidance on what to do when you're faced with an invitation, and you have to decide whether to happily accept or gracefully decline it.

When you receive an invitation to join someone's network of connections and you're not sure whether to accept or decline the invitation, ask yourself these questions:

>> **How well do you know this person?** With any luck, the inviter has included a custom message clueing you in to who she is, in case you don't remember. You can, of course, click the name to read that person's profile, which usually helps trigger your memory. If you don't know or remember this person, you probably don't want to add him to your network just yet. If you do know him, you need to consider whether he's worth adding to your network.

>> **Does this person fit with the goals of your network?** As I mention early in this chapter, it's easier to put together a network when you've established a sense of the purpose you want it to serve. When you're looking at this invitation, simply ask yourself, "Does accepting this invitation help further my goals?"

>> **Is this someone with whom you want to communicate and include in your network?** If you don't like someone or don't want to do business with him, you should certainly not feel obligated to accept the invitation. Keep in mind that these people will have access to your network and can hit you up with introduction messages and recommendation requests (see Chapters 5 and 8, respectively).

If you're thinking of declining an invitation, you can simply ignore the invitation message or click the X button on the screen to ignore the invitation. Optionally, you can respond to the person who sent you the invitation. Some people prefer to respond in order to be professional or polite, for example. If you decide to send a response message, instead of just ignoring the invite, here are some tips to help you do so gracefully:

>> **Respond quickly.** If you wait to respond to the invitation and then decide to go ahead and decline the invite, the other person might be even more offended and confused. Respond quickly so that this issue isn't hanging over anyone's head.

>> **If necessary, ask for more information.** If you feel uncomfortable because you don't know the person well but want to consider the invitation before you decline, respond with a request for more information, such as, "I appreciate your interest, but I am having trouble placing our previous meetings. What is your specific interest in connecting with me on LinkedIn? Please let me know how we know each other and what your goals are for LinkedIn. Thanks again."

>> **Respond politely but with a firm no.** You can simply write something along the lines of, "Thank you for your interest; I appreciate your eagerness. Unfortunately, because I'm not familiar with you, I'm not interested in connecting with you on LinkedIn just yet." Then, if you want, you can spell out the terms in which you might be interested in connecting, such as if the opportunity ever arises to get to know the person better or if he is referred to you by a friend.

Chapter 7

Connecting with and Endorsing Your Network

et's look inward for a moment and think about the basic building block of your LinkedIn network — your relationship with each of your first-degree connections. Each of these relationships has a different identity, from the colleague you just met and added to your network, to a lifelong friend. LinkedIn wants to help you manage the qualities of that relationship, not just the fact that you know that person. This way, LinkedIn becomes more of your hub for managing your professional network and building your own brand and/or business.

In this chapter, I discuss how to properly use two of LinkedIn's important functions, Contacts and Endorsements. I start by discussing how LinkedIn displays and organizes your contacts, and then I walk you through how you can use Contacts as your own personal "Customer Relationship Management" (CRM) system to store notes, tags, and information about how you relate to each contact. Then, I shift gears and focus on LinkedIn Endorsements, where you can give and receive endorsements of others' skills, and how they differ from recommendations. You find out how to endorse your first-degree connections, review the endorsements they give you, and add those endorsements to your profile.

Interacting with Your Network with LinkedIn Contacts

The goal of LinkedIn Contacts is to give users "a smarter way to stay in touch." LinkedIn Contacts lets you sync your address books, e-mails, and calendar entries with your LinkedIn contact information, so LinkedIn can organize your communication with your colleagues and professional friends. By knowing all the information you keep in these various systems (address book, calendar, e-mail), LinkedIn Contacts can group and sort that information to show you a comprehensive history for each connection: how you met, all your LinkedIn conversations, any mutual friends, and all of their LinkedIn updates and activities. Finally, LinkedIn gives you the power to add and store your own private notes for each contact and schedule follow-up or regular interactions with those contacts.

LinkedIn Contacts is a tool to help you manage your professional relationships en masse while still being personal. Here are some of the advantages of using this system:

>> **It stores your contact history.** For each contact, LinkedIn shows you when you connected with that person, and logs each conversation with that person you did through LinkedIn. If you synced other systems (like your e-mail), LinkedIn Contacts shows you a chronological history of those conversations as well, even if you are not yet connected with that person on LinkedIn.

>> **It encourages new and ongoing communication.** Since professionals use LinkedIn to record their career accomplishments, from new jobs and promotions to receiving awards and certifications, LinkedIn Contacts notifies you when someone in your network has a career "event" (for example, a promotion or work anniversary) and encourages you to reach out and communicate, whether it's to say "Congrats" or connect with a common friend who just joined LinkedIn. Contacts also allows you to set reminders so you can follow up with someone at a later date. By encouraging regular communication, LinkedIn helps reduce the awkwardness when you need to reach out to a contact.

>> **It's available at your fingertips.** LinkedIn made sure that the Contacts feature is robust and available not just on its website, but also through a dedicated mobile application. You can download and install the LinkedIn Connected app for your Apple or Android OS system and have the same information at your fingertips, in case you're not in front of your computer.

>> **You can add your own notes.** After LinkedIn catalogs your past and current interactions, it allows you to record your own notes for each person, visible only to you. Your notes are stored on LinkedIn and available anytime. In addition, you can create tags for each contact, allowing you to create your own virtual "groups" of people that you can manage or change at any time.

Understanding how LinkedIn Contacts is structured

The good news is there is nothing to install or pay for in order to use LinkedIn Contacts. Any LinkedIn member, whether he has a free or paid account, sees the same LinkedIn Contacts screen and has access to all the LinkedIn Contacts functions. This capability is available from the moment you join LinkedIn and start adding connections, and it's free to sync any of your other accounts to LinkedIn to store additional information. As of this writing, LinkedIn is able to sync with major e-mail providers such as Gmail, Yahoo! Mail, and Outlook, along with address books like Google Contacts, Yahoo! Address Book, Outlook Address Book, and the iPhone Address Book. In addition, you can sync information with systems such as Evernote and TripIt.

To get started, you click the Connections link in the top navigation bar. You should see the Connections screen, as shown in Figure 7-1. Along the top of the screen, LinkedIn displays a tiled bar of contacts who have either reported a new event or potential new contacts of someone in your network. Each element in that bar has a suggested action, such as "Say Congrats" or "Connect," that you can click, which encourages some interaction with that person. You can also hover your mouse over any of these tiles and click the Skip link at the bottom right of each tile area to bring up another potential contact, or click the See More People to Contact link to bring up another row of contact tiles.

FIGURE 7-1: LinkedIn Connections keeps you in touch with your network.

Below that bar is your list of contacts, sorted by Recent Conversation by default. This way, you see the LinkedIn contacts you've most recently talked to, and next to each name, LinkedIn shows the length of time that has passed since your last interaction.

You can click the down arrow next to Sort By to change the sort order of your contacts. As of this writing, your choices for sorting are:

» **Recent Conversation**

» **First or Last Name** (based on each contact's first or last name)

» **New** (starting with the newest connections to your network or your Contacts system)

Next to the Sort By option is the Filter By option, which is useful if you want to see a certain subset of your contacts list. By default, it's set to All Contacts, but if you click the down arrow, you can set a filter to see only the list of contacts from a certain Company, Location, Job Title, Source, or self-created Tag, instead of the list of All Contacts.

To the right of the Filter By option is a Search link. When you click it, a text box appears that you can use to search your contact list. Simply type the desired first or last name in the box and then press Enter to run the search.

Using LinkedIn Contacts

When you're ready to use all of LinkedIn Contact's capabilities, follow these steps:

1. **From the LinkedIn Connections screen, click the wheel icon on the top right of your screen, as shown in Figure 7-2.**

   You are taken to the Connections settings page, as shown in Figure 7-3.

FIGURE 7-2:
Click the wheel
icon to set up
Connections.

Connections
A healthy professional life starts with healthy relationships

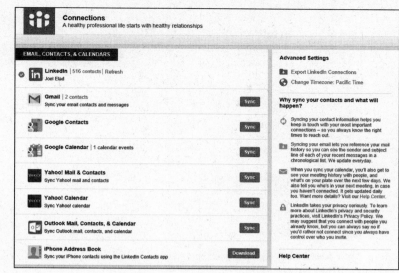

FIGURE 7-3:
Sync your
different
accounts with
LinkedIn.

2. **Click Sync next to the name of your e-mail system and/or address book to sync your e-mail messages with the LinkedIn system.**

   If you've got Gmail, Yahoo! Mail, or Outlook, click the appropriate blue Sync button to start the sync process. In this example, I sync my Gmail and Google accounts.

3. **Follow the prompts to sync your other accounts.**

   In this example, I am prompted to log into my Google account, as shown in Figure 7-4. After I do, I get a Permissions screen, as shown in Figure 7-5, where I click the blue Allow Access button to give LinkedIn the ability to sync with my Google account.

4. **Repeat Steps 2 and 3 for any other accounts you wish to sync with LinkedIn.**

   After each sync, you are returned to the LinkedIn Connections Settings page, where you can pick another e-mail, contacts, calendar, or application provider. In addition, you can import your Outlook, Yahoo! Mail, or Mac Address Book contacts by importing a .CSV (comma-separated values) file created by those applications.

REMEMBER

LinkedIn Contacts stores more information than just your first-degree connections. You can also add someone who's not yet a LinkedIn member or a LinkedIn member who is not yet directly connected to you.

FIGURE 7-4:
Log into your
other accounts.

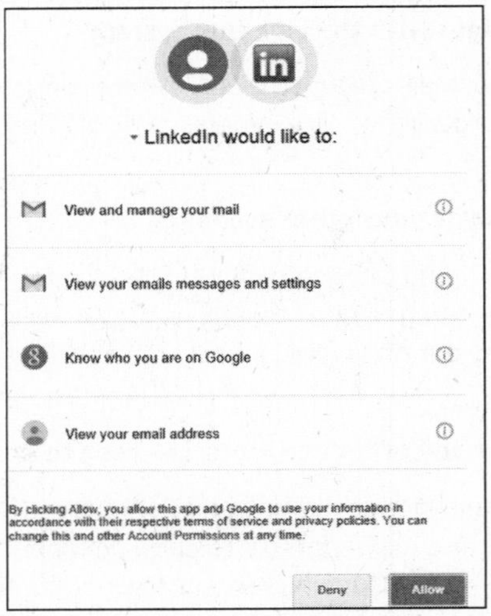

FIGURE 7-5:
Allow access for
LinkedIn to sync.

5. **From the Connections settings page, click the Connections link on the top navigation bar and pick an individual contact by clicking her name on the main Connections screen.**

   To use the Contacts functions for any particular first-degree connection, you need to pull up the person's profile information by clicking his name on the Connections screen. When you reach a contact's profile page, you should see a box with the Relationship and Contact Info tabs, as shown in Figure 7-6. LinkedIn has already populated this box with any LinkedIn messages you've sent to each other.

FIGURE 7-6:
LinkedIn shows
the Relationship
elements.

6. **(Optional) Click the Note link to add a note to yourself about this contact.**

   Think of the Note function as a way for you to record any thoughts about this contact, remind yourself of information that was mentioned in past conversations, or jot down any questions you need to ask this person. When you click the Note link, a text box opens where you can type the note, as shown in Figure 7-7. When you're done, click the blue Save button and the note is added to the log of communications for that contact, as shown in Figure 7-8.

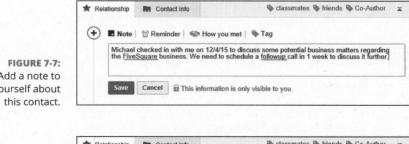

FIGURE 7-7:
Add a note to
yourself about
this contact.

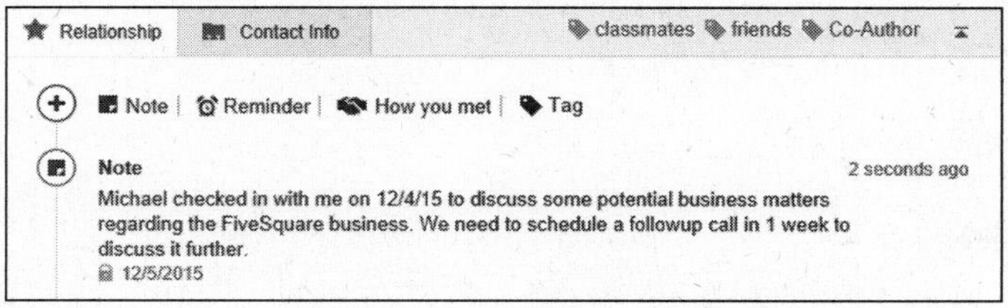

FIGURE 7-8:
The note is
recorded as part
of your communi-
cation with that
person.

7. **(Optional) Click the Reminder link to set up a reminder message from LinkedIn about this contact.**

When you click the Reminder link, a text box opens where you can type the subject of the reminder message that LinkedIn sends you, as shown in Figure 7-9. Using the radio buttons below that text box, decide when you want the reminder message sent to you. Click the blue Save button to create the reminder, and in the designated time frame, LinkedIn sends you a reminder message with the subject line you just entered.

8. **(Optional) Click the How You Met link to record how you met this contact.**

Clicking the How You Met link opens a text box where you can record the details of how you met this contact. When you click the blue Save button, LinkedIn creates a How You Met entry and puts it at the bottom of the Relationship box, as shown in Figure 7-10. This way, this information is always available to you.

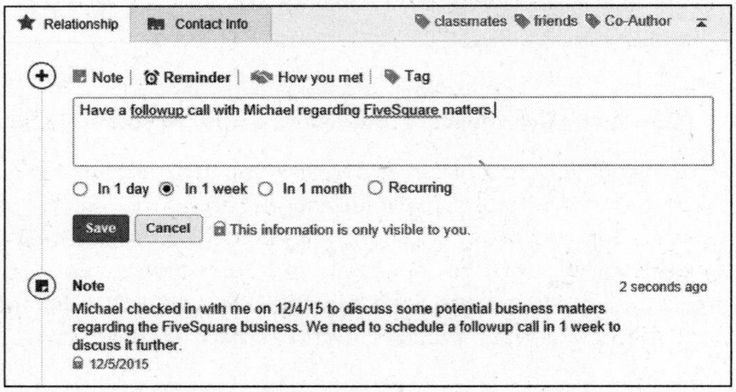

FIGURE 7-9:
Use LinkedIn to remind you of upcoming actions you wish to take for a particular contact.

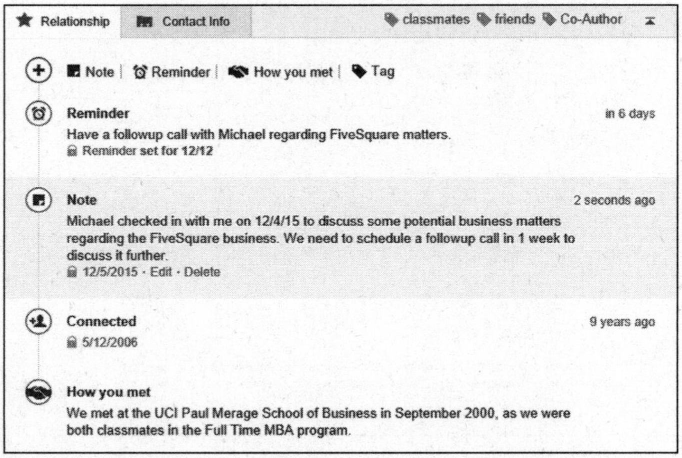

FIGURE 7-10:
Record the details of how you met this contact.

REMEMBER

The information you add with these functions is visible only to you and nobody else, so you can type these notes without the other person (or anybody else) seeing this information.

9. **(Optional) Click the Tag link to identify this contact with your own "category" name.**

   Let's say that you want to tag your LinkedIn connections with whom you shared a certain group in college, in case you want to send messages to only this group regarding a reunion or something similar. Click the Tag link to generate a drop-down list of tags to choose from. You can select the check box next to a pre-determined tag, like colleague or classmate, or click the Add a Tag link to generate a text box to write your own tag, as shown in Figure 7-11.

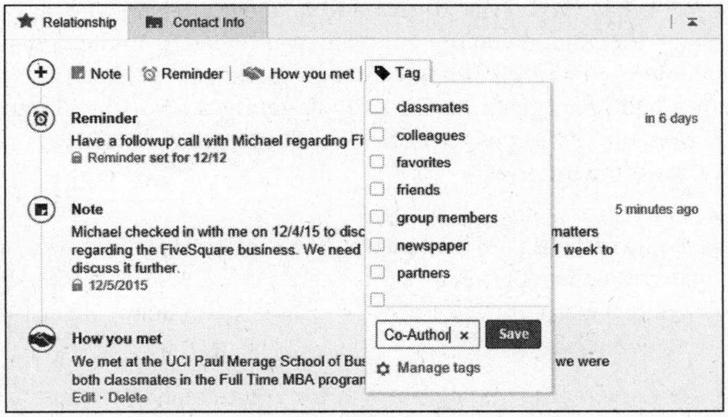

FIGURE 7-11:
Create your own tags to identify the different contacts in your network.

TIP

You can assign multiple tags to the same person — if the same person is involved in more than one category in your life, for example.

10. **Repeat Steps 6–9 for any contacts for whom you want to record any of this information.**

You can add this information whenever you want; it doesn't have to be done all at once. As you use LinkedIn, be aware that these options exist, especially when you're looking at someone's profile page. Make notes while they're still fresh in your mind, or after receiving an e-mail or notification from someone.

Giving and Receiving Endorsements on LinkedIn

Although many people believe "It's not what you know, it's who you know," which is one of the main reasons why LinkedIn is so valuable, many folks (recruiters, hiring managers, CEOs, investors, and more) are very interested in what you know. Logically, the people who know you best are the people in your network, who have observed your work firsthand and can speak to the quality and degree of your skill set. LinkedIn came up with an easier way for users to identify what skills they think their contacts have, and this system is called LinkedIn Endorsements.

Initially, LinkedIn offered this ability through its Recommendations feature (which I cover in Chapter 9), but it wanted to offer a way for users to identify skills in their contacts that was easier to use and less comprehensive (and time-consuming), and so, the Endorsements function was created. Endorsements had only been available a short time when, LinkedIn announced more than 2 billion endorsements had been given on its site, signaling a widespread adoption of this new functionality. So why is LinkedIn Endorsements important to understand and use? Here are a few reasons:

>> **Endorsements are an easier way to recognize someone's skill set.** While a recommendation can be a thorough and positive review of someone's job, endorsing a particular skill can show the community very quickly what skills someone possesses.

>> **Endorsements are a great way for you to highlight important skills.** When you're looking for a job or thinking about your career, having your key skill set show up as endorsements on your profile signals to recruiters and hiring managers that not only do you have the skills to do that job, but other people believe in your skills enough to endorse you. Just like with recommendations, people are more likely to believe other people's testimony about your skills than your own assertions.

>> **Endorsements are independent of any specific position.** When you write a recommendation for someone on LinkedIn, it is tied to one position. When you endorse someone's skill, it's tied to that person's entire profile, not just one job that was held any number of years ago.

>> **Endorsements are faster and more specific.** It's much easier and more precise for your contacts to endorse your specific skills than to write an entire recommendation. Many of your contacts can only speak to certain skills anyway, and with LinkedIn Endorsements, they can "give kudos with just one click."

WARNING

Because of the ease and speed of endorsing someone's skills, coupled with the fact that LinkedIn offers lots of prompts for you to endorse people's skills, there is a very real trap you need to avoid: blindly endorsing skills the other person may not possess (and others endorsing skills of yours they can't verify you possess). It's important that your endorsements are authentic, so put some thought into giving and managing your endorsements.

Each LinkedIn user can have up to 50 skills that can be endorsed by his network, and the top 10 endorsed skills appear on the person's profile page, under the Skills & Endorsements section, as shown in Figure 7-12. The profile pictures of the people who endorsed those skills appear to the right of each skill. While many of the skills that appear on the Endorsements list come from what you entered as your skills and experience on your profile, your contacts can add skills you may not have identified yet. (For example, in Figure 7-12, I was endorsed for SQL and Testing, which were skills I had not yet defined in my profile.)

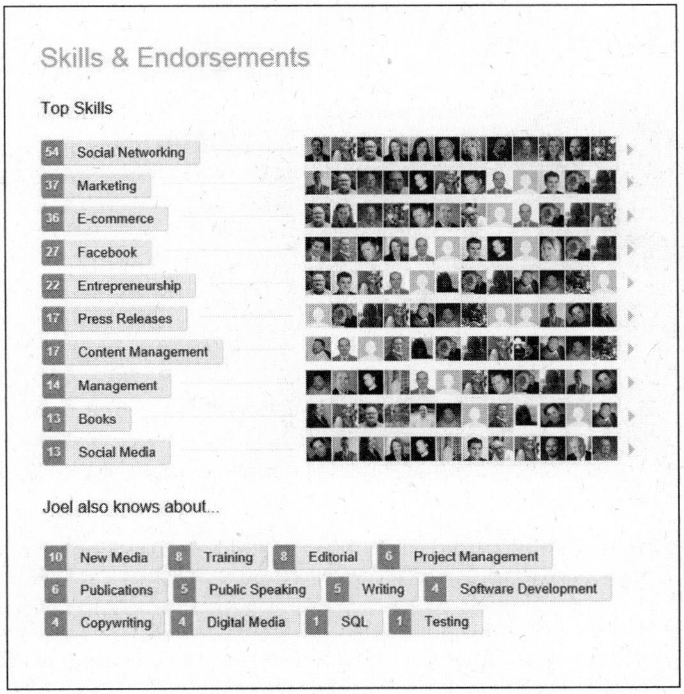

FIGURE 7-12: LinkedIn Skills & Endorsements show your network's beliefs in your skill set.

Endorsing someone on LinkedIn

As you use LinkedIn, you should notice that the system often prompts you to endorse your contacts for specific skills on their profile. LinkedIn built this into its system to make it as easy and automatic as possible to endorse your contacts without you looking for a particular screen or function.

When you are looking at any particular contact's profile, you may be presented with a box asking you to endorse multiple skills for that contact (as shown in Figure 7-13). You can also bring up this box by clicking the down arrow next to the Send a Message button and selecting Endorse.

FIGURE 7-13:
Endorse multiple skills for one contact.

When you see this box, you have several options:

>> You can click the yellow Endorse button to endorse all the skills listed in the box.

>> To remove an individual skill from the list before clicking Endorse, click the X next to the skill name.

>> To add an individual skill to the list before clicking Endorse, simply start typing in the Type Another Area of Expertise area. LinkedIn prompts you with possible skill names that you can click (as shown in Figure 7-14), or finish typing to add that skill to the list.

>> You can click the Skip button (or the X in the top right corner of the box) to stop the process. The box disappears from the screen.

FIGURE 7-14:
You can add skills to your endorsements list for this contact.

After you click Endorse or Skip, you might see a screen that gives you the option to endorse four different contacts for a particular skill, as shown in Figure 7-15. When you see this box, you have several options:

>> Click the View More button to see a new screen of four contacts with a skill to endorse for each one.

>> You can click individual Endorse links (below each profile picture) to select which of the four endorsements you want to give. Each time you click Endorse, a new skill and contact pops up in that box for you to consider.

>> You can click the X in the top right corner of each person's tile to close that option. That box is repopulated with a new contact and a new skill to endorse for that contact.

>> You can click the Close button (or the X in the top right corner of the big box) to stop the process.

At this point, the process is concluded for that particular contact. When you visit another contact's profile page, the process begins again for that contact.

TIP

Think carefully about which skills you can honestly endorse for another person, as you should only endorse skills you truly believe the other person has or that you have witnessed in action. You may also want to consider what skills the other person wants highlighted on her profile, which can be evident from the most endorsed skills she has currently. You should never feel compelled to endorse someone's skill just because LinkedIn prompts you for one particular skill.

FIGURE 7-15:
Endorse multiple contacts for the skills they possess.

If you want to give endorsements for someone's skills without being prompted, simply go to her profile page and scroll down to her Skills & Endorsements section, where you can see her identified skills. When you see an individual skill you want to endorse, hover your mouse over the + sign next to the skill name (as shown in Figure 7-16) and click the Endorse link that appears. You can repeat the process to endorse as many skills as you wish.

Any skills you have already endorsed appear with a blue filled in + sign next to the skill name, and your profile picture is underlined to the right of the skill name. If you want to remove a particular endorsement, hover your mouse over that + sign and click the Remove Endorsement link that appears.

REMEMBER

You can always go back and add more skill endorsements at any time, even after you initially endorse someone's skills.

Accepting endorsements on LinkedIn

LinkedIn does not automatically add any incoming endorsements to your profile; you must accept those endorsements first. When you receive an endorsement, it appears in your Notifications list at the top right corner of the LinkedIn screen (as shown in Figure 7-17), and you also receive an e-mail (depending on your e-mail settings) letting you know who endorsed you and for what skills.

FIGURE 7-16:
Select individual
skills to endorse
for a contact.

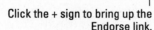

Click the + sign to bring up the
Endorse link.

FIGURE 7-17:
LinkedIn notifies
you when
someone
endorses
your skills!

The easiest way to accept (or reject) these endorsements is to edit your LinkedIn profile. Hover your mouse over the Profile link in the top navigation bar, and then click Edit Profile from the drop-down list that appears. You can also respond to the Notification message that LinkedIn sends you, which takes you to the Edit Profile screen, too. When your profile comes up for editing, you should see a box indicating that your connections have endorsed you for skills and expertise, as shown in Figure 7-18, and now you have to decide whether to add these endorsements to your profile.

FIGURE 7-18:
LinkedIn asks you
whether to add
new endorse-
ments to your
profile.

When you see this box, you have two options:

» Click the yellow Add to Profile button to add all the incoming endorsements to
  your profile. (You can manage your endorsements later, which I discuss in the
  next section.)

» Click the Skip button, or the X in the top right corner of the blue box, to ignore
  this and deal with it later.

If you decide to add these endorsements to your profile, LinkedIn offers you the
chance to give endorsements to people in your network (refer to Figure 7-15).

TIP

After you've accepted the endorsements, an optional step is to contact the person or
people that endorsed you with a quick note to say thanks. Not only does it give you
a valid reason to stay in touch, but it helps cultivate the relationship. You can also
visit the person's profile page and decide to reciprocate by endorsing some of his
skills, but staying in contact is a great networking chance that shouldn't be missed.

Managing your endorsements

Now that you've added endorsements to your profile, you may want to manage
them and make sure you are happy with the ones you've received being displayed
on your profile. Whenever you are ready to manage your endorsements, simply
follow these steps:

1. **Hover your mouse over the Profile link in the top navigation bar and select Edit Profile from the drop-down list that appears.**

   This allows you to edit your LinkedIn profile, which is necessary when you want to manage your skills listings and endorsements.

2. **Scroll down to the Skills & Endorsements section of your profile and click the Add Skill link either next to the Skills & Endorsements header or at the bottom of the section (see Figure 7-19).**

   This opens up a new section below the Skills & Endorsements header to help you manage your settings for Endorsements, as well as your skills listings and endorsements of those skills, as shown in Figure 7-20. There are two options: Add & Remove and Manage Endorsements. Since you have to click Add Skill to edit this section, you see the Add & Remove options first.

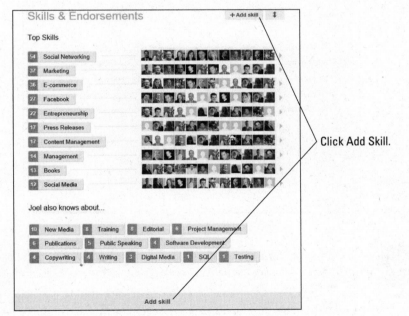

Click Add Skill.

FIGURE 7-19: Click the Add Skill link to edit the section.

3. **Review your settings to make sure you can receive endorsements and leave endorsements for other people. Then, if you want to add a skill to your list (so people can endorse it later) simply type in the name of the new skill and then click Add. When you're done, click the Save button to save your changes.**

   You must click the Save button before doing anything else, like managing your endorsements. Otherwise, any skills you add won't be saved to your profile.

   WARNING

As you start typing the name of your skill into What Are Your Areas of Expertise? text box, LinkedIn automatically prompts you with possible skill names based on other users' profiles, as shown in Figure 7-21. You can click the option that best matches what you want, or finish typing your own skill name.

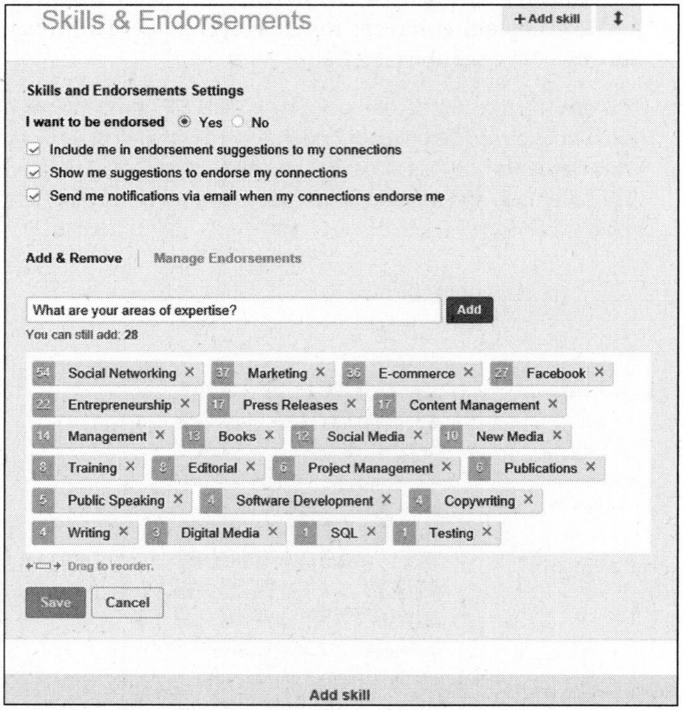

Skills & Endorsements

+ Add skill

Skills and Endorsements Settings

I want to be endorsed ◉ Yes ○ No

☑ Include me in endorsement suggestions to my connections
☑ Show me suggestions to endorse my connections
☑ Send me notifications via email when my connections endorse me

Add & Remove | Manage Endorsements

What are your areas of expertise?   **Add**
You can still add: 28

| 54 Social Networking × | 37 Marketing × | 30 E-commerce × | 27 Facebook × |

22 Entrepreneurship ×   17 Press Releases ×   17 Content Management ×
14 Management ×   13 Books ×   12 Social Media ×   10 New Media ×
8 Training ×   9 Editorial ×   6 Project Management ×   6 Publications ×
5 Public Speaking ×   4 Software Development ×   4 Copywriting ×
4 Writing ×   3 Digital Media ×   1 SQL ×   1 Testing ×

←▭→ Drag to reorder.

Save   Cancel

Add skill

FIGURE 7-20:
Add skills to be
endorsed later.

TIP

You don't have to accept what LinkedIn prompts you for, especially if you are trying to ensure the right keywords come up for your skills profile when other people review it.

4. **To manage your endorsements, click the Manage Endorsements link. Click the name of the skill that was endorsed and then click any person's name to deselect the check box, effectively hiding that person's endorsement from your profile.**

On the Manage Endorsements screen that appears, your skills are sorted by the number of endorsements you've received for each skill, from highest to lowest, as shown in Figure 7-22. Click the arrows next to the number of endorsements to scroll up and down the list of skills, and use the scroll bar on the right side to scroll through the names of your connections that endorsed the highlighted skill.

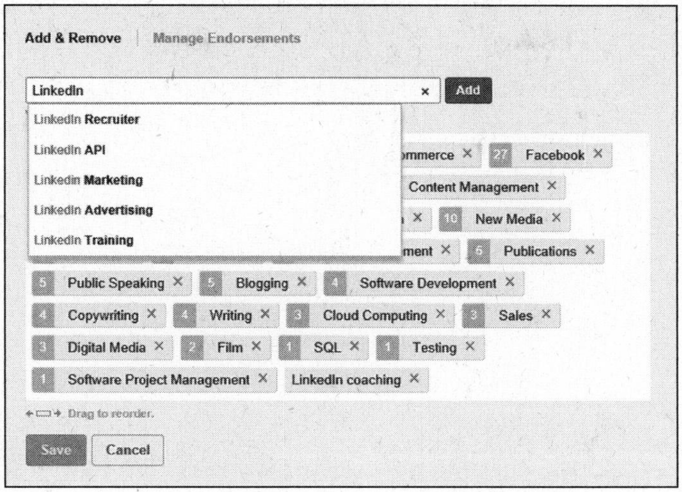

Add & Remove | Manage Endorsements

FIGURE 7-21:
LinkedIn prompts you for new skill names.

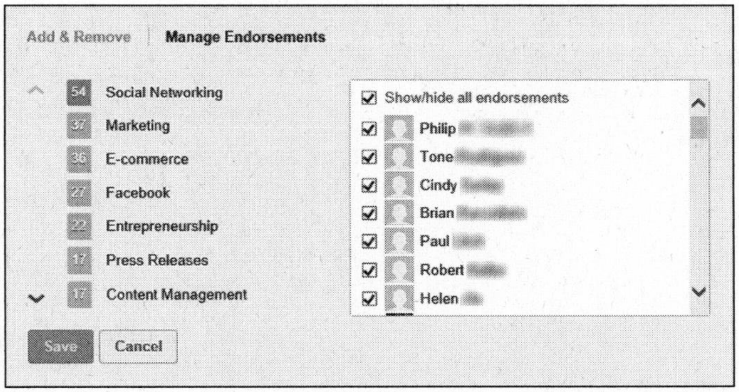

FIGURE 7-22:
You can hide someone's skill endorsement from appearing on your profile.

TIP

If you want to remove all the endorsements for any given skill, simply deselect the Show/Hide All Endorsements check box.

5. **Repeat Step 4 for any other endorsements you want to hide from your profile. When you're done, click the Save button to save your changes.**

After you finish with your changes, you see the Skills list again and the number of endorsements for your skills is updated based on the changes you made.

3

Growing and Managing Your Network

Chapter 8

Staying in the Know with LinkedIn Pulse

As far back as 1597, Sir Francis Bacon said that "Knowledge is power." Today's information age only emphasizes how true that point still is. We are constantly using the tools at our disposal to stay better informed and become better at what we do, for our career and our lives in general. LinkedIn is looking to support that goal for its members, beyond the core tools of networking and advertising your skills with your profile.

Enter LinkedIn Pulse. In 2013, LinkedIn purchased a popular news feed application called Pulse for $90 million and began to integrate the Pulse app into the overall LinkedIn website. Simply put, LinkedIn Pulse pulls together traditional and user-based news for its members to browse, share, and discuss with each other. The goal of LinkedIn Pulse is to create a news feed that's tailored to each of its members, which increases the likelihood that news is shared among this networked community.

In this chapter, I discuss how LinkedIn Pulse works within the website and how you can access it, either on a web browser (by going to `https://www.linkedin.com`) or on your mobile device with the LinkedIn Pulse app. I show you how you can customize your Pulse news feed to get the most use out of it, and how you can create your own "long-form" posts that can be carried on LinkedIn Pulse to other members, as well as how you can interact with any LinkedIn Pulse post.

Understanding LinkedIn Pulse

Imagine if you read a newspaper that only showed you articles that mattered to you. (For that matter, for many of you, imagine the days you might have read a newspaper.) Customized news is possible, and on LinkedIn, it's called LinkedIn Pulse.

All you have to do to bring up LinkedIn Pulse is hover your mouse over the Interests link in the top navigation bar and click Pulse from the drop-down list that appears. You will then see your LinkedIn Pulse home page, as shown in Figure 8-1.

TIP

You can also access LinkedIn Pulse by going straight to the web page: `https://www.linkedin.com/pulse/`.

FIGURE 8-1:
LinkedIn Pulse
shows you
various articles.

You will notice the basic structure of LinkedIn Pulse:

>> **Article headlines:** You will see the article headlines and author names along the left side of the screen; clicking any of these headlines brings the article into view in the middle of your screen.

>> **Author information:** Below every article's cover graphic is the author's name and LinkedIn headline. If you click the name, you are taken to the author's LinkedIn profile page (if he is a LinkedIn member) where you can learn more about the author and interact with him.

>> **Follow button:** To the right of the author's name is a Follow button. If you enjoy this author's article and feel that this type of news fits with what you want to read, click the Follow button to add that person's articles to your sources of news for LinkedIn Pulse.

>> **Publish a Post button:** When you are ready to add your own news to the mix, you would click this button and start your own post or article. I discuss the mechanics of this later in the chapter, in "Writing a Long-Form Post for LinkedIn."

>> **LinkedIn Pulse menu:** If you click the three lines next to the Pulse headline, you will bring up the LinkedIn Pulse menu, (see Figure 8-2), where you can choose from different channels of information to read. It's defaulted to "Top Posts," but you can focus your search on a particular subject, or click the Discover More link at the bottom of this menu to find other sources of information.

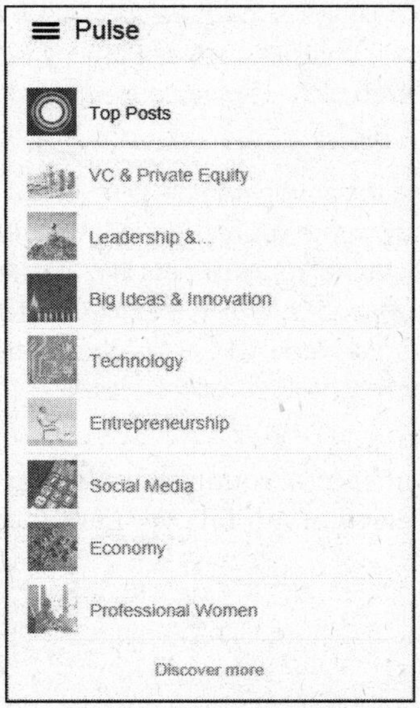

FIGURE 8-2:
Choose your own channel to read on LinkedIn Pulse.

As you scroll down and read an article on LinkedIn Pulse, once you get to the end of the article, you will see the author summary, and the Like and Comment links, similar to the links you see on your update messages. When you click these links, you can interact with the author and other readers. If you keep scrolling down, you will see the next article on your list.

Configuring LinkedIn Pulse

You may wonder how LinkedIn pulls together these relevant articles. The actual algorithm that LinkedIn uses to decide what articles are included on LinkedIn Pulse is not disclosed, but LinkedIn uses this algorithm plus additional variables to match the right content with the right professional. However, we do know of three clear sources that help determine each person's LinkedIn Pulse feed:

>> **Influencers:** Back in 2012, LinkedIn reached out to 500 prominent people around the world, from CEOs like Jack Welch and Richard Branson, to authors like Deepak Chopra, Guy Kawasaki, and Tony Robbins, to popular entrepreneurs like Mark Cuban, to share their wisdom and experience and generate discussions in the business community. These thought leaders' content was published on LinkedIn and given prominent placement. As LinkedIn noticed a high number of members viewing these Influencers posts, as well as Liking and Commenting on them, it decided to expand this program and add more Influencers to share their insights and experiences.

>> **Channels:** Articles that are generated can be categorized and collected by topic, whether it's aspects of your career such as Leadership & Management or Marketing & Advertising; large industries such as Banking & Finance, Big Data, or Social Media; or specialized niches such as Green Business or Customer Experience.

>> **Publishers:** When you're looking to catalog and present lots of publishable information, it helps to go directly to the source. LinkedIn identifies publishers of all shapes and sizes, from traditional news outlets like *The New York Times, The Wall Street Journal,* and *Time Magazine,* to services like Reuters, Yahoo! News, and even niche audiences like National Geographic, Entrepreneur Media, Harvard Business Review, or the TED Talks series.

When you initially set up your LinkedIn account (see Chapter 2) you may have been asked to pick some of these elements to follow, and those show up in your

Pulse feed. At any time, however, you can customize which of these sources you want to follow to add to the mix of articles you see on LinkedIn Pulse.

When you go to your Profile page and scroll down the page, you will find a section called Following (see Figure 8-3) that shows which news items, companies, and schools you are following. The news items in particular influence what shows up in your LinkedIn Pulse feed. When you're ready to change this list, click the Discover More link.

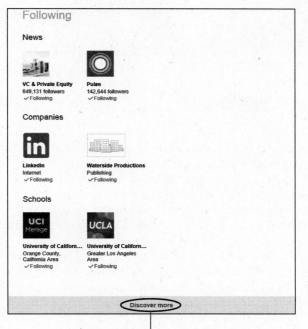

FIGURE 8-3:
See what you're
following on
LinkedIn.

Click this link to pick your news sources.

You'll be taken to the Discover More page, where you can pick which influencers, channels, or publishers you wish to follow on LinkedIn. The top of this page shows an assortment of these three elements called Recommended for You (see Figure 8-4), based on the information in your LinkedIn profile and how you've been interacting with LinkedIn up until now. Below the Recommended for You section, you will find rows of "tiles," or boxes of photos or logos, representing influencers, channels, and publishers you can follow.

FIGURE 8-4:
Discover more
people or
channels to
follow.

You can click any of these tiles to see their own influencer, channel, or publisher LinkedIn page and read the most recent set of articles by them, to help you figure out if this is a news source you wish to follow. As you hover your mouse over any Influencer tile, you will see a link appear with their most recent post on LinkedIn. Clicking the + sign at the top right corner of the tile indicates to LinkedIn that you wish to Follow this source; once you click it, the sign changes to a green check mark.

You can scroll through the screen and pick as many influencers, channels, or publishers as you wish to follow by simply clicking the + sign. If you change your mind, you can click the green check mark in the tile to change Follow to Unfollow and therefore "unsubscribe" from this source in your LinkedIn Pulse feed.

WARNING

As you decide which influencers, channels, or publishers to follow, keep in mind that if you simply click inside the tile and NOT the + or green check mark, you will be taken to their Pulse page and it will not affect your subscription to that source.

When you want to expand your options in each of the sections, simply click the See More link in between the sections (see Figure 8-5) and more rows of tiles for that section will appear of sources you can follow, along with a new See More link below these new rows. You can click the See More link multiple times, as LinkedIn has hundreds of sources in each of these categories, providing you with a rich set of sources with which to customize your news.

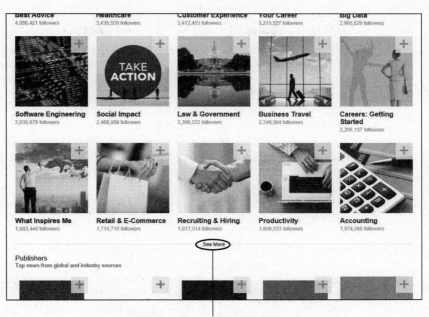

Expand your choices by clicking this link.

Enjoying LinkedIn Pulse on the Go

An important part of the LinkedIn Pulse experience can be found with its dedicated Pulse app, so you can read and interact with the news makers from your mobile device. Although you can use LinkedIn Pulse as a guest or as a LinkedIn member, I highly recommend logging in with your LinkedIn account, so the same content can be seen among all your devices. This way, the LinkedIn Pulse app will know which sources you are following to show you the appropriate content you want to view.

To get started, go to your iOS or Android store and search for "LinkedIn Pulse." Follow the instructions for your mobile device to install this app, and then launch the app to start using it.

WARNING

If you downloaded the original LinkedIn Pulse app before December 31, 2015, and didn't update it, starting it now will result in a black screen. You need to go back to the iOS or Android store to re-install LinkedIn Pulse to get it to work.

When you launch the LinkedIn app, be sure to Sign in with your LinkedIn account. After logging in, you will be presented with the main screen, with stories based on what you are following; what your first-degree connections are reading, sharing, and commenting on; as well as stories related to your current employer and/or industry. With the LinkedIn Pulse app, you will see more of a focus on stories from the previous 24 hours as opposed to older articles from your favorite news sources. The app will feature stories curated by LinkedIn employees, chosen for their context and business focus.

Unlike the desktop version, LinkedIn Pulse on the mobile app wants to learn what you like and don't like from your news source. As you go through each article presented to you on-screen, you can either "swipe right," or swipe your finger on the screen to the right, to indicate you want to save the article to read later, or "swipe left" to indicate you are not interested in having this story on your feed. LinkedIn uses the data from the "swipe left" stories to determine what not to show you in the future.

You can click your profile picture to bring up several tabs. Click the Activity tab to see the articles you have saved, shared, commented on, or sources you decided to follow or unfollow. Click the Saved tab (only visible once you save an article) to read through articles you decided to save by swiping right on the article initially. Click the Following tab to see the list of influencers, channels, and publishers you are following. If you tap the check mark icon, you will unfollow any of these sources.

REMEMBER

If you are logged into the Pulse app with your LinkedIn account, when you unfollow a source using the app, you will unfollow that source on your desktop version of LinkedIn Pulse as well.

You can click the Search icon on the top right of your screen and search through the various Pulse articles by entering keywords into the box provided. You can click the cog (wheel) at the top right of the screen to go to your Pulse settings. You can decide whether to set up Notifications, where messages from the app pop up alerting you to breaking news and new stories coming into your feed, as covered in the following section.

Setting Up Digest Notifications

One way to help ensure that you are always up to date on breaking news is to have the news delivered to you. Instead of the paperboy dropping off your customized newspaper on your doorstep, LinkedIn can send you a digest of your top news articles to your e-mail address.

When you are ready to set up this digest, follow these steps:

1. **Hover your mouse over your profile icon at the top right of any LinkedIn page. When the Account & Settings menu comes up, click the Manage link next to Privacy Settings.**

   This brings up the main settings page, as shown in Figure 8-6.

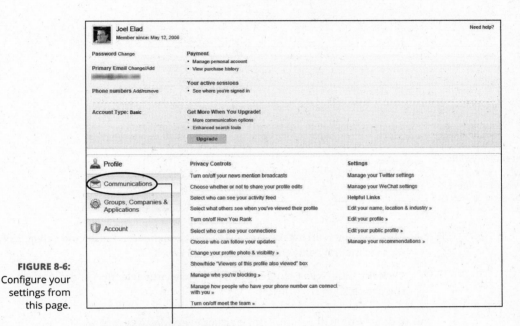

Click the Communications link.

FIGURE 8-6:
Configure your settings from this page.

2. **Click the Communications link on the left-hand side of the page.**

3. **Under the Emails and Notifications header, click the link for Set the Frequency of Emails.**

   This brings up the Email Frequency screen. From this screen, you can decide when and how frequently LinkedIn notifies you of actions related to your LinkedIn account.

4. **Click the pencil icon next to Updates and News to expand that section.**

   You see a number of options, as shown in Figure 8-7.

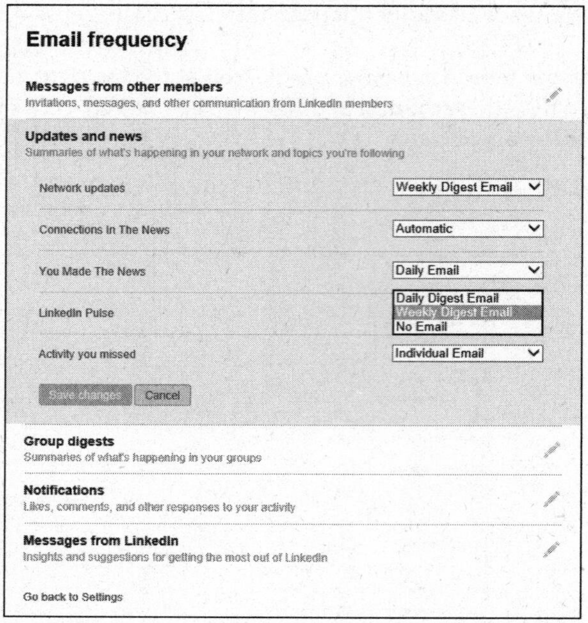

Email frequency

Messages from other members
Invitations, messages, and other communication from LinkedIn members

Updates and news
Summaries of what's happening in your network and topics you're following

Network updates   Weekly Digest Email ▾

Connections In The News   Automatic ▾

You Made The News   Daily Email ▾

LinkedIn Pulse   Daily Digest Email
                                Weekly Digest Email
                                No Email

Activity you missed   Individual Email ▾

[Save changes] [Cancel]

Group digests
Summaries of what's happening in your groups

Notifications
Likes, comments, and other responses to your activity

Messages from LinkedIn
Insights and suggestions for getting the most out of LinkedIn

Go back to Settings

FIGURE 8-7:
Pick the frequency with which you want to receive a digest of news stories.

5. **Click the down arrow for the option next to LinkedIn Pulse, and select Daily Digest Email, Weekly Digest Email, or No Email.**

6. **Click the blue Save Changes button to save your selection and complete the process.**

You're done! You will see an e-mail either every day or every week, based on your selection, giving you the top headlines and a link that will take you straight to your LinkedIn Pulse screen, so you can read more of what's happening in your world.

Writing a Long-Form Post for LinkedIn

Today, LinkedIn offers all members, whether they have a free or premium account, the opportunity to publish information that can reach their entire network, which LinkedIn calls a "long-form" post, or a "post" for short. The gives any LinkedIn member the ability to share useful information with the community at large. There are guidelines to prevent someone from spamming the network with purely promotional information or information that provides no value. LinkedIn catalogs all of its help pages for long-form posts, including its guidelines, on this web page: https://help.linkedin.com/app/answers/detail/a_id/47445/.

There are a couple of ways for you to publish a post. From your LinkedIn home page, you can click the Publish a Post link next to the Share an Update and Upload a Photo links. From the LinkedIn Pulse home page, you can click the Publish a Post button in the top right corner.

When you are ready to write your post, follow these steps:

1. **Click the Publish a Post link from either your home page or the LinkedIn Pulse home page.**

   This brings up the Your Posts page, as shown in Figure 8-8. Along the left side, you will see links for Your Posts and for Writing Ideas to help you come up with topics for your post.

2. **(Optional) Add an image to be associated with your article by clicking the Image icon.**

   LinkedIn allows you to upload an image that helps represent what your post is about. LinkedIn guidelines recommend using an image with a 700-by-400 pixel size for optimal viewing (see https://help.linkedin.com/app/answers/detail/a_id/52988 for details). When you click the Image icon, LinkedIn opens a window for you to find the image file on your computer and upload it to LinkedIn. You can also click the X in the top right corner of this box to remove the option of adding an image.

3. **Write your post headline in the Write Your Headline space.**

When you hover your mouse over the words "Write Your Headline," those words disappear and you can type in your own headline in the space provided. Think of the appropriate headline that captures the essence of your post with an appealing message that will encourage people to click and read it. Write a headline that would appeal to your target audience, and don't forget to use some of the appropriate keywords that'll be picked up by search engines and the human eye. You should save some of your keywords for the body of your post, which you will write next.

4. **Write your post in the window provided.**

You will notice a series of icons above the text area for your post, similar to a word processor like Microsoft Word, as shown in Figure 8-9. Think of this area as your publishing editor. You can copy and paste, or type your text directly into the publishing editor, then use the formatting buttons to format the text as you want it to appear on-screen.

Your Posts		Saved	Publish

Joel Elad
Author, LinkedIn for Dummies; Co-Promoter, So Cal Comic Con

This is the Headline to My Post

h1 h2 66 | **B** *I* U̶ T̶ | ⊟ ⊞ | ≡ ≡ | 🔗 📷 ▶ <>

Here is where you write the text for your post.

You can provide readable information in:

- Multiple
- Bullet
- Format

You can **Bold**, *Italicize*, or <u>Underline</u> your text in this editor.

FIGURE 8-9:
Write your post in the space provided.

TIP

You can add images, videos, presentations, tweets, podcasts, and other kinds of rich media to your post by clicking the < >, or Embed icon, from the row of buttons in your publishing editor.

There is no fixed minimum or maximum length to your posts, but if you want your post to be read and have an impact, you should pick a length that makes the point without becoming an actual novel in length. Daniel Roth wrote a great article for LinkedIn Pulse containing seven tips for writing a killer post, and when it came to length, he stated that "800–2,000 words was the sweet spot," but he also added that the demands of your content should dictate the length of your post, not what statistical data shows. (See more of his tips at `https://www.linkedin.com/pulse/20120906170105-29092-the-7-secrets-to-writing-killer-content-on-linkedin.`) Also, at the bottom of your post, be sure to write a brief biography (one or two sentences) of who you are, what you are doing, and how you can help other people. This can include links to your own website, blog, or even a call to action to gather leads of your own.

TIP

LinkedIn created an informative slide presentation of tips to help you publish a post on its site. You can access it by going to `www.slideshare.net/linkedin/everything-you-need-to-know-about-publishing-on-linkedin.`

5. **Create tags to assign topics to your post so it can be easily found.**

If you want your post to be associated with a specific topic or topics, you can create tags for your post. This way, LinkedIn and the reading public will know what topic(s) this post belongs to, and it will help LinkedIn's algorithms know when and where to display the post. At the bottom of the text area, click the Tag icon and start typing topic keywords. LinkedIn displays applicable tags and you can click the correct one to assign a tag, as shown in Figure 8-10. You can repeat the process by assigning more tags, but be careful: If you assign too many tags, they lose any sense of being a valuable identifier for your post.

6. **When you're ready, click the blue Publish button to publish your post.**

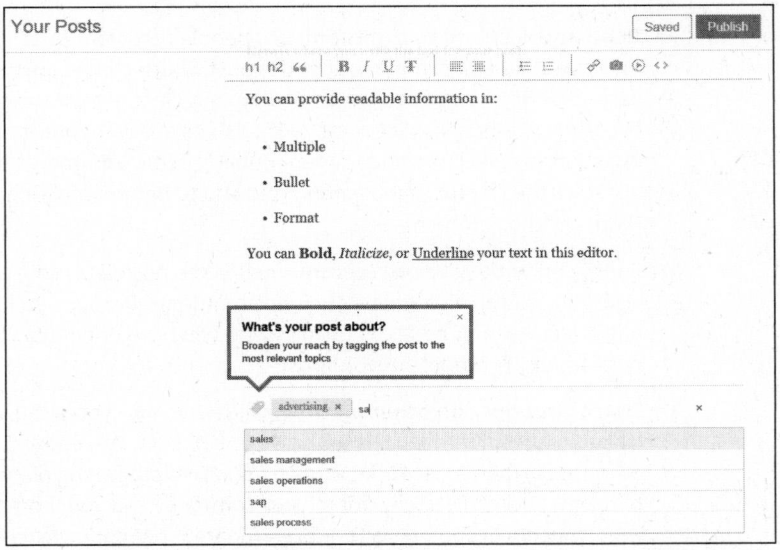

FIGURE 8-10: Create tags for your post to identify relevant topics.

Your Posts   Saved Publish

h1 h2 66   **B** *I* U T   ≡ ≡   ≔ ≔   𝒫 📷 ▶ <>

You can provide readable information in:

- Multiple

- Bullet

- Format

You can **Bold**, *Italicize*, or Underline your text in this editor.

What's your post about?
Broaden your reach by tagging the post to the most relevant topics

🏷 advertising × sa| ×

sales
sales management
sales operations
sap
sales process

That's it! LinkedIn publishes your post, and there will be a section on your LinkedIn profile, entitled Posts, that catalogs and displays your posts. Based on LinkedIn's algorithms, this post could show up in other people's LinkedIn Pulse, and your first-degree connections will see your post in their home page feed, as well as receive a notification that you have published a post.

REMEMBER

If you cannot complete your post in one sitting, click the Save (or Saved) button next to the Publish button. When you come back to this screen later, you will see your saved draft in the Your Posts section on the left side of the screen. As you write your post, you will see this button as Saved when LinkedIn automatically saves your work after a certain amount of time.

Managing Your Post Interactions

Once you click Publish, you may think your job is done, but it's only begun. As more and more people read your post, they can interact with the post and with you as the author. Here are some things to keep in mind after you publish a post:

>> **Monitor the statistics.** When you look at your post, you will see three key numbers: Views, Likes, and Comments. These represent how many people viewed your post, how many people clicked Like for your post, and how many comments were left for your post. As you publish more and more posts, you can start to judge the effectiveness of your posts by seeing which topics generate the most interest.

>> **Read and respond to comments.** As people read your post, they may be inspired to write a comment after the post, which can be anything from "I agree with this" to a question or a comment. On a regular basis, you should check the Comments section of your posts to see if anyone is asking you a question, and feel free to comment publicly in the Comments section. You can also click the link for that user and respond to her privately, depending on the nature of the comment.

>> **Follow up with your own comments.** As the post gets more and more visibility, you can also leave your own comments. Perhaps you want to share any effects of your post, or any follow-up you have done that could be relevant to the readers of your post.

>> **Share your post on other platforms.** Just because you wrote a post on LinkedIn does not mean it is exclusive to LinkedIn. You can share your post on other social media networks, and on your own publishing platforms, like a blog or website. If it's relevant to your company, and your company has its own LinkedIn Company page, you can share it on that page (see Chapter 15).

Chapter 9

Exploring the Power of Recommendations

Endorsements and testimonials have long been a mainstay of traditional marketing. But really, how much value is there in reading testimonials on someone's own website, like the following:

Maria is a great divorce attorney — I'd definitely use her again.
                                                    ELIZABETH T. LONDON

or

Jack is a fine lobbyist — a man of impeccable character.
                                                    EMANUEL R. SEATTLE

Without knowing who these people are, anyone reading the testimonials tends to be highly skeptical about them. At the very least, the reader wants to know that they're real people who have some degree of accountability for those endorsements.

The reader is looking for something called *social validation*. Basically, that's just a fancy-shmancy term meaning that a person feels better about his decision to conduct business with someone if other people in his extended network are pleased with that person's work. The reader knows that people are putting their own reputations at stake, even if just to a small degree, by making a public recommendation of another person.

As this chapter shows you, the LinkedIn Recommendations feature offers you a powerful tool for finding out more about the people you're considering doing business with, as well as a means to build your own reputation in a way that's publicly visible. I walk you through all the steps needed to create a recommendation for someone else, request a recommendation for your profile, and manage your existing recommendations.

Understanding Recommendations

The LinkedIn Recommendation process starts in one of three ways:

>> **Unsolicited:** When viewing the profile of any of your first-degree connections, a Recommend link is displayed when you click the down arrow next to the Send a Message button in the middle of that person's profile, as shown in Figure 9-1. By clicking that link, you can give an unsolicited recommendation.

FIGURE 9-1:
You can start a recommendation with any first-degree connection.

>> **Requested:** You can request recommendations from your first-degree connections. You might send such a request at the end of a successful project, for example, or maybe ask for a recommendation from your boss before your transition to a new job.

>> **Reciprocated:** Whenever you accept a recommendation from someone, LinkedIn gives you the option of recommending that person in return. Some people do this as a thank you for receiving the recommendation, other people reciprocate only because they didn't realize they could leave a recommendation until someone left them one, and some people don't feel comfortable reciprocating unless they truly believe the person deserves one. You decide in each circumstance whether to reciprocate, because there are circumstances where that might be awkward, such as if you get a recommendation from a supervisor or boss.

REMEMBER

After the recommendation is written, it's not posted immediately. It goes to the recipient for review, and he has the option to accept it, reject it, or request a revision. So even though the majority of recommendations you see on LinkedIn are genuine, they're also almost entirely positive because they have to be accepted by the recipient.

LinkedIn shows all recommendations you've received as well as links to the profiles of the people who recommended you. (See Figure 9-2.) This provides that social validation you want by allowing people to see exactly who is endorsing you.

Director of Marketing & Sales
Top Cow Productions

Notify your network?
Yes, publish an update to my network about my profile changes.   Yes

Philip W. [redacted]
Freelance Writer and Graphic Designer. Publisher at Fighting Lion Comics

" Joel did an exceptional job while director of Marketing and Sales at Top Cow Productions, Inc.. Joel is a detail oriented, innovative and careful perfectionist - his ideas, skills, creativity and understanding of the field of, not only comics, but also social and auction media make him an invaluable asset to any organization. He has an extensive knowledge, and his open-... **more** "

May 12, 2011, Philip W. worked with Joel at Top Cow Productions

Janine [redacted]
Seeking New Position

" Joel is a marketing genius! It has been a pleasure to work with him in a multitude of capacities. He is sharp as a tack, has his finger on the pulse of many industries and has a great sense of humor too. "

May 2, 2008, Janine was with another company when working with Joel at Top Cow Productions

Hal [redacted]
VP, Entertainment at Engine Shop Agency

" Joel needs to be commended for his job as Top Cow's sales and marketing maven. I remain impressed to this day how he single handily brought the comic company into the new media space by pioneering a successful web strategy, including a killer eBay business model, while ensuring all comic titles got the proper marketing and promotional attention in and around the industry.... **more** "

May 2, 2008, Hal worked directly with Joel at Top Cow Productions

David [redacted]
Art Lead at TinyCo

" Joel's the most dedicated, hard-working, and nicest guy you'll ever work with. Artists at Top Cow would routinely work well into the AMs, and Joel was right there with us, doing the job of an entire marketing staff, long after other employees went home. "

July 22, 2007, David worked indirectly for Joel at Top Cow Productions

FIGURE 9-2:
Recommendations shown on a profile page.

REMEMBER

The quality of the recommendations matters as well as who they're from. Five very specific recommendations from actual clients talking about how you helped them solve a problem are worth more than 50 general recommendations from business acquaintances saying, "I like Sally — she's cool," or "Hector is a great networker." And any recommendations that heartily endorse the number of cocktails you had at the last formal event probably need revision. Check out "Gracefully Declining a Recommendation (Or a Request for One)," later in this chapter, if you're receiving those kinds of statements.

Writing Recommendations

I suggest you practice making some recommendations before you start requesting them. Here's the method to my madness: When you know how to write a good recommendation yourself, you're in a better position to help others write good recommendations for you. And the easiest way to get recommendations is to give them. Every time you make a recommendation and the recipient accepts it, she is prompted to give you a recommendation. Thanks to the basic desire that most people want to be fair when dealing with their network, many people will go ahead and endorse you in return.

Choose wisely, grasshopper: Deciding who to recommend

Go through your contacts and make a list of the people you want to recommend. As you build your list, consider recommending the following types of contacts:

>> **People you've worked with:** I'm not going to say that personal references are completely worthless, but standing next to specific recommendations from colleagues and clients, they tend to ring pretty hollow. Business recommendations are much stronger in the LinkedIn context. Your recommendation is rooted in actual side-by-side experience with the other party, you can be specific on the behavior and accomplishments of the other party, and the examples you give are most likely to be appreciated by the professional LinkedIn community at large.

>> **People you know well:** You may choose to connect with casual acquaintances or even strangers, but reserve your personal recommendations for people you have an established relationship with (and by that, I mean friends and family). Remember, you're putting your own reputation on the line with that recommendation. Are you comfortable risking your rep on them?

WARNING

Recommend only those people whose performance you're actually happy with. I can't say it enough: Your reputation is on the line. Recommending a real doofus just to get one recommendation in return isn't worth it! Here's a great question to ask yourself when deciding whether to recommend someone: Would you feel comfortable recommending this person to a best friend or family member? If not, well, then, you have your answer.

When you complete your To Be Recommended list, you're probably not going to do them all at once, so I suggest copying and pasting the names into a word processing document or spreadsheet so that you can keep track as you complete them.

Look right here: Making your recommendation stand out

Here are a few things to keep in mind when trying to make your recommendation stand out from the rest of the crowd:

>> **Be specific.** Don't just say the person you're recommending is great: Talk about her specific strengths and skills. If you need help, ask the person you're recommending if there's any helpful elements they think you could highlight in your recommendation.

>> **Talk about results.** Adjectives and descriptions are fluff. Clichés are also pretty useless. Tell what the person actually did and the effect it had on you and your business. It's one thing to say, "She has a great eye," and another to say, "The logo she designed for us has been instrumental in building our brand and received numerous positive comments from customers." Detailed results make a great impression, from the scope of difficulty of a project to the degree of challenge the person faced.

>> **Tell how you know the person.** LinkedIn offers only the very basic categories of Professional or Education. If you've known this person for 10 years, say so. If she's your cousin, say so. If you've never met her in person, say so. Save it for the end, though. Open with the positive results this person provided, or the positive qualities the person exhibited in your interaction; then qualify the type of interaction.

>> **Reinforce the requestor's major skills or goals.** Look at her profile. How is she trying to position herself now? What can you say in your recommendation that will support that? That will be far more appreciated by the recipient. For example, if you read her profile and see that she's really focusing on her project management skills as opposed to her earlier software development skills, your recommendation should reinforce *that* message because that's what she's trying to convey on her profile.

>> **Don't gush.** By all means, if you think someone is fantastic, exceptional, extraordinary, or the best at what she does, say so. Just don't go on and on about it, and watch the clichéd adjectives.

>> **Be concise.** Although LinkedIn has a 3,000-character limit on the length of recommendations, you shouldn't reach that limit. That should be more than enough to get your point across. Make it as long as it needs to be to say what you have to say, and no longer.

TIP

Don't be afraid to contact the requestor and ask for feedback on what you should highlight in your recommendation of that person. He knows his own brand better than anyone, so go right to the source!

Creating a recommendation

Now you're ready to write your first recommendation. To create a recommendation, first you need to pull up the person's profile:

1. **Click the Connections link from the top navigation bar of any page to bring up your list of connections.**

2. **Select the person you're recommending from the connections list that appears.**

    REMEMBER

    Your recommendation goes directly to that person, not prospective employers. Any prospective employer who wants a specific reference can request it by contacting that person directly on LinkedIn.

3. **Visit the profile of the person you want to recommend.**

Before you write up your recommendation, review the person's experience, summary, professional headline, and other elements of his profile. This helps you get a sense of what skills, attributes, or results should be reflected in your recommendation of that person. After all, if the person you want to recommend is trying to build a career as a finance executive, your recommendation will serve him better if you focus on finance instead of his event planning or writing skills, for example.

After you inform yourself a bit more about the person you're going to recommend and have thought about what you are going to say, you can get your recommending groove on. Follow these steps:

1. **Click the down arrow next to the Send a Message button in the middle of his profile page, and then click the Recommend link from the drop-down list that appears.**

    As soon as you click the Recommend link, you're taken to the Give (person) a Recommendation page, as shown in Figure 9-3.

2. **Fill in the text box under Write a Recommendation with the text for your recommendation.**

   Throughout this chapter, I stress staying specific, concise, and professional while focusing on a person's results and skills. Keep in mind that recommendations you write that end up getting accepted by the other party also appear in your own profile in a tab marked Recommendations. Believe it or not, people judge you by the comments you make about others, so read your recommendation before you post it and look for spelling or grammatical errors. (You may want to prepare your recommendation in a word processing program like Microsoft Word, use its Spelling & Grammar check, and then cut and paste your newly pristine prose into the Write a Recommendation field.)

3. **(Optional) Include a note in the Your Message to (person) text box.**

   When you send your recommendation, you have the option to also attach a personal note. If it's someone you're in recent contact with, the note is probably unnecessary — the endorsement should speak for itself. But if it's someone you haven't spoken to in a while, take advantage of the opportunity to reconnect with a brief note. You can keep the boilerplate text, "I wrote this recommendation of your work that you can include on your profile," or you can write your own note, like I did in Figure 9-4. Let the person know why you are writing the recommendation, whether it's because you admire her work, enjoyed working with her, or want to recognize her for a job well done.

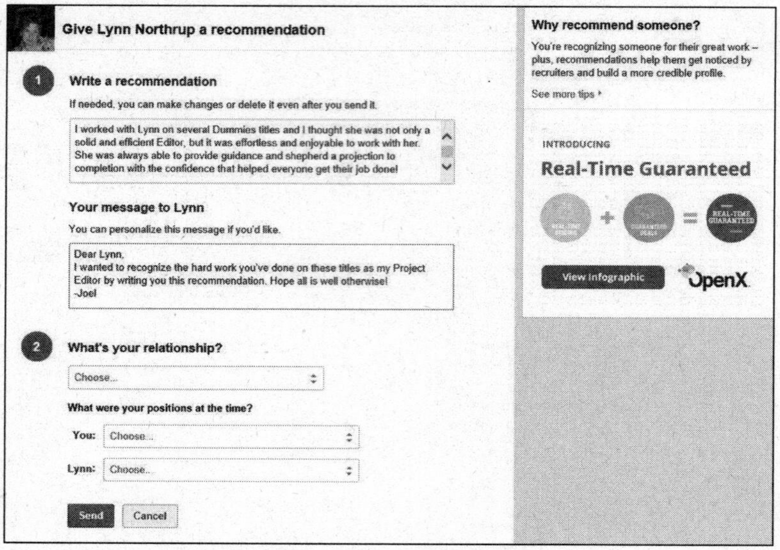

FIGURE 9-4:
Sending a personal note with a recommendation is a good idea.

4. **Define your relationship with the person you're recommending by answering a few questions in the What's Your Relationship? section.**

   Each of the three drop-down boxes asks you to pick an answer from a predefined list. Specifically, you will be asked to

   a. *Define the basis of the recommendation under Relationship.*

      If you're a colleague of the person, LinkedIn wants to know whether you managed or worked side by side with the other person, whether that person was the manager or senior official, or whether you were a client of the other person or the person was a client of yours.

   b. *Define your title at the time.*

      Identify which position you held when you worked with or knew the other person you're recommending. This list is generated from the positions you defined in your LinkedIn profile. If your experience overlaps multiple positions, pick the position that best defines your relationship with the other party.

   c. *Define the other person's title at the time.*

      You have to select at least one position that the other party held to associate the recommendation. You can enter only one recommendation per position, but you can recommend the other party on multiple positions.

   By answering these questions, you inform anyone reading the recommendation about how you know the person you're recommending. Perhaps you were the person's manager at one time.

TIP

After you've written everything out, go back over all the fields one more time to check for spelling or grammatical mistakes, and to make sure the recommendation conveys what you want to say about this person.

5. **Click Send.**

The recommendation is sent to the recipient.

After you send your recommendation, the other person has to accept it before it's posted. Don't take it personally if she doesn't post it, or at least not right away. After all, it's a gift, freely given. The primary value to *you* is in the gesture to the recipient, not the public visibility of your recommendation. And if she comes back with requested changes to the recommendation, by all means accommodate her as long as it's all true and you feel comfortable with it. It's a service to her, not you.

Requesting Recommendations

In an ideal world, you'd never request a recommendation. Everyone who's had a positive experience working with you would just automatically post a raving recommendation on LinkedIn. But the reality is that most likely only your raving fans and very heavy LinkedIn users are going to make unsolicited recommendations. Your mildly happy customers, former bosses whose jokes you laughed at consistently, and co-workers who you haven't seen in five years could all stand a little prompting.

Be prepared, though: Some people feel that recommendations should only be given freely, and they may be taken aback by receiving a recommendation request. So it's imperative that you frame your request with a personal message, not just a generic message from LinkedIn.

TIP

Don't be afraid to consider off-line methods of requesting a recommendation, such as a phone call or a face-to-face meeting, to make the request more personal and more likely for the person to say yes.

Choosing who to request recommendations from

Request recommendations from the same people you might write them for: colleagues, business partners, and service providers. The only difference is that you're looking at it from his point of view.

Relationships aren't all symmetrical. For example, if someone hears me speak at a conference and buys this book, that person is my customer. My customers know my skills and expertise fairly well — perhaps not on the same level as a consulting client, but still well enough to make a recommendation. I, on the other hand, might not know a customer at all. I'm open to getting to know him, and I'm willing to connect, but I can't write a recommendation for him yet.

Creating a polite recommendation request

When you identify the person (or people) you want to write your recommendations, you're ready to create a recommendation request. To get started on authoring your request, follow these steps:

1. **Click the Profile link from the top navigation bar to bring up your profile. Click the down arrow next to the View Profile As button (in your Summary box) and click the Ask to Be Recommended link.**

2. **After the Ask for Recommendations page loads, click the drop-down list (right there at Step 1 — see Figure 9-5) to choose what you want to be recommended for from the list provided.**

   LinkedIn ties this recommendation to a particular position or school attended from your profile, so you need to select the position (or school you were attending) where the recommender observed you and is providing his recommendation.

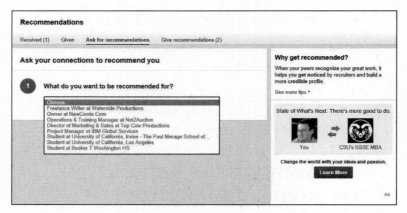

FIGURE 9-5: Select the position to be associated with your requested recommendation.

3. **Under the Who Do You Want to Ask? header, type the name of the person you want to request a recommendation from into the Your Connections text field.**

   You can add the names of up to three people in this text field, and all will get a recommendation request.

As you start typing the name of the person, you should see that name pop up, as shown in Figure 9-6. Clicking the name adds it to the list of names visible in the Your Connections field. You can now type in another name if you would like to send this recommendation request to more than one person.

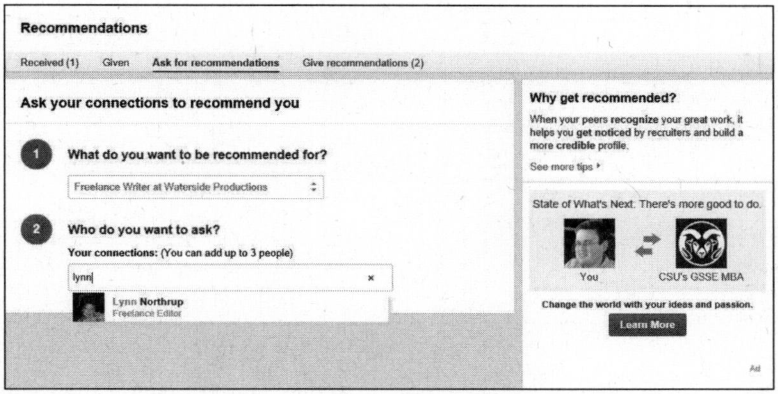

Recommendations

Received (1)   Given   **Ask for recommendations**   Give recommendations (2)

Ask your connections to recommend you

❶ What do you want to be recommended for?

Freelance Writer at Waterside Productions ▼

❷ Who do you want to ask?

Your connections: (You can add up to 3 people)

lynn| _____ ✕

　　Lynn **Northrup**
　　Freelance Editor

Why get recommended?
When your peers recognize your great work, it helps you get noticed by recruiters and build a more credible profile.
See more tips ▸

State of What's Next: There's more good to do.

You ⇄ CSU's GSSE MBA

Change the world with your ideas and passion.

Learn More

Ad

FIGURE 9-6: Confirm the person (or people) to request recommendations from.

4. **Define your relationship with each person from whom you want to request a recommendation in the drop-down boxes provided.**

   Similar to the process of writing a recommendation, LinkedIn will ask you to define the basis of your relationship with this person, either Professional or Educational, that pertains to the recommendation request, as well as the role of the person from whom you are requesting the recommendation. Use the drop-down boxes provided to pick the appropriate responses.

5. **Type your message in the fields provided, as shown in Figure 9-7.**

   The same etiquette is recommended here as in other requests: Don't just accept the boilerplate text that LinkedIn fills in, but rather customize it to create a personal note, like I did in Figure 9-7. You can customize not only the body of your message, but the subject line as well.

   Don't forget to thank the person for the time and the effort in leaving you a recommendation!

TIP

6. **Check your spelling and grammar.**

   You can write your message first using a program like Microsoft Word, run the Spelling & Grammar check, then cut and paste your message into the space provided, if you like.

7. **Click Send.**

   The recommendation request is sent to the intended recipient.

FIGURE 9-7:
A customized recommendation request.

REMEMBER

Giving people some context as to why you're making the request helps motivate them more effectively, especially if they're nervous or unaware about how to use LinkedIn. Let them know you're available for any technical or follow-up help. Also, even though you should be asking only people who would be comfortable recommending you (you are, aren't you?), you still want to give them a gracious way to decline. After all, you're asking a favor. The person you're contacting is in no way obligated, so don't expect anything, and you won't be disappointed.

TIP

There's really no such thing as too many recommendations as long as the quality is good. Once you start accepting mediocre recommendations, though, on the assumption that "something is better than nothing," people will start to think that a lot of them are fluff. LinkedIn doesn't give you control over the display order, either, so you have all the more reason to make sure the recommendations displayed are good quality.

Gracefully Declining a Recommendation (or a Request for One)

Unfortunately, not everyone naturally writes good recommendations, and all your LinkedIn connections haven't read this book, so it's bound to happen eventually: Someone will write a recommendation that you don't want to show on your profile.

No problem. Just politely request a replacement when you receive it. Thank him for thinking of you, and give him the context of what you're trying to accomplish:

> Wei:
>
> Thank you so much for your gracious recommendation. I'd like to ask a small favor, though. I'm really trying to position myself more as a public speaker in the widget industry, rather than as a gadget trainer. Since you've heard me speak on the topic, if you could gear your recommendation more toward that, I'd greatly appreciate it.
>
> Thanks,
>
> Alexa

If he's sincerely trying to be of service to you, he should have no problem changing it. Just make sure you ask him for something based on your actual experience with him.

You may receive a request for a recommendation from someone you don't feel comfortable recommending. If it's because she gave you poor service or was less than competent, you have to consider whether you should even be connected to her at all because, after all, LinkedIn is a business referral system. I discuss how to remove a connection in Chapter 6.

Perhaps you don't have sufficient experience with her services to provide her a recommendation. If that's the case, just reply to her request with an explanation:

> Alexa:
>
> I received your request for a recommendation. While I'm happy to be connected to you on LinkedIn, and look forward to getting to know you better, or even work together in the future, at this time I just don't feel like I have enough basis to give you a really substantive recommendation.
>
> Once we've actually worked together on something successfully, I'll be more than happy to provide a recommendation.
>
> Thanks,
>
> Wei

Managing Recommendations

Relationships change over time. Sometimes they get better, occasionally they get worse, and sometimes they just change. As you get more recommendations, you might decide that you don't want to display them all, or that you would like some of them updated to support your current branding or initiatives.

Fortunately, neither the recommendation you give nor those you receive are etched in stone (or computer chips, as the case may be). You can edit or remove the recommendations you've written at any time, and you can hide or request revisions to those you receive.

Editing or removing recommendations you've made

To edit or remove a recommendation you've made, follow these steps:

1. **Hover your mouse over the Profile link from the top navigation bar and then choose Edit Profile from the Profile drop-down list that appears.**

2. **Scroll down to the Recommendations section and hover your mouse over the Recommendations header, then click the Manage button to the right of the Recommendations header.**

   Doing so brings up a dedicated Recommendations page that contains all the recommendations you've received or given, or requests that are still pending.

3. **Click the page's Given tab.**

   All the recommendations you've made are listed in reverse chronological order, as shown in Figure 9-8.

4. **Click the Edit or Remove link next to the recommendation you want to change or remove.**

   - *Edit:* When you click the Edit link, the screen updates and shows you the Written Recommendation text, as well as a text box where you can send a message to the person along with the updated recommendation, as shown in Figure 9-9. Make the changes to your recommendation in the first box and then write a new message to the recipient in the second box. When you're done, click Send below the two text boxes.

   - *Remove:* Click the Remove link to ditch the recommendation completely. LinkedIn will display a message box asking you to click the Confirm button to remove the recommendation. The message indicates that the person whose recommendation you are deleting will not be notified of the deletion.

An edited recommendation is submitted to the recipient again for approval. If you remove it, it comes off immediately, and the recipient (or is that the *unrecipient*?) doesn't receive any notification.

Handling new recommendations you've received

Every time you receive a recommendation from someone else, you will see it on your Recommendations page, under the Received tab. You can click the pending recommendation to read the full text as shown in Figure 9-10.

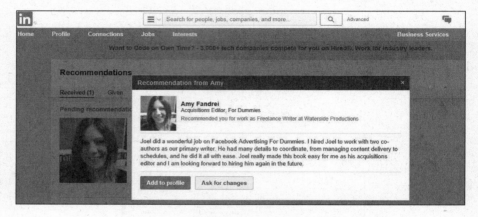

FIGURE 9-10: Here is where you can accept an incoming recommendation.

When you receive a recommendation, you have these options:

>> **Add it to your profile.** Click the Add to Profile button to add this recommendation, as stated, to your profile.

>> **Ask the writer for changes.** If you aren't completely happy with the person's recommendation, click the Ask for Changes button to be given the opportunity to send him a brief note explaining what you would like changed.

>> **Ignore it.** Until you take action, the recommendation will sit in a pending status and will not show up on your profile. Perhaps you don't want the recommendation to become visible until a certain event happens, like applying for a different job. You can return to this screen at any future time to add the recommendation or ask for changes.

Removing a recommendation or requesting a revision

To remove a recommendation you've received or to request a revision, here's what you do:

1. **Hover your mouse over the Profile link from the top navigation bar and then choose Edit Profile from the menu that appears.**

2. **Scroll down to the Recommendations section and hover your mouse over the Recommendations header. Click the Manage button that appears to the right of that header to bring up the Recommendations page. Click the Received tab on the Recommendations page.**

   Doing so takes you to the Recommendations You've Received page.

3. **Scroll down the page to find the position from your Experience list that the recommendation is tied to, and you will see all the recommendations for that position, as shown in Figure 9-11.**

4. **To remove a recommendation, deselect the check box next to the recommendation. This will automatically hide your recommendation. At any time, you can come back to this screen and select the check box to add the recommendation back to your profile.**

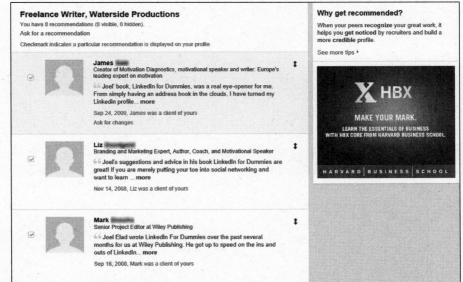

FIGURE 9-11: Remove a recommendation or request a revision here.

5. **To request a new or revised recommendation, hover your mouse over the recommendation text and click the Ask for Changes link that appears.**

   This brings up a new Recommendation message screen (similar to what I covered in "Creating a polite recommendation request," earlier in this chapter), where you can write a brief note explaining why you're requesting a change.

6. **Click Send Message to send the request for changes to your recommendation.**

Negotiating the social graces around recommendations might feel a little awkward at first, but with some practice, you'll quickly become comfortable. By both giving and receiving good recommendations, you'll build your public reputation, increase your social capital with your connections, and have a good excuse for renewing relationships with people you haven't contacted recently.

Chapter 10

Monitoring Your LinkedIn Activities Through Your Home Page

I talk a lot about the different functions available on LinkedIn for you to use, and hopefully you've started to set aside some time on a regular basis to keep track of various tasks as you build up your profile and network. Because of the growing number of functions available on LinkedIn, you should take a look around the site to see how you can manage this new set of tasks most effectively.

In this chapter, I detail the different ways you can access the LinkedIn functions as well as how you can keep track of incoming messages, invitations, and other notifications that require your input or attention. I discuss the functions that you can access from the top navigation bar on the LinkedIn home page. I also discuss the LinkedIn Inbox, where all your messages, invitations, and communication are received. Then, I go over some ways you can set up LinkedIn to communicate with you through e-mail and keep you informed of communication from other LinkedIn users, whether those are Invitations, Recommendations, or other LinkedIn functions.

Using the LinkedIn Home Page as Your Command Console

The LinkedIn home page is, by default, full of information about how you use the site. Think of the home page as your command console for working with LinkedIn. You can get to the home page at any time by clicking the LinkedIn logo or the Home link in the top-left corner of every LinkedIn web page. The home page holds a variety of information. Of course, your home page is unique to your LinkedIn identity, so it will look different from mine (shown in Figure 10-1) or any other user on LinkedIn. And remember that your home page is based on the first-degree connections in your network, the pending messages in your Inbox, and the level of participation with functions, such as LinkedIn Groups or Recommendations, or applications like SlideShare or the Amazon Reading List.

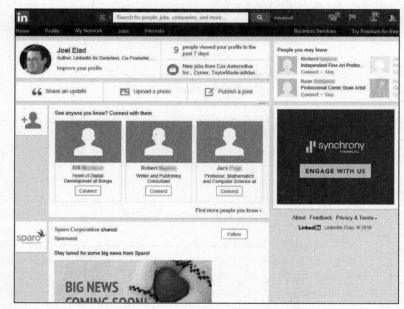

FIGURE 10-1:
Coordinate all your LinkedIn activities through the home page.

First off, check out the menu along the top of the site. I refer to this menu as the top navigation bar. This bar has all the major categories for checking your activities on LinkedIn. Just hover your mouse over each function to expand the menu item to see more options. Figure 10-2 shows the top right corner of the LinkedIn screen, containing four very important icons:

» Messaging/Inbox

» Notifications (flag)

» Grow Your Network (the person with the + sign)

» Your profile icon

If you see a red box with a number next to the Messaging, Notifications, or Grow Your Network icon, it represents the number of unanswered messages, unread notifications, or unanswered invitations, respectively. This method of indicating a numerical "flag" is similar to other social media sites such as Facebook and designed to give you a visual cue on actions you need to take.

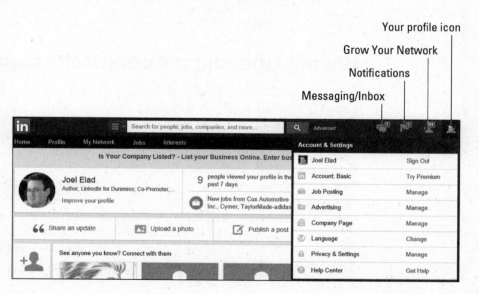

FIGURE 10-2: Review your navigation bar icons.

Scroll down your LinkedIn home page to see modules of other aspects of LinkedIn, such as your Network Activity, along with alerts for potential jobs, connections, and Sponsored Updates (ads). To change any of the settings of your account, simply hover your mouse over your profile icon (in the top-right corner of the screen) and click the Manage link (next to Privacy & Settings) to bring up your settings page, as shown in Figure 10-3.

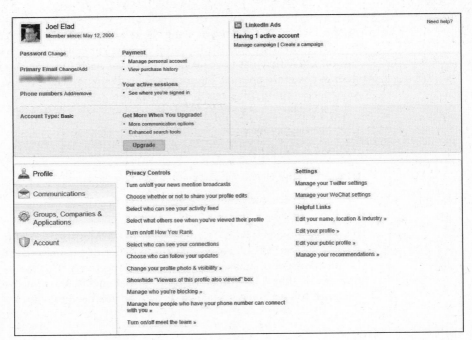

FIGURE 10-3:
See LinkedIn modules on your home page.

Having LinkedIn automatically contact you

Sure, you can do all the footwork by going to the LinkedIn home page and looking around to see what messages or changes have occurred. The true power of staying connected, however, is having LinkedIn automatically contact you with the information you need to stay informed.

As I mention in the preceding section, clicking the Manage link next to Privacy & Settings (after hovering your mouse over your profile icon from the home page) takes you to the settings page, which contains information about your account and your LinkedIn settings. Click the Communications header on the left side of the screen to bring up the Communications settings, as shown in Figure 10-4. This is your hub for controlling how you interact with LinkedIn and how the site communicates with you.

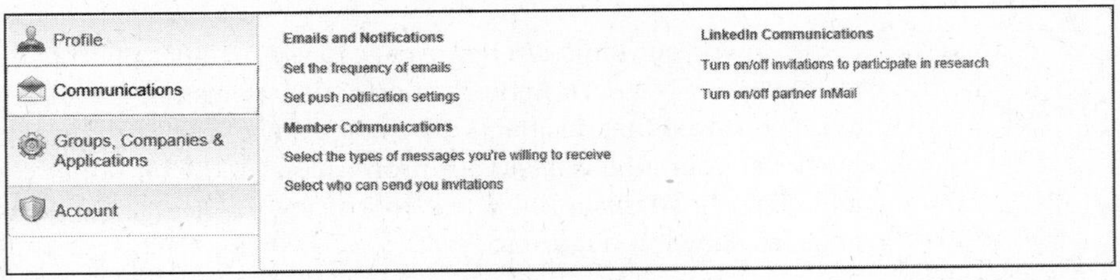

FIGURE 10-4:
Control your LinkedIn settings from the Account & Settings page.

Start by setting preferences in the Emails and Notifications section by deciding when LinkedIn should send you an e-mail to your e-mail account on file with LinkedIn:

1. **On the Account & Settings page, click the Set the Frequency of Emails link in the Emails and Notifications section.**

   You're taken to the Email Frequency page. For each section, like Messages from Other Members, click the pencil icon on the right side to expand the list of options, as shown in Figure 10-5.

2. **Review the list of options and decide how you want to receive your e-mails. Click the drop-down arrow for each row to select:**

   - *Individual Email:* As soon as something occurs in a given category, like introductions, invitations, or job notifications, LinkedIn sends you an e-mail with that one item in the e-mail.

   - *Weekly Digest Email or Daily Digest Email:* Instead of individual e-mails, LinkedIn groups activities in a given category and sends you one e-mail in a digest format, with a summary at the top of the e-mail and the detailed activities below the summary. Note that Daily Digests are for Group updates, while Weekly Digests are available for General and Group updates.

   - *No Email:* Turn off e-mail notification. You can read the message, though, when logged in to the LinkedIn site.

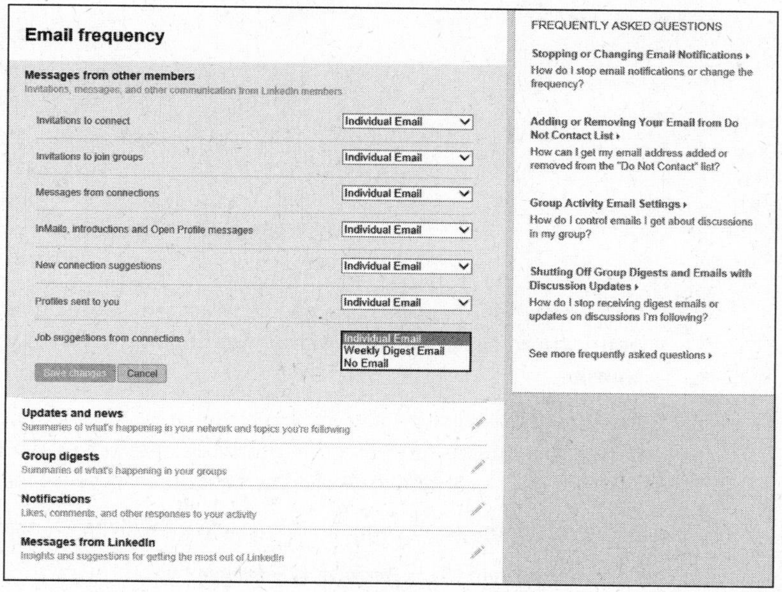

FIGURE 10-5: Decide what e-mails you want to get from LinkedIn and how often.

3. **(Optional) Click the pencil icon next to the Messages from LinkedIn header and select the Individual Email for the Details on New Products, Tips, and Special Offers option to receive information from LinkedIn.**

4. **Scroll down to the bottom of the page and click the Save Changes button.**

   You return to the Account & Settings page.

5. **Click the Set Push Notifications link in the Emails and Notifications section.**

   You're taken to the Push Notification Settings page. For each of the two sections, Messages from other members, or Notifications, click the pencil icon on the right side to expand the list of options, as shown in Figure 10-6 when I expanded Notifications.

6. **Review the list of options and decide when you want LinkedIn to "push a notification" or e-mail you when something that involves you occurs on the website.**

   If you want LinkedIn to notify you when something occurs — when someone shares your update, for example — you would select the check box next to that option. If you don't want to receive the notification, deselect that check box.

7. **After you've made all your selections, click the Save Changes button.**

   You are returned to the Account & Settings page.

8. **Click the Select the Types of Messages You'd Prefer to Receive link from the Settings page.**

   A box pops up offering you several options regarding the types of messages you are willing to receive from LinkedIn members, as shown in Figure 10-7.

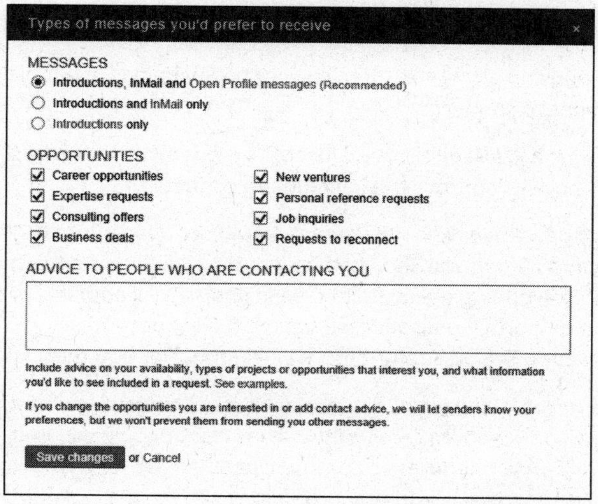

FIGURE 10-7: Decide what messages you want to receive from LinkedIn members.

9. **Pick one of the three options regarding the types of messages you want to receive.**

   As of this writing, you can choose between receiving:

   - *Introductions, InMail, and Open Profile messages:* Choose this if you are willing to allow anyone requesting an Introduction, paying to use an InMail message, or subscribing to the Open Profile system to send you a message that would show up in your Inbox.

   - *Introductions and InMail only:* Choose this if you are only willing to receive Introduction requests or InMail messages.

   - *Introductions only:* Choose this if you are only willing to receive introduction requests.

10. **(Optional) You can select the check boxes indicating which opportunities you are interested in hearing about through LinkedIn, and you can advise people on how you want them to contact you.**

    LinkedIn provides eight options, such as Career Opportunities and Business Deals, that you can select, but the advertising of these opportunities has been limited by LinkedIn. Type any instructions in the Advice to People Who Are Contacting You text box to let people know how to best contact you.

WARNING

Any information you put in the Advice to People Who Are Contacting You text box will be advertised on your profile for your network to see, so don't include sensitive or private information in this box.

11. **After you've made all your selections, click the Save Changes button.**

You are returned to the Account & Settings page.

12. **Click the Select Who Can Send You Invitations link.**

A box pops up giving you three choices of what types of people can send you invitations to connect:

● *Anyone on LinkedIn:* This is LinkedIn's recommended setting. After all, you still have to approve the invitation to connect.

● *Only people who know your email address or appear in your "Imported Contacts" list:* If you choose this option, LinkedIn will either prompt the person sending the invite to type in your e-mail address, or it will check that person's e-mail address against the list of contacts you imported to LinkedIn. This will occur before LinkedIn sends you the invitation.

● *Only people who appear in your "Imported Contacts" list:* Choose this option if you only want to receive invitations from people you imported from your e-mail or address book into LinkedIn. This way, even if someone knew your e-mail address, he couldn't send you a LinkedIn invitation.

13. **Click the radio button next to the option you prefer and then click Save Changes.**

The pop-up box disappears, and you are back on the Account & Settings page.

14. **(Optional) If you want to receive invitations to participate in LinkedIn's research efforts, click the Turn On/Off Invitations to Participate in Research link. You can also click the Turn On/Off Partner InMail link if you want to opt in to offers from third-party companies that partner with LinkedIn.**

This completes your options when it comes to Communications. You can always click Profile, Account, or Groups, Companies & Applications to control more of your LinkedIn experience.

Understanding your Inbox

The best hub for your communications is the LinkedIn Inbox, which you can access by clicking the Messaging icon in the top navigation bar. You go to the list of messages in your Inbox, as shown in Figure 10-8.

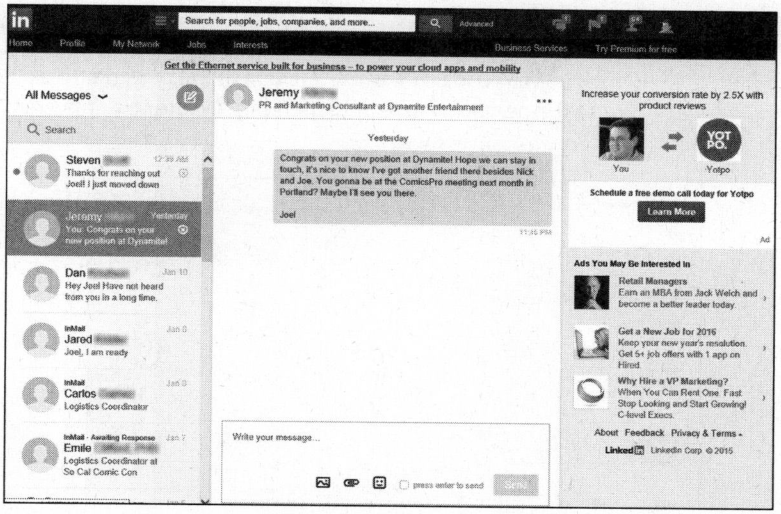

FIGURE 10-8:
Review the action items in your Inbox.

Here are some things to keep in mind when navigating your Inbox:

>> **Starting a new message:** Click the round blue button with the pencil icon to start a new conversation. The middle of the screen displays a message box. In the top line, type the name of the LinkedIn member to whom you want to send a message, and then type the message into the Message portion of the box.

>> **Using the icons on the bottom of the reply window:** You can click the icons along the bottom of the reply window to attach an image to the conversation, attach a file to the conversation, or post an emoji icon (like the Cool Icon in Figure 10-9) into your reply. In addition, by clicking the Press Enter to Send check box, your reply will work like a chat window, where every press of the Enter key sends your reply. (When it's check-marked, as in Figure 10-9, the Send button disappears.)

>> **Using the filters:** By default, when you're looking at your Inbox, you see all messages. If you click the down arrow next to the All Messages heading (above your first item), you can pick a specific category (such as My Connections, InMail, Unread Messages, or Blocked Messages).

>> **Taking action on the conversation:** After you read your message, you can click the three dots next to the person's name in the main window, to bring up action items for this conversation, as shown in Figure 10-10. You can add people to this existing conversation, mark it as unread, mute the conversation (which turns off e-mail notifications to you when new comments are made in this conversation), forward the conversation to another LinkedIn member, report the message as spam, or delete the conversation.

>> **Deleting a conversation:** If you don't want to keep a message, click the X icon in the subject header along the left side of the screen or click the three dots next to the person's name, and then click Delete this Conversation.

FIGURE 10-9:
Add chat-like
elements to your
conversations.

Attach a photo   Post an emoji picture

Attach a file

FIGURE 10-10:
Take action on
your existing
conversations.

Tracking Your InMail Messages

Although many of your communications with immediate first-degree LinkedIn connections take place through your own e-mail system, communications with people *outside* your network of first-degree connections need to be tracked and responded to via LinkedIn. So take a look at how you can track InMail messages through your LinkedIn Inbox.

To go directly to your list of InMail messages, click the down arrow next to All Messages from your Inbox and select the InMail option. This takes you to the InMail page shown in Figure 10-11.

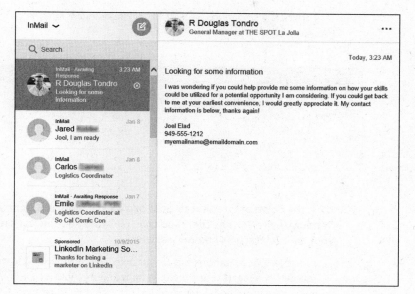

FIGURE 10-11:
Take a look at the InMail you've received.

Tracking Invitations

As you grow your network, you need to keep track of the invitations you sent to your connections as well as any incoming invitations. I cover invitations in Chapter 2, and I talk about setting up your notifications for receiving e-mail about invitations in "Having LinkedIn automatically contact you," earlier this chapter. The following sections tell you about monitoring your invitations on the LinkedIn website.

Tracking sent invitations

The last thing you want to do is send repeat invitations to the same person because you didn't monitor your sent invitations. Also, you might want to review your sent invitations to see whether someone has responded; if not, you can send that person a follow-up e-mail either through LinkedIn or via your own e-mail account. As of this writing, there is no running list, so you have to go through your Inbox to see which sent invitations have been accepted or not.

Here's how to track your sent invitations:

1. **Click the Grow Your Network icon from the top navigation bar of any LinkedIn page, then click the See All link next to Pending Invitations.**

   This opens the screen for viewing all your pending invitations, as shown in Figure 10-12.

Search for people, jobs, companies, and more...
Advanced
Pending invitations (46)
Pending invitations
Sent invitations
Blocked invitations
Annie
Business Analyst at Toshiba America Information Systems, Inc
Jeff
Stay at home Father of 3

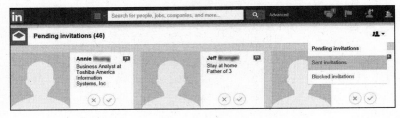

FIGURE 10-12: Use this page to track pending invitations.

2. **Click the down arrow next to the People icon along the right side of the Pending Invitations header, and then click the Sent Invitations link to pull up your sent invitations and messages.**

   You see the Sent Invitations page, as shown in Figure 10-13. The date of each invitation is displayed above the invitation and multiple invitations sent on the same day are grouped by name, as indicated in the figure. Note the radio button next to each person's name.

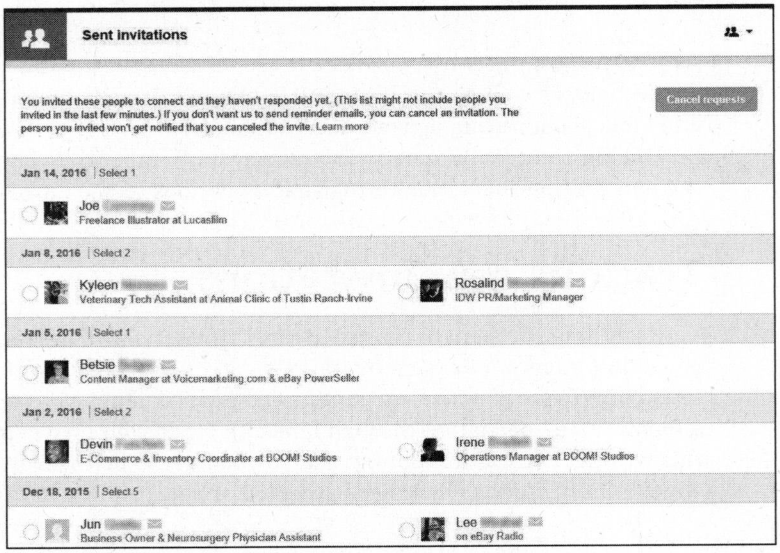

Sent invitations
You invited these people to connect and they haven't responded yet. (This list might not include people you invited in the last few minutes.) If you don't want us to send reminder emails, you can cancel an invitation. The person you invited won't get notified that you canceled the invite. Learn more
Cancel requests
Jan 14, 2016 | Select 1
Joe
Freelance Illustrator at Lucasfilm
Jan 8, 2016 | Select 2
Kyleen
Veterinary Tech Assistant at Animal Clinic of Tustin Ranch-Irvine
Rosalind
IDW PR/Marketing Manager
Jan 5, 2016 | Select 1
Betsie
Content Manager at Voicemarketing.com & eBay PowerSeller
Jan 2, 2016 | Select 2
Devin
E-Commerce & Inventory Coordinator at BOOM! Studios
Irene
Operations Manager at BOOM! Studios
Dec 18, 2015 | Select 5
Jun
Business Owner & Neurosurgery Physician Assistant
Lee
on eBay Radio

FIGURE 10-13: See your sent invitations and the dates you sent the requests.

3. **To view an invitation, hover your mouse over the Envelope icon next to the person's name. To cancel the invitation request, click the radio button next to the person's name, and then click the blue Cancel Requests button.**

   When you hover your mouse over the envelope, you see a copy of your invitation message, like the one shown in Figure 10-14. You can click the radio button next to one or more people to cancel your invitation request. When you cancel the request, no message is sent to the other person.

Tracking received invitations

When growing your LinkedIn network, you should be responsive to others who want to add you to their LinkedIn connections lists. To review your received invitations, follow these steps:

1. **Click the Grow Your Network icon from the top navigation bar and then click the See All link next to the Pending Invitations link from the drop-down list that appears.**

   You're taken to a list of your received invitations, as shown in Figure 10-15. You can hover your mouse over the blue quotation marks to see the person's incoming message with his invitation request, and, with a click of the mouse, see his profile.

2. **To accept a pending invitation, click the check mark (Accept) button. To ignore the invitation, click the X (Ignore) button.**

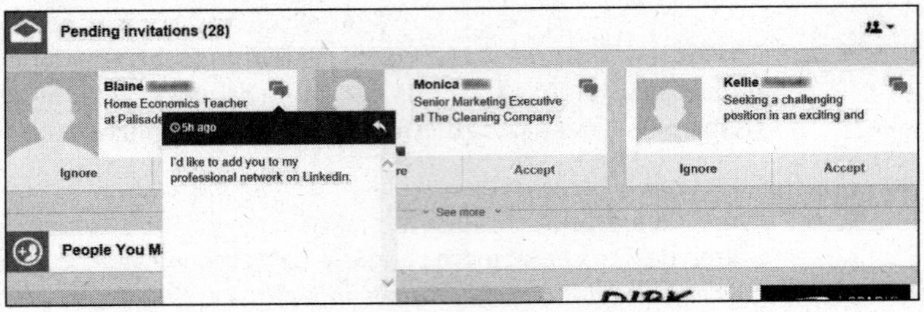

FIGURE 10-15:
Review your
received
invitations here.

If you want to reply to the person without immediately accepting that invitation (say, to get clarification in case you don't recognize the person), click the person's name to see his profile and either send him InMail, or send a message to any first-degree connections who know the person and can pass along your message to him. You can also click the X (Ignore) button to remove this invitation from your list. (See Chapter 6 for tips on growing your network.)

After you click the Accept or Ignore button, that invitation disappears from your view and, if there are additional invitations that require action, one of those invitations will appear.

3. **Continue to act on each invitation in your list until there are no more new invitations.**

Chapter 11

Using LinkedIn with Your Internet Activity

This chapter delves in to how you can use LinkedIn as a part of your overall presence on the Internet, especially when it comes to communication. Specifically, I focus on two aspects of your Internet experience: your e-mail account with and without your Internet web browser.

LinkedIn makes it convenient for you to exchange information between your e-mail program and your LinkedIn profile and to enhance your World Wide Web browsing experience with specialized LinkedIn functions. LinkedIn offers the capability to import your contacts list from programs such as Microsoft Outlook. You can also do the reverse: Export your LinkedIn contacts list to a variety of e-mail programs, including the Mail program that's part of Mac OS X.

Importing Contacts into LinkedIn

One of the most popular (and necessary) activities people use the Internet for is e-mail. Your e-mail account contains a record of e-mail addresses of everyone you regularly communicate with via e-mail. And from your established base of communications, LinkedIn offers a way for you to ramp up your network by importing a list of contacts from your e-mail program. Importing your e-mail contacts into LinkedIn eliminates the drudgery of going through your address book and copying addresses into LinkedIn. The next sections show you how to generate a list of contacts and import that list into LinkedIn to update your connections.

Importing a contacts list from Outlook

Microsoft Outlook is one of the most popular e-mail programs out there. This section shows you how to import your Microsoft Outlook contacts list into LinkedIn. To do so, follow these steps:

1. **On the main Outlook screen, click Contacts to bring up your contacts list (similar to that shown in Figure 11-1).**

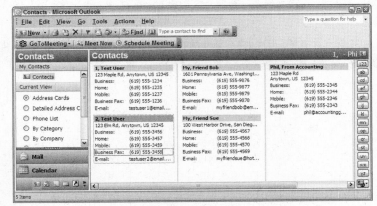

2. **Choose File ⇨ Import and Export.**

   The Import and Export window appears.

3. **Select the Export to a File option, click the Next button, and then select a file type in the Export to a File window.**

   You see a list of options, including Comma Separated Values (DOS), Comma Separated Values (Windows), Microsoft Access, and so on.

4. **Select the Comma Separated Values (Windows) option and then click Next.**

   The Export to a File window appears. Here, you're asked to pick a folder that you want to export, as shown in Figure 11-2. Look for the contacts folder, which contains your list of contacts through Microsoft Outlook.

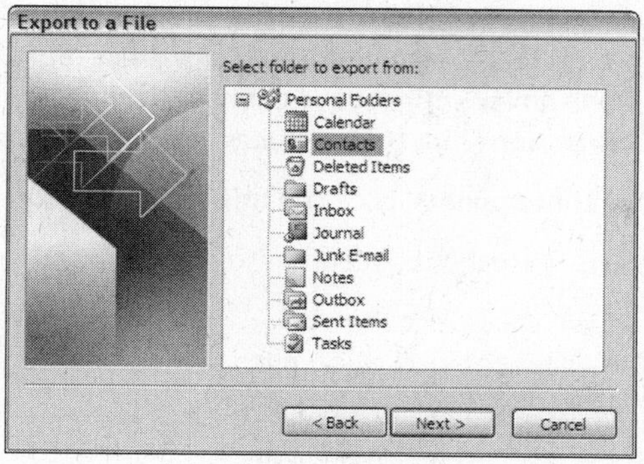

FIGURE 11-2:
Select your
contacts folder
to export.

5. **Select the contacts folder to export and then click Next.**

   If you created categories within your Outlook contacts list, you can select one of those subcategories under the main contacts folder and export just those contacts.

   TIP

6. **In the next Export to a File window that appears, enter a suitable file name, click the Browse button to locate a folder for storing the new (exported) file, and then click Next.**

   In the Export to a File window, Outlook displays the action it's about to take, as shown in Figure 11-3.

   Note the filename and location of your exported contacts file because you need this information in a few steps. Pick a memorable name and save the file to a commonly used folder on your computer.

   REMEMBER

7. **Click Finish to start the export of your Outlook contacts file.**

   Depending on the size of your contacts list, the export process might take a few minutes. When the export is complete, the status indicator disappears, and you're ready to go to the next step.

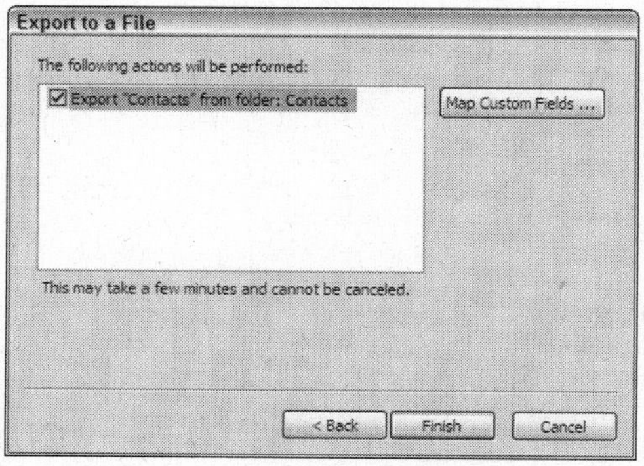

FIGURE 11-3:
Outlook verifies
the export action.

8. **Using your web browser, go to LinkedIn and log in to your account; then, on the top of the page, hover your mouse over the Connections link, and then click the Add Connections link that appears from the drop-down list.**

9. **On the new page that appears, click the Import File button.**

   The upload contacts instructions appear on-screen, as shown in Figure 11-4.

TIP

   If you have a Mac, you should see the Open window appear after clicking the Import File button. When this occurs, navigate to the exported contacts file so it can be read by LinkedIn.

10. **Click the Browse button (or paperclip icon) to locate the contacts file you just exported from Microsoft Outlook. When you locate that file, click the Upload File button to start the process.**

   After LinkedIn reads your entire contacts list, it displays the names of contacts from your list, as shown in Figure 11-5; and then, below those names where the person is already on LinkedIn, it shows how long they've been a member of LinkedIn.

WARNING

   When LinkedIn imports the list, it usually drops the middle name from each person's full name when creating the imported contacts. You might need to edit your contacts to add the appropriate information.

11. **Review the names, deselect any check box for someone you don't wish to invite, and then click the Send Invitations button to complete the process.**

   If the names you see on the screen aren't correct (perhaps LinkedIn did not read the file properly and everyone's first and last names are reversed, for example), you can click Cancel to abandon the process.

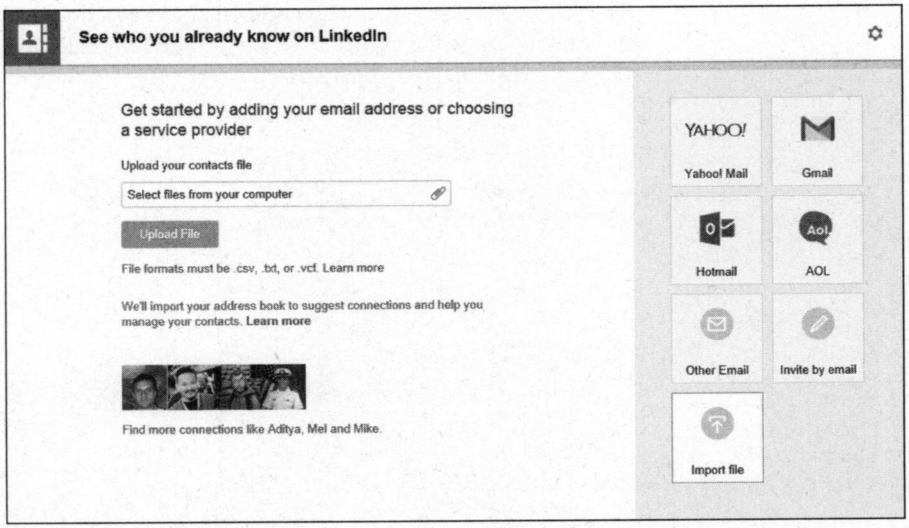

FIGURE 11-4:
LinkedIn is ready to accept your Outlook contacts list.

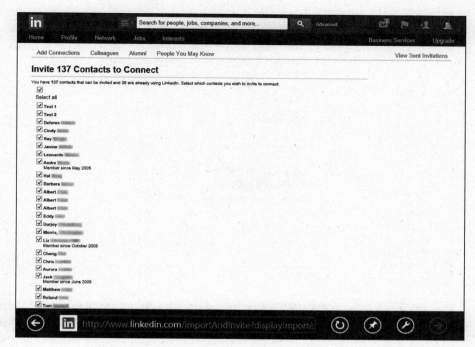

FIGURE 11-5:
LinkedIn asks you which names from your contacts list should get an invitation.

Importing contacts from a web-based e-mail program

Many people use a web-based program (*webmail*) to send and receive e-mail. Gmail (from Google), Yahoo! Mail, and Hotmail are among the most popular of these programs. Just like Outlook, you can import your webmail program contacts list and feed it into LinkedIn to expand your network. For the example in this section, I use Yahoo! Mail, but the other systems work similarly for importing contacts.

To import a webmail contacts list, follow these steps:

1. **Using your web browser, go to LinkedIn and log in to your account.**

2. **Hover your mouse over the Connections link at the top of any LinkedIn page, and then click Add Connections from the drop-down list to bring up the Add Connections window.**

   The See Who You Already Know on LinkedIn page appears, as shown in Figure 11-6.

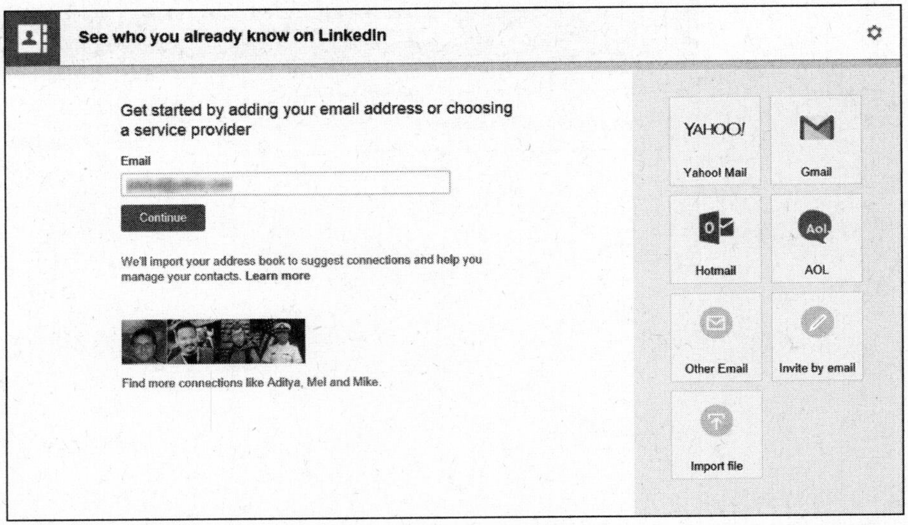

FIGURE 11-6:
LinkedIn can check your webmail program for contacts.

3. **Click the appropriate webmail button, enter your e-mail address into the Email text box (and your password, when prompted), and then click the Continue button.**

   LinkedIn opens a new window in which you can connect with your webmail program. (You are asked for your webmail e-mail password, so LinkedIn can log in to your account for you.)

4. **Follow the instructions to access your webmail account.**

   For this example, I used my Yahoo! account, which took me to the Yahoo! login screen. After I was logged in to my account, Yahoo! requested my permission to let LinkedIn access my Yahoo! contacts, as shown in Figure 11-7. You must click the Agree button if you want LinkedIn to import your contacts. After you do, LinkedIn automatically goes into the account and starts importing contacts, and you're returned to the LinkedIn website.

5. **Review the imported contacts and who you want to invite to your LinkedIn network.**

   LinkedIn may select all your contacts who aren't yet connected to you via LinkedIn and offer to send them an invitation, as shown in Figure 11-8. If that is the case, deselect the check box next to each person you don't want to invite. For some e-mail systems, you will see your imported contacts and have to manually select which contacts you want to invite by selecting the check box next to each person you want to invite. When you are ready, click the Add to Network button to send invitations to the contacts you wish to add to your network.

6. **When you're done, close the newly opened window that was created back in Step 3 when you started the import process.**

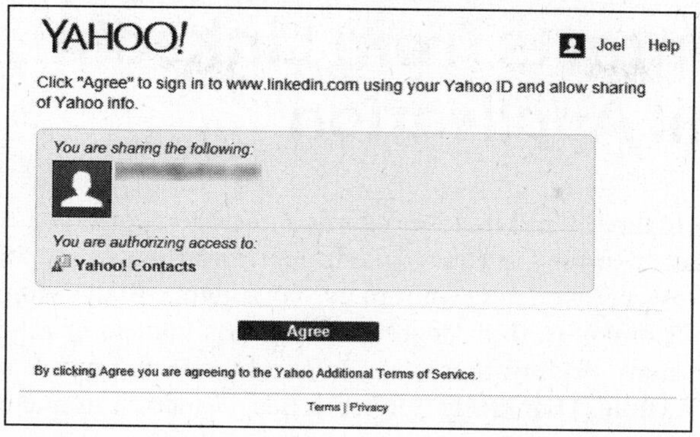

FIGURE 11-7:
You need to allow LinkedIn to read your webmail address book.

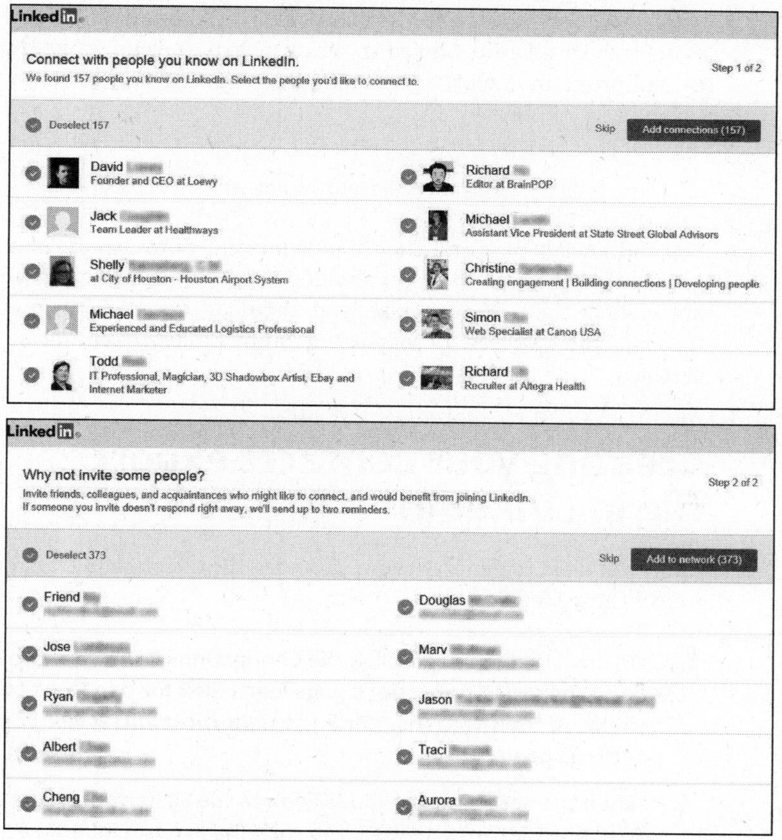

FIGURE 11-8:
From your imported address book, decide who gets invited to your network, or who gets invited to LinkedIn and then your network.

Exporting Contacts from LinkedIn to Your E-Mail Application

As you use LinkedIn and build up your contacts network, you might end up with more contacts "on file" in your LinkedIn network than stored away in your e-mail program. However, you may want to use your own e-mail system to communicate with all your LinkedIn first-degree connections instead of relying on LinkedIn's message system. Adding these people one by one to your e-mail address book could take a while. Thankfully, LinkedIn has a function to make this easier.

In essence, your list of LinkedIn connections is similar to a list of names in any e-mail program's address book. And just like you can import contacts from an e-mail program into LinkedIn, you can export your LinkedIn contacts to your e-mail program. Exporting is a simple process that amounts to the following:

1. You export your LinkedIn connections into a contacts file.

2. You import the contacts file into your main e-mail program.

You can always pick and choose which contacts to export, and your e-mail program should be able to detect any duplicates — meaning that if you try to import any names that already exist, you should get a warning message. I walk you through the process of exporting your LinkedIn contacts in the next few sections.

Creating your contacts export file in LinkedIn

First, you need to generate your exported file of contacts from LinkedIn. To do so, follow these steps:

1. **On any LinkedIn page, click the Connections link in the top navigation bar. When the Connections page loads look for two icons to the right of the word "Connections." Click the right-most wheel icon to load the Settings page.**

2. **When the Settings page loads, look to the right of the page and, under the Advanced Settings header, and click the Export LinkedIn Connections link.**

   You'll be taken to the Export LinkedIn Connections page, as shown in Figure 11-9. From the drop-down list provided, pick the e-mail program to which you want to export your contacts.

3. Click the Export button to generate your contacts file.

First, you are asked to enter the text of a security image into the box provided. Then, either your file will automatically download to your computer, or the File dialog box will appear, asking whether you want to open or save the file. If that box appears, click Save to save the file to your computer. Give it a custom name, if you like, but remember the filename and location because you need that information when you load this file into your e-mail program, which I discuss in the next sections.

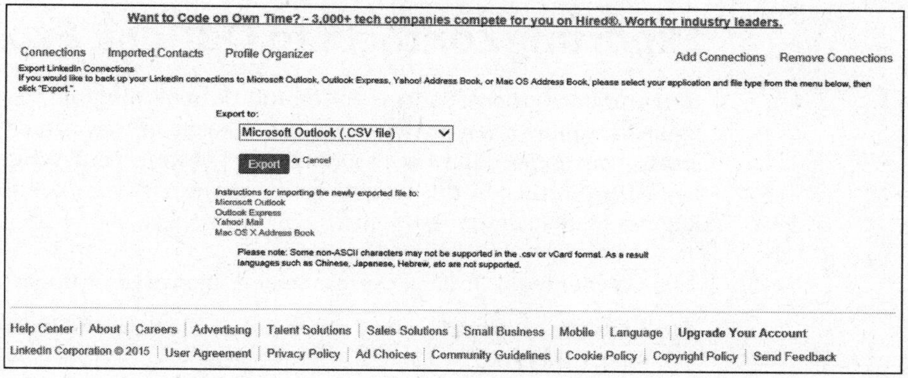

FIGURE 11-9:
Pick your e-mail program and create an exported file of contacts.

Exporting contacts to Outlook

Now that you've created your contacts file, it's time to import it into your e-mail program. For my first example, I'm going to use Microsoft Outlook, but the procedure is similar with other e-mail clients. The next few sections give you an idea of how to handle other e-mail clients.

After you create your LinkedIn export file and are ready to export your LinkedIn contacts to Microsoft Outlook, follow these steps:

1. On the main Outlook screen, choose File ➪ Import and Export.

The Import and Export window appears.

2. Select the Import from Another Program or File option and then click Next.

3. When Outlook asks you to select a file type to import from, select the Comma Separated Values (Windows) option and then click Next.

4. When Outlook asks you for the file to import, enter the path and filename of your exported file, or click the Browse button to find the file on your computer. Be sure to select the Do Not Import Duplicate Items option and then click Next.

If you don't select the Do Not Import Duplicate Items option, you risk flooding your Outlook account with multiple e-mail addresses and names for the same people, which will make your life more difficult and flood your connections with unnecessary e-mail messages.

5. **When Outlook asks you to select a destination folder, click the contacts folder and then click Next.**

6. **Verify that you're importing your contacts file into Outlook and then click Finish to start the process.**

Exporting contacts to Outlook Express

If you prefer Outlook Express to the full Outlook program, you're in luck: Your LinkedIn contacts can go live there just as easily as they can elsewhere. After you create your export file (as described in "Creating your contacts export file in LinkedIn," earlier in this chapter), you can export your connections to Outlook Express by following these steps:

1. **On your main Outlook Express screen, choose File ⇨ Import.**

2. **In the Import window that opens, select the Other Address Book option and then click Next.**

3. **When Outlook Express asks you to select a file type to import from, select the Text File (Comma Separated Values) option and then click the Import button.**

4. **When Outlook Express asks you for the file to import, enter the path and filename of your exported file, or click the Browse button to find the file on your computer. Click Next.**

5. **Verify the fields that you're importing into Outlook Express (click the Change Mapping button if you want to change how the information is being imported) and then click Finish to start the process.**

Exporting contacts to Yahoo! Mail

If you're using a web-based mail program, like Yahoo! Mail, you can follow this basic procedure to take your exported LinkedIn contacts and import them into your webmail program. After you create your export file (as described in "Creating your contacts export file in LinkedIn," earlier in this chapter), you can import those connections to Yahoo! Mail by following these steps:

1. **Using your web browser, go to Yahoo! Mail and log in. Click the Contacts tab to go to the Yahoo! Contacts page.**

   You see a page similar to that shown in Figure 11-10.

FIGURE 11-10:
Start at your Yahoo! Contacts page.

2. **Click the Import Contacts button.**

   A new screen appears, as shown in Figure 11-11.

3. **Click the From File button.**

   The Upload from File screen appears.

4. **Click the Browse button to find the file on your computer, as shown in Figure 11-12.**

5. **Click the Upload button to send the LinkedIn contacts file to your Yahoo! account.**

On the next screen, you see a summary page of the number of contacts that were successfully imported or not imported, and the number of duplicate contacts that were found. Click the View Contacts button to see your new contacts list, or click the Done button to finish the process.

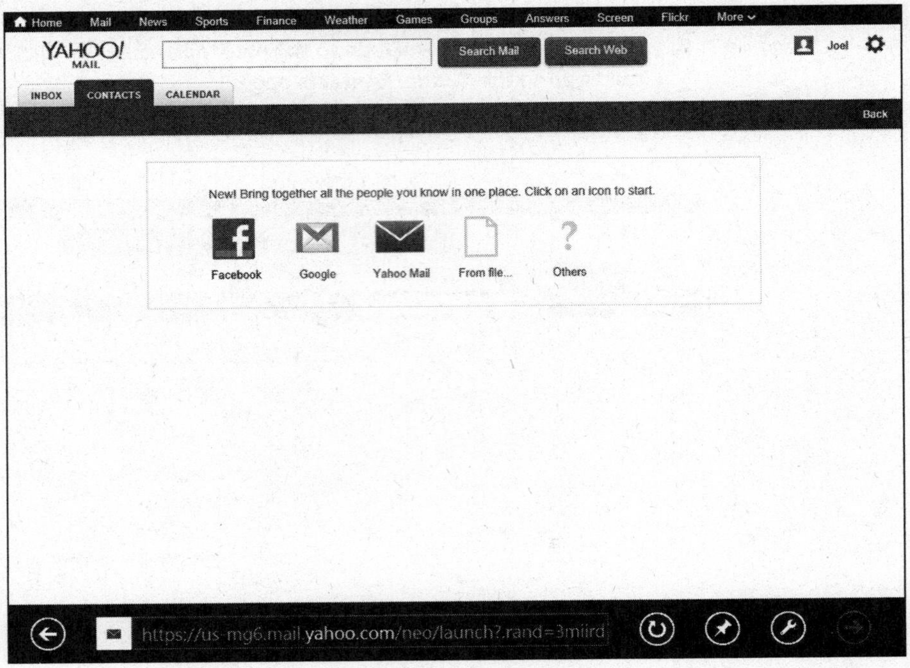

FIGURE 11-11:
Yahoo! asks you from where you want to import contacts.

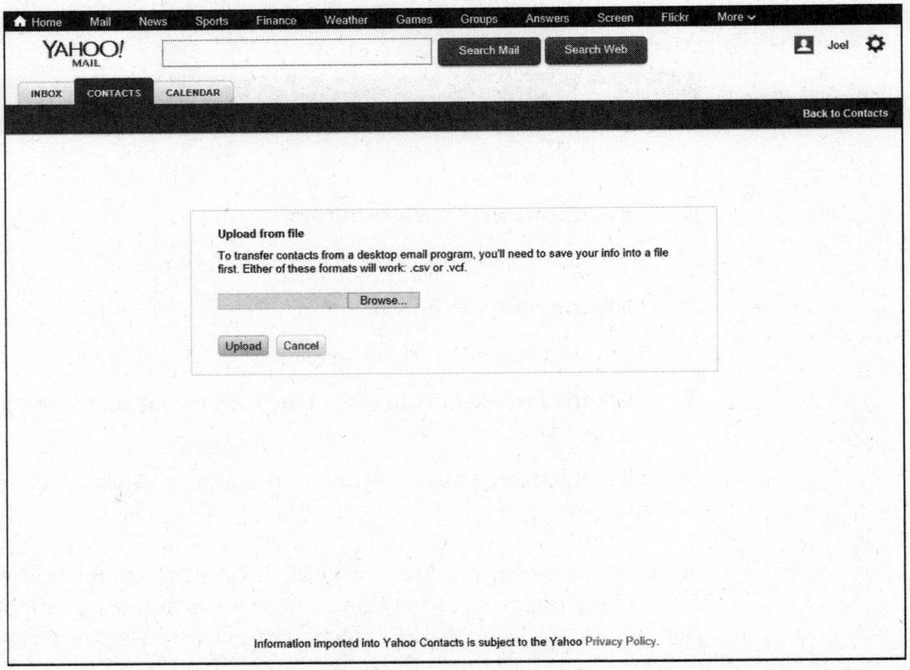

FIGURE 11-12:
Find your exported file to import your contacts.

Exporting connections to Mac OS X Contacts book

After you create your export file (as described in "Creating your contacts export file in LinkedIn," earlier in this chapter), you can export your connections to Mac OS X Contacts book by following these steps:

1. Locate your Mac OS X Contacts Book icon in either the Dock or the Applications folder, and open it up.

2. Look for the contacts file you created in the previous section.

3. In the Contacts book, click File and then Import from the drop-down menu.

This should start the importing of contacts from your LinkedIn contacts file.

Chapter 12

Accessing LinkedIn with Your Mobile Devices

Mobile devices seem to be everywhere these days. Smartphones, tablet devices, wearable devices like the Apple Watch, and whatever portable devices are being invented as I type this sentence, are having increased usage, especially as more people prefer to use their mobile device as their main (or only) gateway to Internet content. Because of this shift, companies of all sizes are paying more and more attention to developing their own mobile applications, or "apps" for short, that give their user base an easier way to interface with the company than having the user open up the web browser for their device and surf over to the company's website.

LinkedIn is no exception, and its mobile strategy has been evolving for years. Assisted by some outside purchases, such as LinkedIn's acquisition of the news site Pulse in 2013, LinkedIn has evolved to provide its user base with a suite of mobile apps that cater to general and specific uses of the LinkedIn website and its functions. In late 2015, LinkedIn launched a major redesign of its flagship mobile app to simplify the experience and encourage users to access LinkedIn through the app when they are on the go, perhaps on the way to a client meeting or expanding their personal network at a conference.

In this chapter, I detail LinkedIn's presence in the mobile app space. I discuss the different apps available as of this writing, and then talk about installing an app on your mobile device. I then analyze the main LinkedIn app and detail the functionality currently available in that app. Finally, I talk about how your activity on the app affects your use of LinkedIn on the desktop or laptop.

Surveying the Different LinkedIn Apps

As more and more people use their mobile devices to access the Internet and do their daily tasks, companies such as LinkedIn have been aggressively ramping up their mobile app development to meet the needs of their device-toting user base. The look and design of the apps have evolved over time to give LinkedIn users a clear picture of the data they are trying to retrieve in an easy-to-read format.

In addition, the number of LinkedIn apps has increased over time to keep the user experience simple and effective. Rather than having one bloated app that forces users to access all the different LinkedIn functions, the company decided to develop stand-alone mobile apps that focus on a specific function to allow users to better use these functions on their mobile devices. These can be used separately or in conjunction with LinkedIn's main mobile app. You can always look at LinkedIn's different mobile offerings by checking out their mobile page at `https://mobile.linkedin.com`, as shown in Figure 12-1.

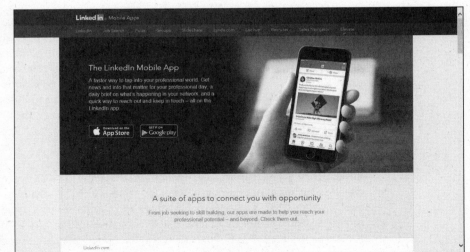

FIGURE 12-1:
Learn about the different LinkedIn mobile apps.

As of this writing, LinkedIn currently offers apps in these areas:

» **LinkedIn mobile app:** The main LinkedIn app allows you to interact with LinkedIn the same way you would when using your desktop or laptop computer. You can view your news feed of friends' stories, update your profile, talk to your connections, add new people to your network, or search for more information.

» **LinkedIn Job Search:** This targeted app allows you to search and filter the job openings on the LinkedIn job board to find jobs where you can apply. This app also includes the functionality that lets you see who you know at the company you're applying to, as well as information about the person who posted the job opening. You can apply for jobs through the app with a couple of taps, and track the jobs that you've looked at, applied, or saved. You can set up notifications on your mobile device to hear when jobs become available to apply for or if a targeted job posting is about to expire.

» **LinkedIn Groups:** If you're a big user of LinkedIn Groups, then this app is for you. It allows you to monitor and contribute to the discussions in the LinkedIn Groups where you are a member, as well as give you the ability to post new discussions to those groups from your mobile device.

» **LinkedIn Lookup:** This app is designed for use by workers in medium to large companies, and is meant to help you find, learn, and connect with co-workers in your own company, regardless of whether that co-worker is in your first-degree network. The app allows you to search by the person's title, skills, expertise, name, and more. You can review any co-worker's profile and contact her directly using the information in the app.

» **LinkedIn Pulse:** Stay up to date on the news and information that matters to you. Read up on the influencers, companies, and industries you are following with this Pulse app. You can also see what your peers are viewing. The mobile app goes further than the desktop, allowing you to save stories with a swipe of your finger to read at a later date. You can "swipe left" to indicate to Pulse that you didn't like that content, which will help Pulse tailor future news feeds for you. You can also set up Smart Notifications that let you know when your connections are mentioned in the news.

» **LinkedIn SlideShare:** This app gives you mobile access to over 18 million slide presentations, information graphics, and videos that have been uploaded by LinkedIn members around the world. Learn about various topics from your network and leading industry professionals, all from the ease of your mobile device.

» **Lynda.com:** In April 2015, LinkedIn acquired Lynda.com, a subscription-based online learning website. While part of the LinkedIn family, Lynda.com developed its own stand-alone mobile app, which is available to its subscribers and allows users to access Lynda's vast library of educational presentations to learn about thousands of different skills. Learn from the experts while on the go and advance your skills and career with Lynda's monthly subscription and this app. You can also download this content to your mobile device for future viewing.

When you are on either the iTunes App Store or Google Play store, you can look for apps owned by LinkedIn by looking for apps where the developer is LinkedIn Corporation. You can see from Figure 12-2 the variety of apps available for different devices for Apple iOS devices, for example.

FIGURE 12-2:
Download different LinkedIn apps to your iOS device.

REMEMBER

There are other apps available to premium users, targeting specific users like recruiters and sales professionals. Consult the LinkedIn mobile page at https://mobile.linkedin.com for more information about these apps.

Installing a LinkedIn Mobile App

WARNING

As of this writing, LinkedIn apps are only available for mobile devices running the Apple iOS operating system or the Android operating system, and not every app will work on every device. For example, as Figure 12-2 demonstrated, while there are ten apps for an iPhone, only four of those apps work on an iPad device. Consult the app store for your device to see what you can install.

When you're ready to install an app, follow these steps from your mobile device (for the purposes of illustration, the figures in this process demonstrate how I use an iPad to install the main LinkedIn app):

1. **Pull up your main source for installing mobile apps. For example, if you've got an Apple device, start up the App Store; if you've got an Android device, start up the Google Play Store.**

    You can also go to LinkedIn's mobile page at https://mobile.linkedin.com, find the app you want to install, and then click either the App Store or Google Play Store button, depending on your device.

2. **On the search screen, type in the word LinkedIn (and any additional words, if you want one of the specialized LinkedIn mobile apps, like LinkedIn Job Search or LinkedIn Pulse).**

    This should bring up a results screen of apps similar to Figure 12-2 from the previous section. Click the appropriate icon to bring up the app info screen.

3. **When you see the name and description of the app you want, click the Get or Install button to start installing the app, as shown in Figure 12-3.**

    Your device may prompt you to log into your iTunes or Android account at this point. In addition, some apps, like the main LinkedIn mobile app, offer in-app

FIGURE 12-3:
Click the Get or Install button to start the installation process.

purchases, which means that either Apple or Google will want to verify your billing method in case you buy something inside the app.

WARNING

There may be requirements for the level of operating system you need on your device before you can install this app. If your operating system needs to be updated, your mobile device will warn you of this and stop the installation process. You will need to update your OS and then reattempt this installation.

4. **Once the app is fully installed, you should see an icon on your screen. Tap that icon to start the LinkedIn app.**

You should be taken to a login screen, as shown in Figure 12-4, where you can sign in with your LinkedIn account or join LinkedIn with a new account.

FIGURE 12-4:
Sign in to your LinkedIn account from the app.

5. **The first time you open the LinkedIn app, you will be asked to log into your LinkedIn account. Click Sign In, type in your LinkedIn user id and password into the boxes provided and then click the Next button.**

Once you've signed into your LinkedIn account, the first thing the app will ask you is whether to enable notifications, where the app can send a message to your device's screen when certain actions occur. When you see the box pop up (see Figure 12-5), you can click the OK button to turn on notifications, or click Don't Allow to keep notifications turned off. At any time you can go into the app's settings to change this setting.

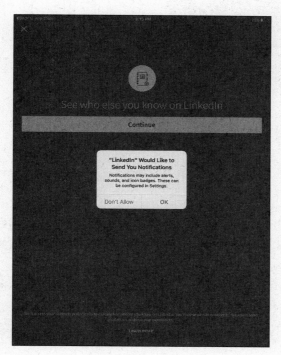

FIGURE 12-5:
Decide whether you want the mobile app to send notifications to your device.

Congratulations, you've installed the app! Repeat this process with any other app you want to install on your device.

Once you've installed the LinkedIn app, there may be a shortcut to bringing the other LinkedIn apps onto your device. Bring up the LinkedIn app, make sure you are on the home screen, and see if you have a grid of dots in the upper right corner. If you can see those dots, tap on that grid to bring up an "app launcher" sidebar (see Figure 12-6), where you can tap one of the menu items to install other apps on your device.

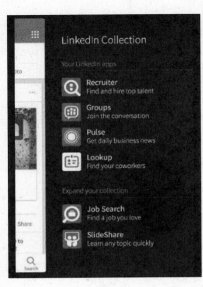

Breaking Down the Sections of the LinkedIn Mobile App

After you install the main LinkedIn mobile app and sign in to your LinkedIn account from the app, you are ready to start using the app. Before you do, though, it's important to understand the capabilities now at your fingertips.

When you use the LinkedIn mobile app, you will notice a series of buttons along the bottom of the screen. These buttons allow you to easily reach the different sections of the LinkedIn app.

The five core sections of the LinkedIn mobile app are organized by these headers:

>> **Home:** This section (see Figure 12-7) mirrors your home page news feed, integrating elements from your first-degree connections and the news sources you follow on LinkedIn, as well as news items and blog posts that LinkedIn thinks you may like, plus job recommendations. LinkedIn takes advantage of the interactivity with your mobile device by allowing you to swipe (with your finger) stories in this section to indicate whether you find them valuable or not, and then remembers your choices and learns over time to help present a finer-tuned list of elements more to your liking.

FIGURE 12-7:
See your feed elements from LinkedIn on the home screen.

>> **Me:** This section mirrors the Notifications list that LinkedIn provides you on the website (see Figure 12-8), showing you when and where you are being mentioned, and who is reading your profile or your posts. You can also easily update your profile from this section so your professional brand can stay strong or get a much-needed refresh. Finally, you can update your settings from this section, by clicking the cog wheel at the top right of the screen. This is particularly important to mobile users because you can set push notifications from the settings screen, allowing you to see pop-up notifications on your device like an incoming text message so you don't miss a new item of interest.

WARNING

As of this writing, you cannot edit every section of your profile in the LinkedIn mobile app. If you do not see the capability to edit that section, then you know you will have to edit it on the desktop version of LinkedIn.

>> **Messages:** This section mirrors your LinkedIn Inbox, allowing you to message or chat with your connections on LinkedIn. This way, you can initiate a new conversation while on the go or follow up on existing communications while away from your desk. You can change your notifications for any given conversation or delete any conversation from the screen.

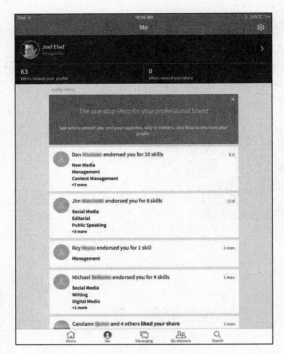

FIGURE 12-8:
See who's viewed
your profile and
how you're
interacting with
your network.

>> **My Network:** This section works very similar to the feed you see on the LinkedIn website home page, where you will see a rundown of activities from people you are connected with on LinkedIn. If you look at Figure 12-9, you will see a stack of "cards" where you can interact with people's updates. You can like or comment on updates from your connections, congratulate a contact on a work anniversary or job change, and see suggestions to stay connected. You go through the elements of this section by swiping and clicking.

You can see any incoming connection requests and act on them by clicking the People icon from the top left corner of the screen without having to log into the website. Finally, this section offers you the ability to sync with your calendar — so LinkedIn can prompt you to review a profile of someone you have a scheduled meeting with that day, for example — making you better prepared for that meeting.

>> **Search:** This section mirrors the general LinkedIn search experience, where you can search for people, jobs, groups, companies, news items, or more. When you type keywords in the search bar at the top, options pop up that give you suggested search result groupings.

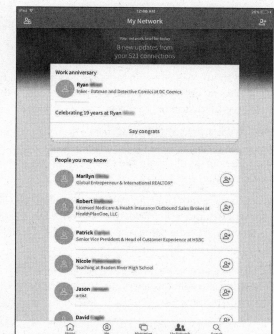

FIGURE 12-9:
Interact with your network through the mobile app.

When you search for people, you will notice that LinkedIn will try to "guess" what you are looking for by studying variations of a name you type in, coupled with your network of connections and list of companies you are employed at, to promote the most likely results at the top of the search results list. You can also type in a collection of keywords (someone's name and employer, job skills, or alma mater, for example) to help find the person on LinkedIn.

Connecting Your App Usage with Website Usage

After you've installed one or more of the LinkedIn mobile apps, and you start using the apps interchangeably with your desktop or laptop when you use LinkedIn, you should notice a synergy where all your actions are captured and available regardless of platform. Many of your actions are replicated or transmitted to your main LinkedIn account and will be reflected when you log onto the LinkedIn web-site with your PC or Mac:

>> Communication will show up in LinkedIn Messages, and you will see the same order of conversations on both the app and the website, where the most recent conversation is at the top of the screen.

>> Any profile updates you made with the app will be stored in the profile you see through the website and vice versa. Depending on your profile settings, your network will be notified of any profile changes you make on either the app or via the website.

>> Any interactions you have with LinkedIn members, whether you like or comment on someone's update, participate in a Groups discussion, or accept or reject an invitation, will be the same whether you did it through the app or the website.

>> When you swiped stories from the mobile app news feed, those choices will be remembered when LinkedIn displays your home page news feed when you access the LinkedIn website on your PC or laptop.

Similar to the settings available from the LinkedIn website, you can update a number of your settings through the LinkedIn app by clicking the Me button, and then clicking the Settings icon (cog wheel) in the top right of that screen. Any settings updated with your mobile device will be reflected when you next log onto the desktop version of LinkedIn. As of this writing, only some settings are acces-sible through the app, and they are divided into three categories:

>> **Account settings:** You can update the list of e-mail addresses on your account, add a phone number, change your password, sync your contacts, or review the active sessions you have where you're logged onto LinkedIn from your various devices.

>> **Privacy settings:** From the app, you can choose whether your network gets notified when you make profile changes and you can choose who can follow you. You can change the setting where you are visible or private when viewing someone else's profile and manage the list of who you're blocking. You can change your advertising preferences and choose who can find your profile by typing in your phone number.

>> **Communication settings:** You can decide which, if any, mobile push notifications you receive from LinkedIn. This way, you can decide what you want the LinkedIn app to notify you about, which only works on a mobile device.

4

Finding Employees, Jobs, and Companies

Chapter 13
Finding Employees

When you have a handle on the key elements of improving your LinkedIn profile and experience, it's time to look outward toward the LinkedIn network and talk about some of the benefits you can reap from a professional network of tens of millions of people.

Whether you're an entrepreneur looking for your first employee, a growing start-up needing to add a knowledgeable staffer, or a part of a Fortune 500 company filling a recent opening, LinkedIn can provide a rich and powerful pool of potential applicants and job candidates, including the perfectly skilled person who isn't even looking for a job! When it comes to looking for an employee, one of the benefits of LinkedIn is that you aren't limited to an applicant's one- or two-page resume and cover letter. Instead, you get the full picture of the applicant's professional history, coupled with recommendations and his knowledge and/or willingness to share information. Even if you find your candidate outside LinkedIn, you can use the site to perform reference checks and get more information about him. This information can augment what you learn from the candidate during the hiring process and from the references he provides. LinkedIn cannot replace your hiring process, but it can help you along the way.

In this chapter, I cover the basics of using LinkedIn to find an employee for your company or start-up. I begin with the basics of how you can post your job listing on LinkedIn and review your applicants. I then move on to the Reference Search function, where you can use LinkedIn to screen potential candidates, and I finish the chapter with search strategies you should employ to find the right person.

Managing Your Job Listings

LinkedIn offers a Business Solutions page for companies to manage their job listings. Hover your mouse over the Business Services link on the top navigation bar on the home page, and select Business Solutions from the drop-down list that appears to see the Business Solutions home page, as shown in Figure 13-1. This is where you start the process of creating a job listing, reviewing the applicants you get, and paying LinkedIn to post the listing.

FIGURE 13-1:
LinkedIn offers a Business Solutions page to manage your job listings.

As of this writing, the cost for one standard, 30-day job listing on LinkedIn varies by location, with the average cost ranging between $195 and $299. LinkedIn also offers packs of five or ten job credits (one job credit allows you to post one job listing) that reduce the per-listing cost by up to 35 percent or so. You can pay for your job listing with PayPal or a major credit card such as Visa, MasterCard, American Express, or Discover.

TIP

If you know you're going to need multiple or ongoing job postings on LinkedIn, you might want to consider LinkedIn Corporate Recruiting Solutions to get discounts on multiple credits for job postings and InMail. You can get more information by completing a request at `https://business.linkedin.com/talent-solutions`.

You can choose to renew your listing at the end of the 30-day window. Your *date posted* (the date you set up the job listing) is updated with the renewal date instead of the original posting date, so the listing appears at the top of search results. The cost for renewing a job listing is the same as the initial job posting cost.

WARNING

You can advertise only one open position per job listing. If you solicit applications for more than one position within a single job listing, LinkedIn removes your listing or requires you to purchase multiple job credits.

Posting a job listing

To post your job opening, follow these steps:

1. **Hover your mouse over the Business Services link on the top navigation bar, and select Post a Job from the drop-down list that appears.**

You see the Build Your Job Posting screen, as shown in Figure 13-2.

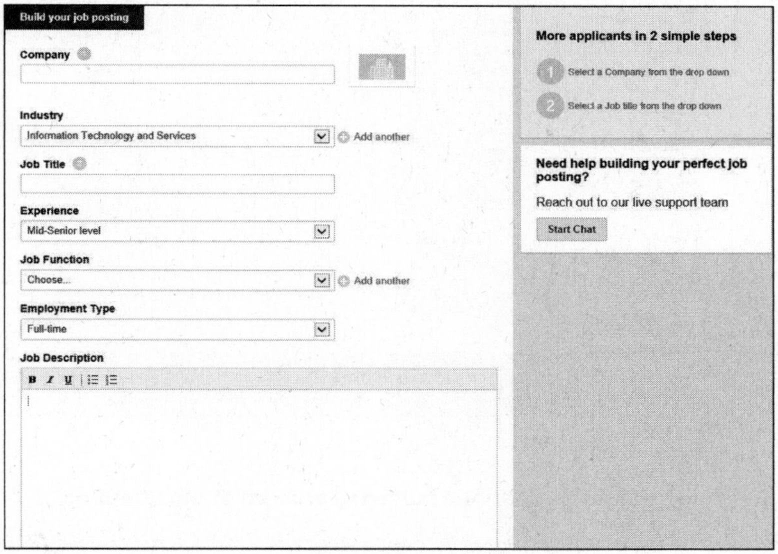

Build your job posting

Company

Industry
Information Technology and Services ▾ ⊕ Add another

Job Title

Experience
Mid-Senior level ▾

Job Function
Choose... ▾ ⊕ Add another

Employment Type
Full-time ▾

Job Description
B *I* U | ≔ ≔

More applicants in 2 simple steps

① Select a Company from the drop down

② Select a Job title from the drop down

Need help building your perfect job posting?

Reach out to our live support team

Start Chat

FIGURE 13-2:
Start composing your job posting here.

2. **Using the text boxes and lists provided, enter the required information about your company and the job you're offering.**

When it comes to your company, LinkedIn asks for your company name and the industry your company represents. As for the job posting itself, you need to specify the job title, employment type, experience level, and function. When you're done with that, you can scroll down and compose your job description in the text box provided (refer to Figure 13-2) or copy the description from another source and paste it into the box. Just make sure any formatting (spacing, bullet points, font size, and so on) is correct after you paste the text.

3. **Scroll down and fill in the How Candidates Apply and Job Poster sections, as shown in Figure 13-3.**

LinkedIn automatically offers you the ability to receive applications at one of your existing e-mail addresses, but you can decide which e-mail address should receive applications, or whether applicants should use a direct URL to apply to your job position. In addition, you can decide whether you want your profile summary to appear with the job listing by selecting the appropriate check box.

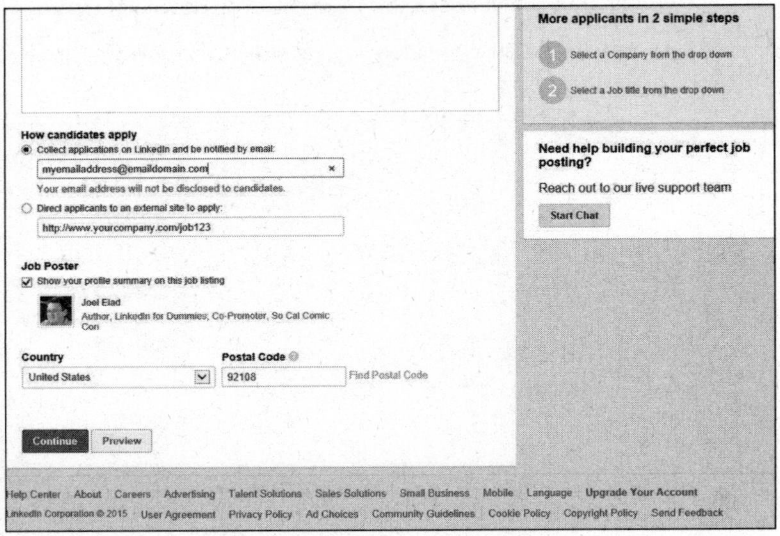

FIGURE 13-3:
Set your information for candidate routing and job location here.

4. **Click the Continue button to proceed to the final step.**

LinkedIn analyzes your job listing and looks for matches, but first, it asks if you want to pay money to "Sponsor" your job listing to show up at the top of search results, which is optional. Second, it needs your billing information, which is mandatory. You are prompted to decide how many job post credits you would like to purchase (see Figure 13-4) based on the job listing you just created. After picking the number of credits, scroll down and make sure you have either a major credit card or PayPal account to pay for the job credit(s). Complete all the fields required and then click the Review Order button. Review all the info on the next screen (see Figure 13-5) and then click the blue Post Job button to post your listing.

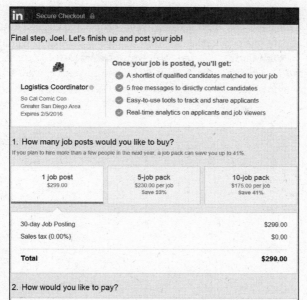

FIGURE 13-4:
Decide on the number of job credits you wish to buy.

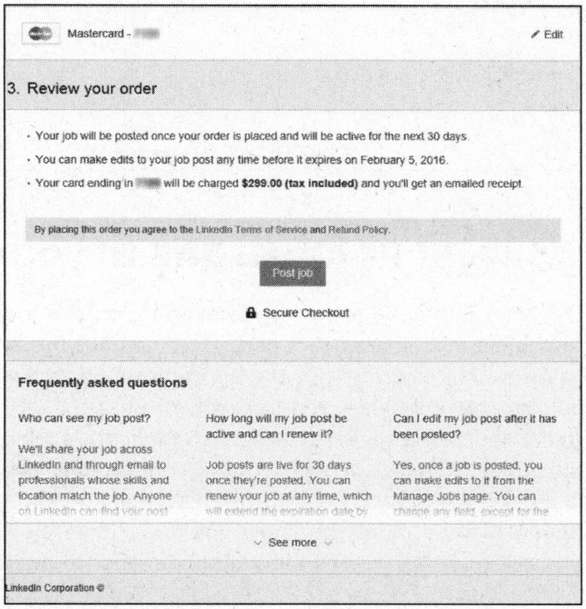

FIGURE 13-5:
Confirm the details for your job listing.

That's it! You have completed the all-important first step: You posted your job listing, and LinkedIn shows you the receipt for your purchase, as shown in Figure 13-6. This listing is available through LinkedIn's Jobs home page, which you can get to by clicking the Jobs link (in the top navigation bar) and looking in the Your Jobs box along the right side of your Jobs home page.

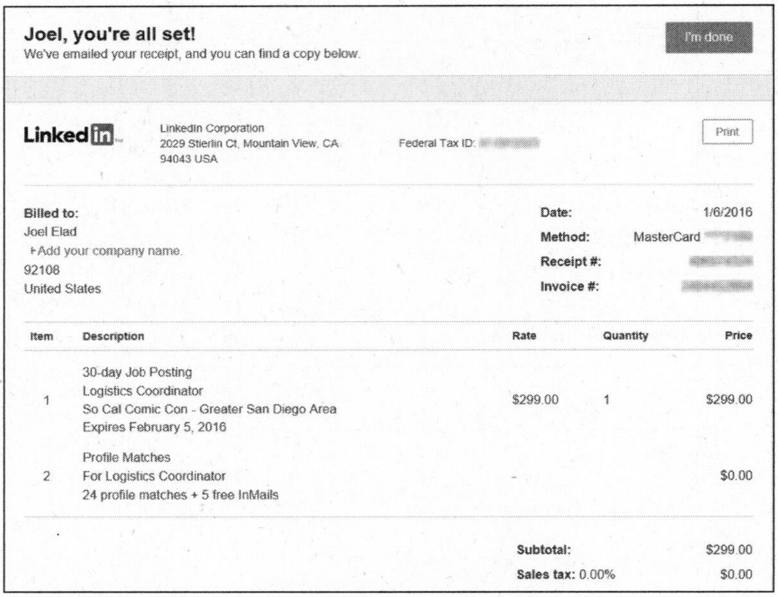

Joel, you're all set!
We've emailed your receipt, and you can find a copy below.

I'm done

Linked in.   LinkedIn Corporation
              2029 Stierlin Ct, Mountain View, CA.   Federal Tax ID: Print
              94043 USA

Billed to: Date: 1/6/2016
Joel Elad   Method: MasterCard
 ⊦Add your company name.   Receipt #:
92108   Invoice #:
United States

Item	Description	Rate	Quantity	Price
1	30-day Job Posting Logistics Coordinator So Cal Comic Con - Greater San Diego Area Expires February 5, 2016	$299.00	1	$299.00
2	Profile Matches For Logistics Coordinator 24 profile matches + 5 free InMails	-		$0.00

Subtotal: $299.00
Sales tax: 0.00% $0.00

FIGURE 13-6: Keep the receipt for your new LinkedIn job listing.

Advertising your job listing to your network

Traditionally, when someone posted a job opening on the Internet using one of those ubiquitous job search sites, that person would hope the extensive pool of job seekers would find the posting and the appropriate parties would submit their resumes and cover letters. When you use LinkedIn to fill a job, however, you still benefit from the pool of job seekers who search LinkedIn's Jobs page, but you have a distinct advantage: *your own network.* You're connected to people who you know and trust, people who you have worked with before so you know their capabilities, and most importantly, people who know you and (hopefully) have a better idea than the average person as to what kind of person you would hire.

LinkedIn offers you the chance to "Share" your job listing using social networking sites like Facebook and Twitter, and it allows you to send all or some of the people in your network a message, letting them know about your job opening and asking them if they, or anyone they know, might be interested in this job. When you're ready to advertise your job listing, follow these steps:

1. **Hover your mouse over the Account & Settings button (your profile photo, on the top navigation bar on the right) and select Manage (next to Job Posting) from the drop-down list that appears.**

   After you've posted your job, you should see the position listed in the Manage Jobs window under Active Jobs, as shown in Figure 13-7.

2. **Hover your mouse over the Share link (above the Post Job button, as indicated in Figure 13-7) and click the LinkedIn icon to generate a LinkedIn message.**

   LinkedIn automatically generates a Share box, as shown in Figure 13-8, that you can send to your LinkedIn network in a variety of ways. You can generate an automatic network update by selecting the Share an Update check box. If you belong to a LinkedIn Group that might be right for this job, select the Post to Groups check box and specify the LinkedIn Group(s) to be notified. You can also select the Send to Individuals check box. Feel free to edit the text in the message box to make it sound like it's coming from you, or just leave the default message in place.

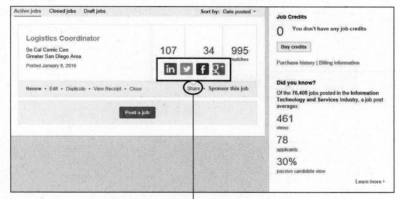

FIGURE 13-7:
See key information about your new job listing.

Click Share and then click an icon to utilize
social media for this job listing.

3. **If you select the Send to Individuals check box to forward this job listing to your connections, start typing names in the To box to decide who will get this message from you.**

   As you start typing the name of a first-degree connection, LinkedIn automatically displays its best guesses as to the correct name and headline right there below the To box. When you see the name you want, click it, and it appears in the To box. Continue to type additional names, up to a recommended maximum of ten people.

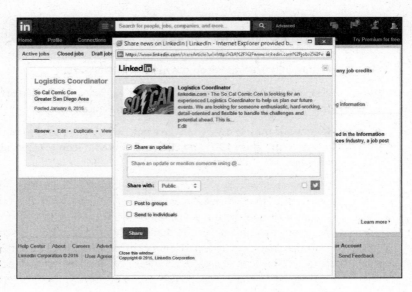

FIGURE 13-8:
LinkedIn lets you
ask your network
for help.

4. **Look over the subject line and text in the window again, make sure you have the right people selected, and when you're ready, click the Share button (see Figure 13-9).**

FIGURE 13-9:
Proofread your
message and
then send it!

Your LinkedIn connections will receive a message in their LinkedIn Inboxes and, depending on their notification settings, an e-mail with this message as well. They can click a link from the message to see the job listing and either apply themselves or forward it to their contacts for consideration.

5. **Hover your mouse over the Share link again and select another icon to generate a message for that social network.**

As of this writing, you can click either a Facebook icon, a Twitter icon, or a Google+ icon. In any case, a new window pops up that interfaces directly with the social network in question and allows you to draft your own update, or tweet and click to send it out directly to your network. (You will be prompted for your login information for any of these networks first.)

Reviewing applicants

After you've posted your job listing on LinkedIn, you should expect to get some applicants for the position. Every time someone applies for that job, you receive an e-mail from LinkedIn notifying you of the application. In addition, LinkedIn records the application in the Applicants number of the Active Jobs window. (Refer to Figure 13-7.)

When you're ready to review the applicants for your job, follow these steps:

1. **Hover your mouse over the Account & Settings button (on the top navigation bar on the right) and then select Manage (next to Job Posting) from the drop-down list that appears.**

   You should be taken to the Active Jobs screen, as shown in Figure 13-7 in the previous section. Click the job title of the job listing you wish to review, which brings you to the Overview screen, as shown in Figure 13-10.

2. **Hover your mouse over each entry in the Applicants section to access the links for viewing the applicant's resume (if attached) or to take other actions.**

   You can click Share to share the person's application with other people, such as other members of a hiring committee. You can click the Message link to send the applicant a message, or you can label her as a Great Fit, Good Fit, or Not a Fit. Once applicants are labeled, you can view only the people you marked Great Fit, for example, as shown in Figure 13-11.

FIGURE 13-10:
Review your open job listings to see who has applied.

Use these links to process the application.

FIGURE 13-11:
Filter through the applicants for the job.

3. **You can click the Filter link in the top middle of the Overview screen to reduce the number of potential matches with filters such as keywords, company, title, or years of experience. You can also click any applicant's name to see his LinkedIn profile and read up on his experience.**

Click the Send InMail or Send a Message button to contact the applicant, as shown in Figure 13-12.

FIGURE 13-12:
Review all your
applicants' data,
such as their
resume.

4. **Scroll down to the Profile Matches section to see additional potential applicants for this job.**

   In this example, LinkedIn analyzes the job listing and then looks through LinkedIn member profiles to see what is a match for the position based on the job description and skill requirements. When I scroll down to the Profile Matches section, as shown in Figure 13-13, LinkedIn displays the name, headline, photo, and location of each potential applicant. You can click the Filter link in the top right corner of the Profile Matches box to reduce the number of potential matches with filters such as years of experience, location, school, or current or past company.

   At this point, you could go through these results and look for applicants you'd want to approach to see if they'd be interested in the position. There are links under each person's name to share their info with your team, label the potential applicant as a Great Fit, Good Fit, or Not a Fit, or send the potential applicant an InMail message. (As of this writing, each job posting gives you five free InMail credits to contact people.) If someone is a second- or third-degree network member, that degree is shown next to their name. Scroll to the bottom of the page and click the Show More link to see more search results.

5. **Click the name of an applicant and contact her to see if she'd be interested in the job.**

   When you click any name in the search results, you bring up the person's profile. If you think an applicant is worth pursuing for your job opening, you can use InMail or an introduction to send him a message (I cover both in Chapter 5) and inquire about his interest in the job.

FIGURE 13-13:
See who in the LinkedIn network might be a good fit for this position.

Screening Candidates with LinkedIn

After you use LinkedIn to post a job request, you can continue to use LinkedIn to assist you in the screening part of your hiring process. In addition to asking for references from the applicant, or possibly ordering a background check from a services company, you can use LinkedIn to verify information in your applicant's resume and application at any stage of the process, without paying a dime!

Here are some strategies to keep in mind:

>> **Start by thoroughly reviewing the applicant's LinkedIn profile.** When you review an applicant's profile, compare it with her resume, cover letter, and application. Is she consistent in how she presents all of her experience?

>> **Read through the applicant's recommendations and follow up.** If your candidate has received recommendations, go through them, pay attention to the date the recommendation was written, and see whether any are applicable toward your open position. Pay particular attention to recommendations from former bosses or co-workers. If necessary, ask your candidate whether you can contact the recommender through InMail and use that person as a reference.

>> **See whether you're connected to your candidate.** When you pull up your candidate's profile, you see whether she is a second- or third-degree network member, which would mean there are one or two people who connect you with the candidate. If so, contact that person (or ask for an introduction to reach the correct party) and ask for more information about the candidate. Chances are good that you will get a more honest assessment from someone you know rather than the recommendations provided by the candidate. Understand, however, that while the two people may be connected, they may not know each other that well, or their connection may be outside the professional expertise you're looking to learn about from this job candidate.

>> **Evaluate the candidate's total picture.** If your candidate mentions any websites, blogs, or other online presence in her LinkedIn profile, click the link and see how it's involved. Take a look at the listed interests and group affiliations and see whether they add to (or detract from) your picture of the job candidate.

Because most LinkedIn users have already defined each company where they worked and the years of employment, you can get a sense for their abilities, what they have handled in the past, and depending on the completeness of their profile, examples of their past accomplishments.

TIP

As helpful as LinkedIn can be when reviewing a candidate, don't be afraid to use other Internet websites and searches to gain a well-rounded view of the candidate in question.

Using Strategies to Find Active or Passive Job Seekers

One of the powers of LinkedIn is its ability to find not just the active job seeker, but the passive job seeker or someone who doesn't even realize she wants a new job! You can tap an extensive network of professionals who have already identified their past experiences, skill sets, interests, educational backgrounds, and group affiliations.

The best piece of advice, in my opinion, for this type of search comes from Harvey Mackay and the book he wrote back in 1999, *Dig Your Well Before You're Thirsty:* You should be building a healthy network and keeping your eye on potential candidates before you have a job opening to fill. The earlier you start, and the more consistent you are with the time you spend on a weekly or monthly basis expanding your network, the easier it is to identify and then recruit a potential candidate to fill your opening.

There are specific steps you should take to make your strategy a reality. Whether you start this process in advance or just need to fill a position as soon as possible, here are some tactics to consider:

» **Perform detailed advanced searches.** If you want the perfect candidate, search for that candidate. Put multiple keywords in the Advanced Search form, look for a big skill set, narrow your search to a specific industry, and maybe even limit your range to people who already live close to you. If you come up with zero results, remove the least necessary keyword and repeat the search, and keep doing that until you come up with some potential candidates.

» **Focus on your industry.** If you know that you're probably going to need software developers, start getting to know potential candidates on the LinkedIn site and stay in touch with them. Look for people to connect with, whether they share a group affiliation with you, and actively network with these people. Even if they say no to a future job opportunity, chances are good that someone in their networks will be more responsive than the average connection. While Software Developer A may say no, that person probably has several software developers in his network who could respond favorably.

» **Start some conversations in the LinkedIn Groups section.** After you've found some LinkedIn Groups full of like-minded or interesting professionals, start exchanging information! Pose a question or start a group discussion that you would ask in an interview to potential candidates, and see who responds. Better yet, you'll see *how* the people respond, and you'll be able to decide from their answers who to focus on for a follow-up. You'll be able to see the public profiles of the people who provide answers and send messages to those people.

Chapter 14

Finding a Job

One of the most important ways that LinkedIn has benefitted people is how it helps improve their job search experience. Before LinkedIn, everyone remembers what was involved when you had a job search — making lots of phone calls and visits (and some e-mails) to people you knew, asking them whether they knew anybody who was hiring, asking whether they knew somebody at Company X who might talk to you, or asking something else related to your search. It was a tedious and inefficient process, and LinkedIn has improved it. Understand, however, that LinkedIn hasn't replaced the entire process. You still need to have some face-to-face meetings and make phone calls, but LinkedIn can help you find the right person before you pick up the phone. One of the most potent aspects of LinkedIn and a job search is the speed with which you can connect with people and find opportunities.

In this chapter, I discuss some of the ways that you can use LinkedIn to help find a job, whether you're an active job seeker (I need a job right now!) or a passive job seeker (I don't mind where I'm at, but if the right opportunity comes along, I'm listening). I start by talking about LinkedIn's job board and how you can search for openings. Then I move into more strategic options like improving your profile, devising specific strategies, searching your network for specific people, and targeting specific companies when you search.

Using LinkedIn to Search for a Job

LinkedIn offers lots of tools that can help you look for a job. The most direct way is to search for open positions on the LinkedIn job board, which I cover in the following section. There are other things to keep in mind when looking for a job, which I cover in the later sections, like improving your visibility and optimizing your profile. Part of the success of finding a job is to have an appealing LinkedIn identity so hiring managers can find you and want to contact you with an opening. According to *Forbes* magazine, 90 percent of employers are using social media sites to recruit employees, with LinkedIn being the most used of those sites. After all, the best search is when someone comes to you with an opportunity without you sweating the details.

Searching for an open position

The most obvious way to look for a job is to look through LinkedIn's advertised job openings. After all, someone is getting hired when a company runs a job listing, so why can't that candidate be you? When you search for a job on LinkedIn, you can see what skills seem attractive to companies these days, which you can keep in mind as you refine your job search and LinkedIn profile.

When you're ready to search for a job opening, follow these steps:

1. **Click the Jobs link from the top navigation bar.**

   The Jobs home page appears, as shown in Figure 14-1.

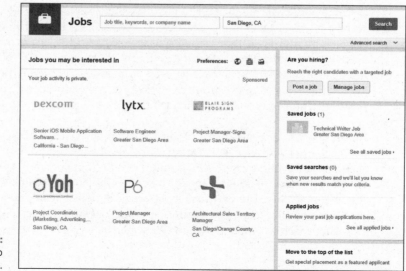

FIGURE 14-1: Look for a job on LinkedIn.

2. **Enter keywords describing the job you want in the Job Title, Keywords, or Company Name text box.**

   To be more precise in your search, you can click the Advanced Search link below the Search button to bring up some Advanced Search additional criteria, such as Industry, Function, or Salary level.

3. **Click the Search button.**

   You're taken to a LinkedIn Jobs results screen like the one shown in Figure 14-2, where you see the basic components of the job listings, such as Company, Title, and Location.

   To refine your job results, enter additional keywords or scroll down the left-hand side of the screen to use additional filters like the name of the company, how long the job posting has been online, and the location of the job.

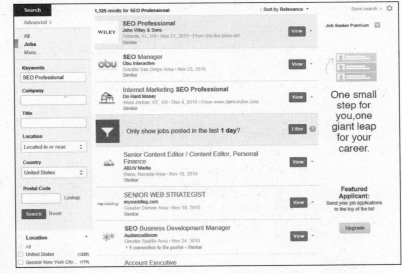

FIGURE 14-2: See your job search results.

4. **Click an individual job title to see the details of that job posting.**

   You see the detailed write-up on the next screen, as shown in Figure 14-3, where you can find out more about the job and the job poster. If the person who posted the job is in your network and has opted to show her name, you will see who in your LinkedIn network can refer you to that person. In the example in Figure 14-3, you can see that two different first-degree connections, like Laura., can introduce me to the job poster, who is a second-degree network member.

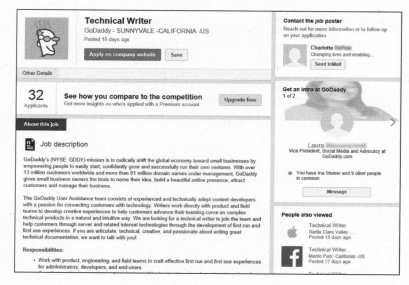

FIGURE 14-3:
Find out more about a specific job listing.

5. **When you see a job you want to apply for, click the Apply button.**

   LinkedIn may display a pop-up window, Apply with Your Profile, as shown in Figure 14-4, where your profile information is used instead of a resume. (In some cases, you're taken to the company's specific applicant tracking system — for example, any job from Google does this. In those cases, simply follow the instructions displayed to apply for that job.)

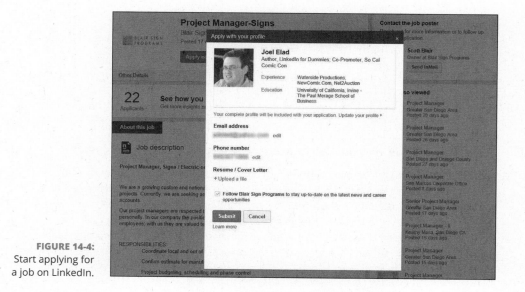

FIGURE 14-4:
Start applying for a job on LinkedIn.

6. **Verify your contact information, then upload a cover letter (which you'll write from your word processing program) in the Resume/Cover Letter section.**

   Include a brief summary of why you feel you are qualified for the job in your cover letter. The cover letter is a great chance for you to expand upon your experience and education to clarify to the employer why you are perfect for the job.

   If you like, you can update and reuse an older cover letter you've used to apply to a similar job: Simply open a word processing program (such as Microsoft Word), find the letter, copy the contents into your new letter, update it with the specific details of this job, and save it as a unique file, which you can upload to LinkedIn. (Be sure to check the letter using your program's spell checker before you upload it.)

   TIP

   If the job poster is in your extended network, I recommend that you read her profile first, see what common interests you have, and incorporate that information into your cover letter. If you have the time, approach that person first with a LinkedIn message or InMail to get more information about the job posting before you apply. (I discuss these at length in Chapter 5.)

7. **Click the Submit button.**

   Off your application goes! Repeat Steps 2–7 to keep looking and applying for jobs.

TIP

When you are looking at a job posting that you like, scroll down until you see the Similar Jobs section, shown in Figure 14-5. LinkedIn shows you jobs from other companies that are similar to the one you're viewing so you can compare positions.

Improving your visibility and attractiveness

When you're looking for a job, manually scanning job listings and sending resumes are only part of the process. You also have to prepare your job-seeking strategies. The most obvious examples of these are your resume (or CV) and your cover letter. When you include LinkedIn in your job search, you need to prepare your total LinkedIn profile and network in order to get the optimal job search experience.

Although no strategy can guarantee the job of your dreams, these strategies can improve your odds of getting the attention of the right contact person, an interview, or extra consideration for your job application that's in a stack of potential candidates.

FIGURE 14-5:
See similar job
postings to the
one you're
reviewing.

Here are some strategies to keep in mind:

>> **Connect with former managers, co-workers, and partners.** This might
seem like an obvious strategy, but let me elaborate. Part of getting the job is
communicating (to your future employer) your ability to do the job. Nobody
knows your skills, potential, work attitude, and capability better than people
who have worked with you and observed you in action. Therefore, make sure
you have connected with your former managers, co-workers, and so on.
When these people are part of your network, the introductions they can
facilitate will carry extra weight because they can share their experience with
the person you want to meet. You can encourage them to provide referrals
for you to express to the entire community your capability and work ethic.

>> **Look at your colleagues' LinkedIn profiles.** Using the search functions or
your first-degree connections in your network, try to find people with goals
and work experience similar to yours. When you see how they describe their
work experience on their profiles, you might get some good ideas on how to
augment your profile.

>> **Look at profiles of LinkedIn members who hold the job title you are
seeking.** One of LinkedIn's newest features for employers is the ability to find
job candidates based on an "ideal employee"; typically, the person currently
holding the job they want to fill. LinkedIn searches for candidates based on

the profile an employer selects as the model. Therefore, study the profiles of people doing similar work to see what keywords, skills, and other elements they put in their profile that may be applicable to you.

>> **Contact people when they change jobs.** LinkedIn lets you know when someone in your immediate network has changed positions. This is an excellent opportunity for you to connect and congratulate that person. As she begins her new job, it's likely she may bring other contacts with her, or will know of advertised or unadvertised opportunities at this new company. Start with a short congratulatory e-mail to help remind the person of your past work together, and then follow up occasionally.

>> **Get referrals from past bosses and co-workers.** After you add your past bosses and co-workers to your network, keep in contact with them, let them know your current job search goals, and ask for an appropriate referral or introduction. They can use their knowledge of your work history and their expanded networks to make more powerful introductions or requests than just a friend asking another friend, "Hey, can you hire my friend, Joel?"

Don't be afraid to provide extra information to your past bosses or co-workers to help them make an effective referral. Before the Internet, when job seekers asked a past boss or co-worker to write a letter of recommendation, it was acceptable to include some bullet points of stories or points you hoped they would cover in their letters. The same is true in the LinkedIn world. Guide your contact to emphasize a work quality or anecdote that would be effective in the referral or introduction.

>> **Collect your recommendations.** Nothing communicates a vote of confidence from your network quite like a recommendation. When anyone reads your LinkedIn profile, he can see exactly what other people have said about you. Because he knows that you can't alter a recommendation, he's more likely to trust the content and believe you're the right person for the job. (See Chapter 9 for more information on how to get more recommendations.)

Checking your profile visibility settings

If you're currently employed but decide to quietly start looking for a new position, you should consider what you are broadcasting to your LinkedIn network before getting ready to make a change. You don't want your current employer or co-workers to see a flurry of activity that's typically a sign of moving on to greener pastures!

To check your visibility settings, hover your mouse over the profile photo at the top right corner of any LinkedIn page, then click Manage next to Privacy and Settings. On your Profile settings page (see Figure 14-6), pay careful attention to the following three options:

>> **Choose Whether or Not to Share Your Profile Edits:** When you click this option, deselect the Let People Know When You Are Changing Your Profile check box. That way, your boss or co-workers won't see a flurry of activity about you updating your profile or following companies that could become your new employer.

>> **Select Who Can See Your Activity Feed:** Typically, this option is set to "Your Connections" so your first-degree connections can see all of your activity on LinkedIn. You can change this option to "Only You" so your boss or co-workers don't see you joining a host of LinkedIn Groups or other actions that could indicate a job search.

>> **Select Who Can See Your Connections:** Again, typically, this option is set to "Your Connections" so your first-degree connections can see your other connections. However, you can change this option to "Only You" so your boss or co-workers can't see you adding a bunch of recruiters or competitors to your network, for example.

Pay attention to these settings when looking for a job.

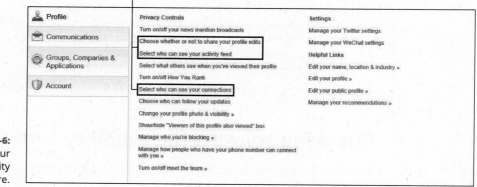

FIGURE 14-6: Manage your profile visibility here.

Optimizing your LinkedIn profile

The core of your LinkedIn presence is your profile, which is included with every job application you make on LinkedIn. Odds are good that prospective employers are going to check your LinkedIn profile when evaluating you for a job, so you want to make sure your profile is optimized to make you as appealing as possible.

Now that you've checked your settings, here are some things to keep in mind when bulking up your profile for a job search:

>> **Complete all the sections in your profile with as much accurate information as possible.** It's easy to put up a skeleton of your employment history and never get around to fully completing your profile. Unlike a resume (where you could feel confined in terms of page length), you can be as expansive as you want with your LinkedIn profile. You never know what part of your profile will get you included in someone's search result, but the more information you provide, the better chance someone will find you. Most important, make sure your most recent positions are filled out, because many employers focus on those positions first.

>> **Focus on accomplishments rather than duties.** I've seen a lot of people prepare their LinkedIn profiles in the same way they do their resumes, focusing solely on the duties they performed at each job. Although you want to give people an idea of what you did, hiring managers want to know the *results* of what you did, and the more concrete the example, the better. Saying you "organized procurement processes in your division" may demonstrate a skill, but saying that you "cut procurement costs by 16% in your first year" makes a bigger impact. Go back and talk to past co-workers or bosses, if necessary, to get whatever specifics they can provide on your performance.

>> **Add all relevant job search keywords, skill sets, and buzzwords to your profile.** When prospective employers are searching for someone to hire, they may simply search for a core set of skills to see who can fill the position. Therefore, just stating your job titles is not enough. If your profile says "Software Developer," prospective hiring managers could assume that you're qualified, but the only way you'd be considered is if these managers ran a search on those keywords. Say that a hiring manager does a search for the programming languages C++, Java, Perl, and Python. If all those keywords are not somewhere in your profile, you won't show up in the list to be considered at all. If you're unsure about what keywords to use, consider asking people in your field or researching the profiles of people who have the job title you are seeking.

>> **Use an appropriate and professional profile photo.** It's been said before but it's worth repeating: LinkedIn is designed for you to be a professional, and your profile photo is an important part of that process. Ditch the party photo best suited for Facebook. LinkedIn provides 5 Tips for Picking the Right LinkedIn Profile Picture on its talent blog. Read more at `https://business. linkedin.com/talent-solutions/blog/2014/12/5-tips-for-picking-the- right-linkedin-profile-picture`.

TIP

Use a photo of yourself rather than the generic icon supplied by LinkedIn. According to research done by LinkedIn Talent Solutions, if you have a profile photo, your profile is 14 times more likely to be viewed by other members.

>> **See how other people position themselves.** Imagine if you could get a book of thousands of resumes from current employees that you could then use as models to position yourself. Do a search for people with a job, education, or skill set similar to yours and see how they've worded their profiles or how they put their experiences in context. Use that insight to adapt your profile to make it clearer to others.

>> **List all your job experiences on your profile, not just full-time positions.** Did you do any short-term or contract jobs? Were you an advisor to another company? Perhaps you're a board member for a local nonprofit group or religious organization. Your LinkedIn profile is designed to reflect all of your job experiences, which is *not* limited to a full-time job that provided a W-2 slip. Document any work experience that adds to your overall profile, whether you were paid for that job/experience or not. LinkedIn even has sections in which you can highlight any volunteer or nonprofit experience.

WARNING

Make sure that every experience you list on your profile helps contribute to your overall career goals. After all, employers might not care that you were a pastry chef one summer — and will question why you thought it was so important that you listed it on your profile.

Implementing Job Search Strategies That Involve LinkedIn

When you're looking for a job, there are many potential ways you can include LinkedIn as part of your overall job search, beyond the direct task of searching jobs database listings and e-mailing a job request to your immediate network. In this section, I discuss various job search strategies you can implement that involve LinkedIn to some degree and can help add information, contacts, interviews, and hopefully some offers to your job search. Use one or use them all, but pick the methods you feel most comfortable with implementing.

REMEMBER

A job search should be considered as a time commitment, even with the power of LinkedIn. Some of these strategies apply to working or unemployed people and might not instantly result in multiple offers.

Leveraging your connections

One of the biggest benefits of LinkedIn is being able to answer the question, "Who do my contacts know?" It's important to think of LinkedIn as not only the sum of your first-degree connections, but also as your extended network of second- and third-degree network members that your colleagues can help connect you with for information, referrals, and hopefully, a new career.

Therefore, keep these second- and third-degree network members in mind so you can best leverage your connections to achieve progress. Consider these points when you're working on your job search using LinkedIn:

» **Look for connections to the job poster.** When searching for a job, pay attention to job listings where you see "X Connections to the Poster," such as the results screen shown in Figure 14-7. You can click those links to see who in your extended network can refer you directly to the employee who posted that job.

» **Ask for referrals whenever possible.** Exchange information first and then work your way up to request a referral.

» **Get your friends involved.** Let your immediate network know about your goals so they can recommend the right people for you to talk to — and hopefully, they'll generate the right introductions for you as well.

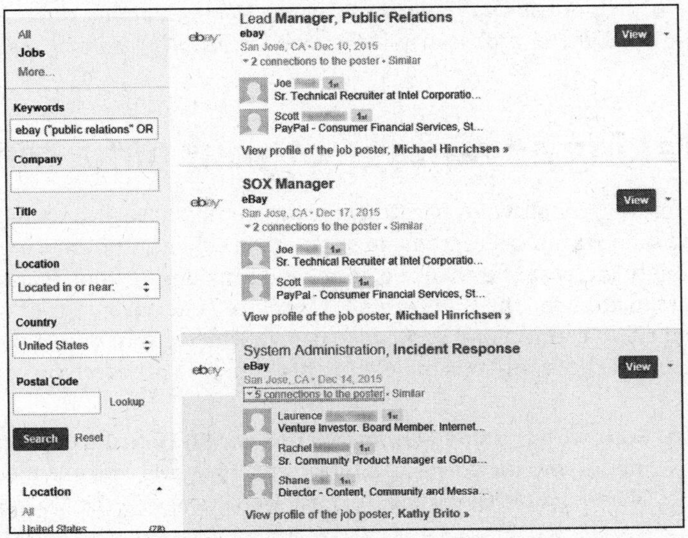

FIGURE 14-7: See which connections can refer you to the job poster.

Finding people with the same or similar job

If you're looking for a specific job, one way to approach your job search is to ask this question: "Who out there could possibly know more about the job I'm interested in than those folks doing that job right now?" The answer to that question is "no one." This means one source of help should be people with the same (or very similar) job title or responsibilities. Although these people might not have hiring authority, they can help give you the right perspective, share the right insider tips about what the job truly entails, and let you know what skills or background the hiring manager considered when they were hired.

Because these people are already employed and not your direct competition, they're more likely to offer help and advice. They have practical knowledge of what it takes to do that job and what qualities will best help someone succeed in that position. When you're ready to implement this strategy, keep these points in mind:

>> **Perform an advanced search for people with a similar job title as the one you're applying for.** Put the job title in either the keywords section or the title section.

>> **Narrow and clarify your search by industry.** For example, Project Manager of Software Development is very different than Project Manager for the Construction industry. Pick multiple industries if they are similar enough.

>> **When you find someone who has the job title you'd like to have, see whether she's interested in meeting for an informational interview (or if she's outside your geographic area, having a phone conversation).** Asking outright for a job lead will most likely not result in anything positive.

Taking advantage of your alma mater

Typically, people who share a school in common have an ongoing affinity, whether the school is an undergraduate or graduate college, or even a high school. You can rapidly increase the chance of someone considering your request if you and that person attended the same school. Therefore, take advantage of your alumni status and try to connect and work with people who went to one of the same schools as you. Here are some tips to help further this type of search by using LinkedIn:

>> **Start with the Find Alumni function within LinkedIn.** If you hover your mouse over the Connections link on the top navigation bar, then click Find Alumni, you will go directly to the university pages within LinkedIn. From here, you can search the alumni, see which are the most popular companies that hire these alumni, and learn other key facts.

>> **Search for alumni association groups of any school you attended. Click Interests and then click Groups from the top navigation bar — and then go ahead and join those groups.** This gives you access to the member list of that group, so you can see other alumni, regardless of graduation year, and communicate with them.

>> **Connect as a former classmate and ask for information first, referral second.** Your shared alumni status helps open the door, but don't expect a handout right away. Be ready to offer one of your contacts in exchange for the former classmate's help or consideration.

>> **Check the connection list of any of your contacts who attended school with you.** This is a good safety check to look for any classmates on your contacts' lists who you might not have initially considered. (I discuss connection lists in Chapter 6.)

>> **Try doing an Advanced People search with the school name as a keyword, and if necessary, try different variations of the school name.** For example, try the school name with and without acronyms. When I look for classmates from the University of California, Irvine, I search for *UCI* as well as *University California Irvine*. (I talk more about doing advanced searches in Chapter 4.)

>> **If your school has changed or updated its name, do an Advanced People search for both the old and new names as keywords.** For example, because my department name at UCI has changed from the Graduate School of Management, or GSM, to the Paul Merage School of Business, I search for the old and new search terms because my classmates may have defined their educational listings differently.

Finding target company referrals

Sometimes your job search involves a specific company and not necessarily a job title. Suppose you know you want to work at one of the top computer database software companies. Now you can use LinkedIn to help you find the right people at those companies who can help you. Here are some points to consider:

>> **Make a list of the ten companies you'd like to work for and do an individual Advanced People search for each company to find potential contacts at these companies.** Type the company name in the search box at the top of the LinkedIn home page and then click the Search button. You should see a list of people on the Search results page that have the Company name in their titles who are in your extended network. For larger companies, you need to search for a specific department or industry area to find the right contact. Ask these people you've identified for referrals to someone in your

target organization, like a hiring manager. You can also refine your search by relationship by searching for any combination of first-degree connections, second- or third-degree network members, or LinkedIn Group members.

>> **Follow the companies themselves.** LinkedIn allows you to "follow" companies through their Company page, so be sure to "Follow this company" after you're looking at the right Company page within LinkedIn Companies. When you know what companies you want to follow, simply hover your mouse over the Interests link in the top navigation bar, and click Companies. Then, type in the name of each company into the search box provided, click Search Companies, and when you find the company in the Search results list, click the Follow button next to the Company listing. Once you are following all your target companies, spend some time each week to review each Company page for news, information, job openings, and useful contacts.

>> **If you can't find someone who currently works at your target company, look for people who used to work there and see what advice they can give you.** You do this through an Advanced People search, where you make sure the option under Company is set to Past. Many times, past employees still maintain contacts at their old company, and they can definitely attest to the work environment and corporate culture.

>> **Get some information from the person you're replacing.** Find the person at the company whose job you're taking and ask her opinion of it, information about the hiring manager, company, and so on. (Understand, of course, that this person might not have left under the best of circumstances, so you may not always get a good or useful response.) If you can't find the person you're replacing, try looking for people with a past position like the one you're interviewing for.

Chapter 15

Following Companies on LinkedIn

Two of the main reasons why people search the LinkedIn network are to find a job and to find a new employee. In both cases, LinkedIn users are trying to learn more about the company, not just the job seeker or hiring manager. Millions of self-employed people who use LinkedIn to promote not only themselves, but also their services, are always looking for a way to expand their brand and look for new business opportunities. LinkedIn organizes all these efforts under its Company pages.

LinkedIn maintains a directory of Company pages that allow people to learn about each company's products, services, and job opportunities. Each Company page has at least one administrator who can add his company to the directory, edit the information, connect his employees to the Company page, and provide company updates to the LinkedIn community. LinkedIn members can "follow" their favorite companies to get company and industry updates, and see how each member's network is connected to the employees of each company they follow.

In this chapter, I cover how you can search Company pages, follow different companies, and, if you are an employee or owner of your own company, create and update your own Company page.

Searching for Companies

When you need to learn more about your current industry or find a potential business partner for a big deal, your first step is to do some research. LinkedIn's Company pages allow users to explore companies of interest, whether it's a for-profit or nonprofit company, and receive company updates and industry news, as well as research each company's products and services — and, of course, learn about job opportunities the company has to offer. You can follow multiple companies and the news, updates, and posts they make will show as part of your News feed and help populate the Pulse news items you see.

To search for a Company page, follow these steps:

1. **Click the down arrow next to the search box at the top of any LinkedIn page and then select Companies from the drop-down list that appears.**

2. **Enter the keywords for your company search into the search box at the top of the screen and then click the blue Search button next to the search box.**

   The Companies Search results page appears, as shown in Figure 15-1. (In this example, I simply searched "Internet" as a keyword.)

FIGURE 15-1: Start a simple company search here.

3. **In the left pane, use the Relationship, Location, Industry, and other filters to refine your search.**

Let's say I'm looking for an Internet company in the United States where at least one person in my first-degree network is employed. Figure 15-2 shows the 40 companies that show up in my refined search.

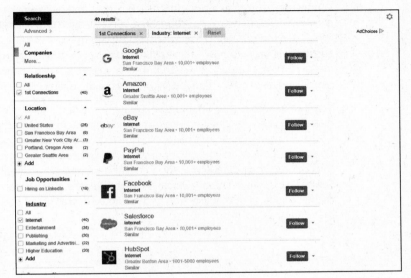

FIGURE 15-2:
See companies that match your search results.

If you plan on using any keywords in your search, enter those words first into a search before using the filters to narrow your search. Otherwise, any time you enter keywords into the top navigation bar search box, you will automatically reset your search filters, like Relationship, Industry, or Location.

After you reach a page loaded with potential companies, use the following tricks to find the one that's just right for you:

>> **Click the Follow button to keep track of that company.** When you click the Follow button next to any company listing, you add that company to your list of companies that you are following. This means you will see all the company updates in the Companies section of your LinkedIn page.

>> **View the Company page and study your connections.** To see the Company page, either click the name of the company, or hover your mouse over the down arrow next to the Follow button and then click the View link. You can

study the information on that page before deciding whether to follow the company. You can also view how you're connected to people inside the company.

For example, I'm looking at the John Wiley and Sons Company page, as shown in Figure 15-3. On the right side of the page, under the How You're Connected header, I can see how many people in my immediate network, or first-degree connections, are associated with that company, and by extension, how many second-degree network members (that is, a colleague of a colleague, or a friend of a friend) I would have at that company. If I click the See All link in that section, I get a list of how I'm connected to people in that company, as shown in Figure 15-4. This page is a search results screen, so I can add more keywords or filters to get a defined list of how I relate to any given company.

>> **You can search based on location.** Let's say you're thinking of moving to a new city and are looking for potential companies to interview with in that city. Click the Location filter and either pick the Region that matches your destination, or click the +Add link and input your city. LinkedIn automatically pops up the region in their database associated with that city. (For example, if I type **Seattle**, LinkedIn eventually displays Greater Seattle Area.) When you see the correct region, click that listing to get a targeted search list of companies in that area.

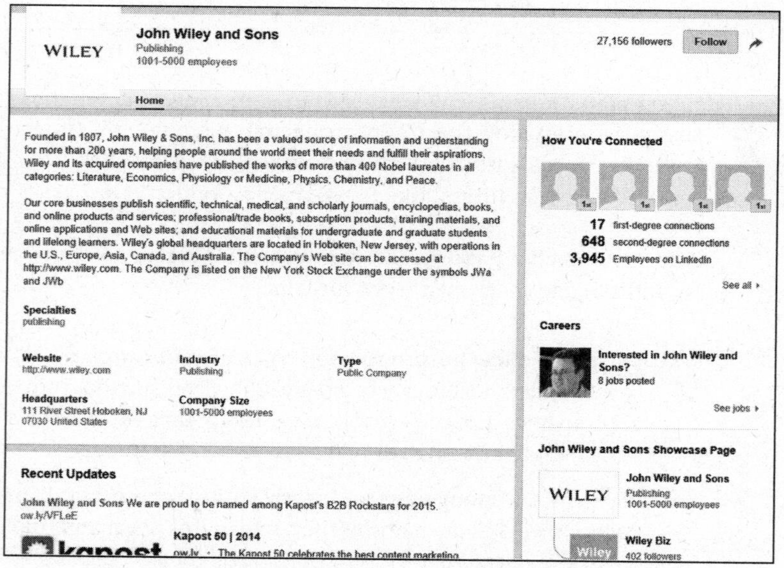

FIGURE 15-3:
See how you're connected to a given company.

FIGURE 15-4:
See a full list of
connections to
search further.

Your search can include multiple locations, so you can select multiple regions, and the results list will include companies headquartered in at least one of those regions. Be aware that if you only want one specific region, you need to deselect your country filter, like United States, for example, and select only the region.

>> **Decide who to follow by studying the number of followers.** If you've got a lot of options for companies, you can use the Followers filter to refine your search based on the number of members who are currently following that company and show you the most-watched companies for your search criteria. Choosing the option 5001+, for example, shows only those companies that currently have more than 5,000 people following them.

TIP

A search filter below Location called Job Opportunities can help you with a job search. When you click the check box next to Hiring on LinkedIn, you see a filtered list of companies that have posted job listings directly on LinkedIn, where you can apply directly through LinkedIn's job board.

Putting Your Company on LinkedIn

The flip side of LinkedIn Company pages is to use them on behalf of the company itself. Companies are always looking at ways to tell their story and engage interested members who want to follow their activities in a way that encourages word of mouth, highlights their products and services, and advertises career opportunities. LinkedIn Company pages allow companies to do all this as well as allow their customers to offer recommendations, which are spotlighted on the Company page.

As of this writing, there are more than 4 million Company pages on LinkedIn, and the number grows every day. The millions of LinkedIn users who follow these companies are current and potential customers, interested job applicants, business partners, and even curious industry watchers who want to hear the latest news, see the latest products and services, and reach out and interact with company leaders, managers, and employees. LinkedIn bills their Company pages as a "central hub" where millions of LinkedIn users can "stay in the loop" of company news and activities.

TIP

You can read more about the benefits of Company pages at `https://business.linkedin.com/marketing-solutions/company-pages/get-started/`.

Requirements for a Company page

When you decide to list your company on LinkedIn Company pages, understand that there are some requirements to protect the quality of this directory while making it accessible to companies of all sizes. Here are some things to keep in mind:

» **Your profile must show you're a current employee.** In your LinkedIn profile Experience section, you must have a position that defines you as a current company employee, manager, or owner. If you don't have a position defined, you will need to create that position in your profile before continuing with this process.

» **Have a company e-mail address defined in your account.** You are allowed to associate more than one e-mail address with your LinkedIn account, so make sure that one of your e-mail addresses for your profile is a company e-mail with the company domain name. This e-mail does not need to be your primary address for LinkedIn for you to have a Company page.

» **Your company's e-mail domain must be unique to your company.** One way LinkedIn controls the integrity of its Company page directory is to make sure that each e-mail domain can only be used once to create a Company page. Free e-mail providers like Yahoo! Mail, Gmail, and Hotmail are too generic to be associated with any one company (besides the e-mail provider itself), so an e-mail address from one of those providers is not sufficient.

TIP

If your company doesn't have its own e-mail domain, consider creating a LinkedIn Group for your company, instead of a Company page, so that your employees, customers, and business partners can stay in touch.

» **Your LinkedIn Profile Strength must be rated Intermediate or All Star, be at least one week old, and show your true identity.** LinkedIn uses a system called Profile Strength to rank its users' ability to create a robust profile, based on the number of sections a LinkedIn user has defined on her profile and network. LinkedIn wants its Company page administrators to have a strong understanding and ability to use LinkedIn so they can manage their page properly, so the Profile Strength rating must be Intermediate or All Star in order for them to create a Company page. In addition, your profile has to be at least seven days old and your profile must use your true first and last names.

» **You must have several first-degree connections on LinkedIn.** Company page administrators on LinkedIn need to be part of the LinkedIn community in general, so LinkedIn requires that administrators have more than just one or two LinkedIn connections before they can create a Company page.

Adding a Company page to LinkedIn

After you've met the requirements for creating a Company page on LinkedIn, it's time to get started by adding the Company page to LinkedIn's system. To create or update your Company page, follow these steps:

1. **Hover your mouse over the Interests link from the top navigation bar and then click the Companies link from the drop-down list that appears.**

2. **On the Companies page that appears, click the Create button (on the right side of the screen, under the Create a Company Page header).**

    You're taken to the first step in the process, the Add a Company page (see Figure 15-5).

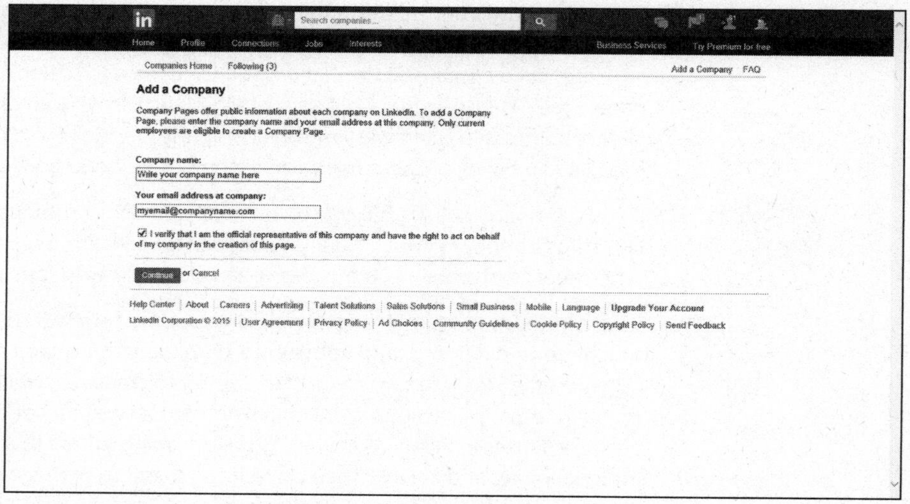

FIGURE 15-5:
Define your
Company page
on LinkedIn.

3. **Enter the company name and your company e-mail address in the fields provided, and then select the check box verifying you are the official representative of your company.**

   REMEMBER

   Make sure the e-mail address you are providing is your company e-mail address, with the unique e-mail domain for your company, and that your company e-mail address has been added and verified to your LinkedIn personal account first.

4. **Click the Continue button.**

   You're taken to the edit mode for your Company page (see Figure 15-6).

5. **Fill in the information in the fields provided: Company Name, Company Description, Company Type, Company Website URL, and so on. Be sure to complete any field with a red asterisk, because those are required pieces of information for a Company page.**

6. **If you want to add another administrator for the Company page, enter his name into the field below the Designated Admins header. If you scroll down the page past the Designated Admins header, you can also list any Direct Sponsored Content Posters — LinkedIn members who are allowed to create sponsored content for your Company page.**

   REMEMBER

   The person you name as a page administrator must already be one of your first-degree connections on LinkedIn.

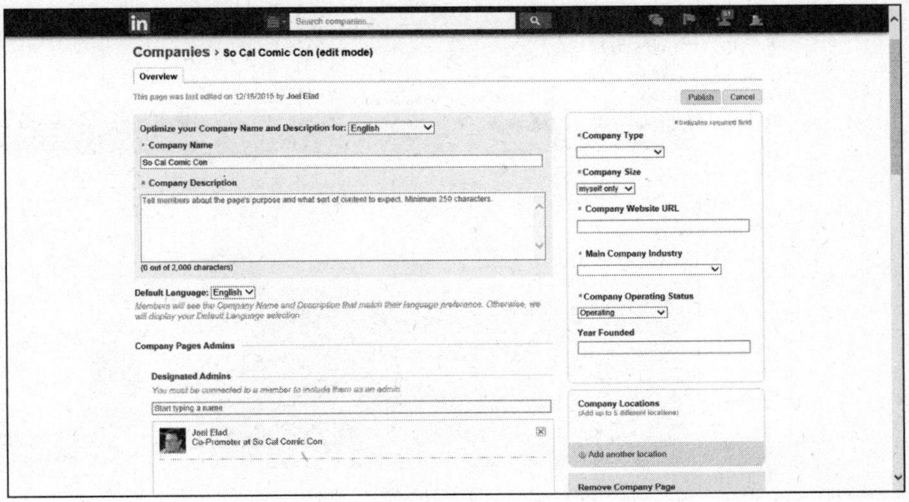

FIGURE 15-6:
Fill in the details for your Company page.

7. **(Optional) Scroll down and provide a company image or a standard logo (300 by 300 pixels or larger is required). List any company specialties and LinkedIn groups that are relevant to your company in the fields provided.**

8. **When you are done entering the information, scroll back to the top of the page and click Publish.**

   Your Company page has been successfully created or updated, as shown in Figure 15-7. Now you can start to provide company updates, add products or services, or edit your page.

REMEMBER

After your page is created, you should click the Follow button so your company has at least one follower. It's also a good check to see how company updates are showing up on a LinkedIn member's page (in this case, your page).

Now that you've created your Company page, think about incorporating your page management duties into your normal LinkedIn activity schedule. While it's important to properly set up your LinkedIn Company page, you'll want to spend some time on an ongoing basis to make sure you're properly communicating and responding with your followers and the community in large.

Here are some tips on how to proceed with administering your Company page:

>> **Follow your competitors.** Not only will you gain insight into what your competitors are doing, you can see how they are using their LinkedIn Company page, which may give you ideas on how to position your Company page and what updates to share with your followers.

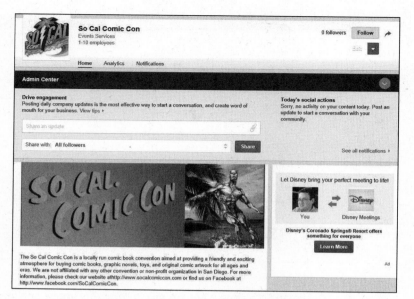

FIGURE 15-7:
Your Company page has been created!

>> **Add Showcase pages.** Providing your basic company information is the first step. Next is defining the aspects of your business that deserve their own page, called a Showcase page, so prospective customers can receive targeted messages and focused content about the part(s) of your business that are relevant to them. Think about highlighting the right keywords and features that your customers want to see when defining your Showcase pages on LinkedIn.

As of this writing, you are limited to 10 Showcase pages per parent Company page. However, you can contact LinkedIn and request additional pages.

TIP

>> **Consider writing Sponsored Updates for your company.** Similar to sponsoring a status update on Facebook with an ad budget, you can sponsor a company update on LinkedIn, which will allow that update to be shown on people's LinkedIn news feeds, whether or not they are following your company on LinkedIn. Sponsored Updates allow you to expand the reach of your company's message and help your company gain more followers on LinkedIn.

>> **Gain insight into the social actions on LinkedIn regarding your company.** When you click the Notifications tab (located near the top of your Company page, below the Company name, next to the Home and Analytics links), you can see some overall sets of information, such as the amount of Likes, Comments, Shares, and Mentions regarding your company and any company posts or updates, for the current day, week, and month. You will also see a list of any notifications of people trying to reach your company through LinkedIn.

>> **Keep an eye on the analytics.** LinkedIn provides a lot of information about how its members are viewing and interacting with Company pages. Click the Analytics tab (located near the top of your Company page, below the Company name, between the Home and Notifications links) to see how your followers are viewing and responding to your updates, as well as how many people you are reaching through your Company page — and how engaged they are with your Company page.

5

Using LinkedIn for Everyday Business

Chapter 16

Getting Connected with LinkedIn Groups

When it comes to the reasons why people get to know each other, there's more to a professional's life than colleagues and classmates. People have always been drawn to groups based on common interests, backgrounds, or goals, and this natural tendency to join together can be seen from sports teams to Boy/Girl Scouts, from social action organizations to nonprofit charity groups. Naturally, LinkedIn also offers a way for people to connect with each other as a group — LinkedIn Groups.

In this chapter, I discuss the value in LinkedIn Groups, from information and exposure to growing your network, and cover the overall idea and structure of LinkedIn Groups and what you can expect to find. I then talk about how to search for existing groups on LinkedIn, and I walk you through the steps necessary to join that group. Finally, if you see that there should be a group for something on LinkedIn but it doesn't already exist, I discuss how to start your own LinkedIn Group and how to invite others to join it.

Reaping the Benefits of LinkedIn Groups

When people who are familiar with other social networking tools are first exposed to LinkedIn Groups, they see some similarities. The group interaction in LinkedIn Groups — discussion threads, job postings, and so on — feels just like discussions or groups on most other social networking sites. And yet, being a member of a LinkedIn Group has extra benefits over other networking sites:

>> **Connections:** Group members share a special sort of connection. Although you don't have access to their extended networks, you're considered "connected" to them in that you can see their profile and send them a message through LinkedIn, and they can appear in your search results even if you aren't within three degrees of everyone in the group. Your search results can include fellow group members as well as your first-degree connections and second-degree network members.

WARNING

LinkedIn imposes a monthly limit on the number of messages you can send to group members outside your network, so use this feature sparingly or your LinkedIn account may be suspended or cancelled.

>> **Visibility:** By joining several groups — particularly large, open ones — you can increase your visibility in the LinkedIn network without having to add thousands of contacts by participating in groups and sharing your knowledge and expertise with people who are not yet in your network.

>> **Knowledge:** LinkedIn Groups share information and expertise among their members through the Discussions page of the group, which you can benefit from as a group member. Because there are thousands of groups for most industries and fields, LinkedIn Groups can be a valuable source of knowledge.

>> **Recognition:** Employers like to see that you are connected with professional groups because it shows the desire to expand your knowledge base, stay current in your industry or field, and be open and eager to network with like-minded people.

>> **Group logos:** The logos of the groups you're in are displayed on your profile. This is a sort of visual branding, reinforcing your association with those groups without a lot of words. For example, Figure 16-1 shows how the profile for a LinkedIn member who belongs to several groups might appear.

Some LinkedIn Groups are extensions of existing organizations and others are created on LinkedIn by an individual or business as a way to identify and network with people who share a common interest. In either case, groups are useful tools for growing your network and leveraging your existing affiliations.

FIGURE 16-1:
Group logos
displayed on a
profile.

Understanding the Two Types of LinkedIn Groups

Over the years, LinkedIn Groups have evolved to provide a quality place for inter-actions and content while fighting attempts for spam or promotional content to flood the group. Therefore, LinkedIn Groups are now private, "members–only" groups, which means that you cannot join a group without approval or an invita-tion, and the conversations in a group are not visible to the outside world (includ-ing search engines), so only members of the group can see and contribute to the conversations.

Today, there are two main types of LinkedIn Groups:

>> **Standard:** These groups are the most common form of LinkedIn groups, as they show up in search results and allow any current member of the group to invite and approve their first-degree connections to join the group. Membership in this group is displayed on each member's profile page, and the group's summary page shows up in search engine results, but not the conversations within the group.

>> **Unlisted:** These groups are basically "Invitation-Only" groups because the only way you can join this group is to be invited by the group owner or

manager. These groups do not show up via a LinkedIn search or any search engine, and non-group members cannot see the group logo on any member's profile page. Examples of ideal unlisted groups include employee-only groups for a company, customer-only groups to handle customer service or new product ideas, or focus groups to share and collaborate on new ideas or discuss potential upcoming products for a company.

Joining a Group

When you look at the LinkedIn Groups out there, one of the most important things to keep in mind is that you should join only those groups that are relevant to you. Although you might think it's fun to join another alumni association group besides your alma mater, it won't really help you in the long run. That said, if you are self-employed or in sales, for example, you may consider joining groups that appeal to your customers or prospects, in order to gain better perspective on what they need, or to share your expertise with a market that could appreciate and use the knowledge you've gained. On an individual level, though, groups are best intended for networking with colleagues or like-minded individuals to share knowledge and grow from each other's experience.

As you use LinkedIn more and decide that you want to get involved by joining a LinkedIn Group, you have a couple of options for getting started:

>> Use the Discover function on the LinkedIn Groups page to see groups that your first-degree connections are currently using.

>> Use the Groups search function along the top of any LinkedIn page to find groups based on keywords.

>> Click the Group logo found on the profile of one of your first-degree connections to join the group yourself.

>> Search the LinkedIn Groups Directory (https://www.linkedin.com/directory/groups) to find a group that interests you, then click the logo to join the group.

The third option may come about when you're browsing your first-degree connections list, and you see a group that you're interested in joining. After you click the logo, you simply click the Ask to Join button on the next page that you see, and you've completed your part of the process. Keep in mind that some professional groups have special requirements and you may not be eligible to join due to your particular educational or professional experience.

If you plan to seek out a group to join, follow these steps:

1. **From the top navigation bar, hover your mouse over the Interests link and then click the Groups link in the drop-down list that appears.**

   You're taken to your Groups page on LinkedIn, as shown in Figure 16-2.

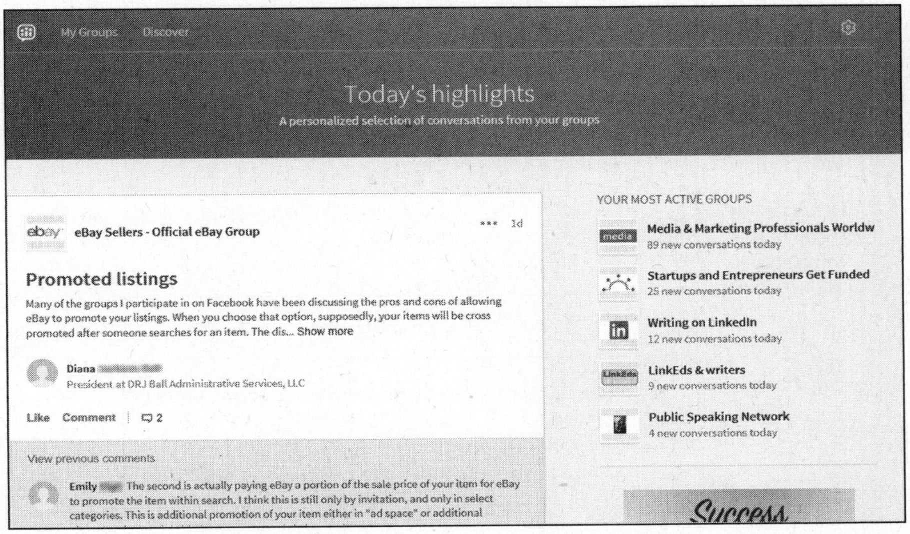

FIGURE 16-2:
You can see your specific LinkedIn Groups activity here.

2. **Click the Discover link near the top of the Groups page to see potential groups you can join.**

   LinkedIn's Group Discover page (shown in Figure 16-3) is filled with groups that your first-degree connections have joined and therefore may appeal to you. Additionally, LinkedIn has created a special group entitled "Getting Started with Groups" that you can join to get guidance from LinkedIn on how to fully utilize its groups.

3. **Click the Ask to Join button for any group you wish to join from the list provided.**

   As you scroll down the page, you will see group summaries along with the list of your first-degree connections who are already in the group, as shown in Figure 16-4. You can click the Ask to Join button next to any group, and LinkedIn automatically updates the screen with the Ask to Join button becoming Request Pending. You can keep scrolling down the same page to look for more groups.

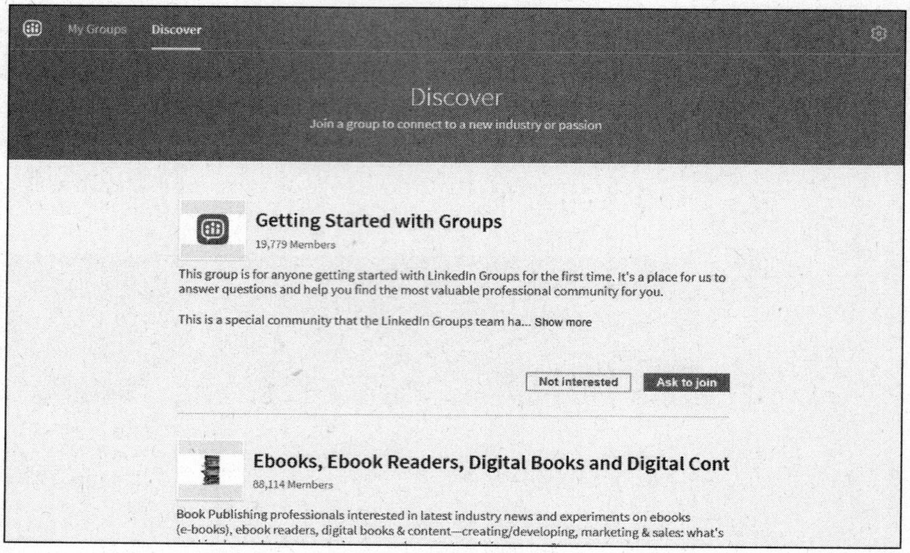

Discover

Join a group to connect to a new industry or passion

Getting Started with Groups
19,779 Members

This group is for anyone getting started with LinkedIn Groups for the first time. It's a place for us to answer questions and help you find the most valuable professional community for you.

This is a special community that the LinkedIn Groups team ha... Show more

Not interested   Ask to join

Ebooks, Ebook Readers, Digital Books and Digital Cont
88,114 Members

Book Publishing professionals interested in latest industry news and experiments on ebooks (e-books), ebook readers, digital books & content—creating/developing, marketing & sales: what's

FIGURE 16-3:
LinkedIn helps you discover groups to join.

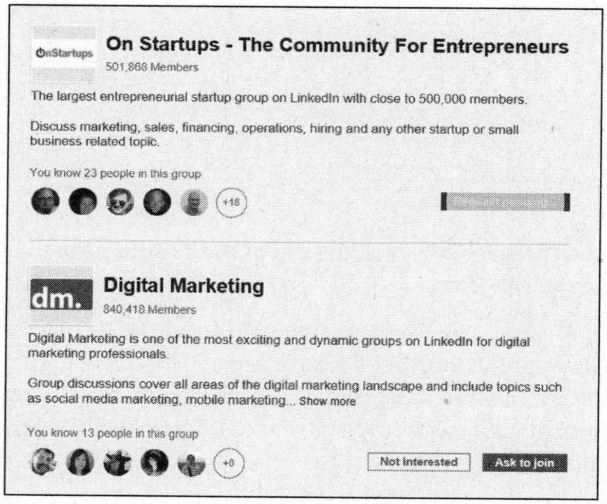

On Startups - The Community For Entrepreneurs
501,868 Members

The largest entrepreneurial startup group on LinkedIn with close to 500,000 members.

Discuss marketing, sales, financing, operations, hiring and any other startup or small business related topic.

You know 23 people in this group

+18

Digital Marketing
840,418 Members

Digital Marketing is one of the most exciting and dynamic groups on LinkedIn for digital marketing professionals.

Group discussions cover all areas of the digital marketing landscape and include topics such as social media marketing, mobile marketing... Show more

You know 13 people in this group

+8   Not interested   Ask to join

FIGURE 16-4:
Read about and join groups that appeal to you.

4. **Once you explore the Discover page, you can find more groups to join by searching LinkedIn for groups. Click the down arrow next to the search box at the top of the page, and select Groups from the drop-down list that appears. Enter keywords in the text box at the top of the page for groups that you are seeking to join.**

Use keywords to describe the group that interests you. If you're looking to join a group that promotes public speaking, for example, type **public speaking** into the text box.

5. **Review the list of potential groups that are prompted as you type your keywords and pick an option that meets your interests.**

   Go through the results list, as shown in Figure 16-5, click a group from the list, and read the description of the group that you picked from the list. You will see that group's summary page, which contains the group's About statement and the administrator(s) for the group. From this page, you can also click the group administrator name to see his profile and send him a message requesting a few details about the group.

FIGURE 16-5:
Review a list of potential groups to join.

6. **Click the Ask to Join button to join the LinkedIn Group.**

That's it! Your request has been sent to the group manager for approval. You see the button change to Pending or Request Pending, as shown in Figure 16-6. As mentioned before, your request may not be approved depending on the criteria for that group.

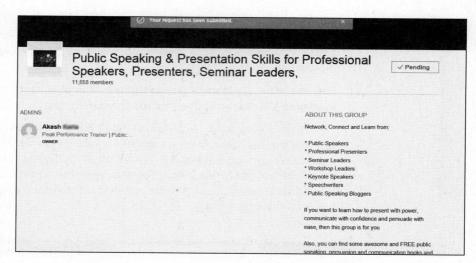

Public Speaking & Presentation Skills for Professional Speakers, Presenters, Seminar Leaders,
11,658 members

✓ Pending

ADMINS

Akash ▨▨▨▨
Peak Performance Trainer | Public...
OWNER

ABOUT THIS GROUP

Network, Connect and Learn from:

* Public Speakers
* Professional Presenters
* Seminar Leaders
* Workshop Leaders
* Keynote Speakers
* Speechwriters
* Public Speaking Bloggers

If you want to learn how to present with power, communicate with confidence and persuade with ease, then this group is for you

Also, you can find some awesome and FREE public speaking, persuasion and communication books and

FIGURE 16-6:
Read the summary of your LinkedIn Group before you join.

Starting and Participating in Group Discussions

The core of LinkedIn Groups is to start and maintain conversations among group members that aid in sharing content and job postings, making business or professional connections, finding answers, and establishing industry experts.

As you look at a typical LinkedIn Groups conversation, as shown in Figure 16-7, you can choose to interact with each entry similar to what you can do on other social media sites:

>> **Like the conversation.** By clicking the Like link, you are signaling that you found the post useful. Some group members may assess whether to participate in any given discussion based on the amount of Likes that the discussion has received.

>> **Comment on the conversation.** By clicking the Comment link and adding a comment to the discussion thread, you unlock the true power of group conversations by adding your own viewpoint, replying to the original point, or replying to an existing comment.

>> **Reply privately to the group member.** When you read a conversation or another comment from a fellow group member, you can simply click the three dots (. . .) next to the conversation or below the comment to bring up a short menu, and then click Reply Privately. This generates a LinkedIn message you can use to communicate with the group member directly, without the group viewing your communication. Perhaps you want to offer individualized help or use this as a form of lead generation.

» **Report the post or comment.** If you're interested in keeping the group as spam-free as possible, you can click the three dots (. . .) either at the top of the conversation post or below any individual comment, and then click the Report link to report the post or comment as inappropriate. Once you do that, the group administrator will be notified and can review the item for further action.

Click here to like or comment on the conversation.

Click the dots to report the person or reply to her privately.

After you join a group, it's recommended in the beginning to understand the dynamics of how the group operates, so start by participating in existing discussions and then decide how you can best contribute with your own posts.

When you are ready to start a conversation, follow these steps:

1. **From the top navigation bar, hover your mouse over the Interests link and then click the Groups link in the drop-down list that appears. From your Groups page, click the My Groups link to bring up a page of groups you manage or are a member of. From that page, click the name of the group to bring up that group page.**

   By default, you should arrive at the Conversations tab of that group (as shown in Figure 16-8) and you should see a box with your profile photo entitled "Start a Conversation with Your Group."

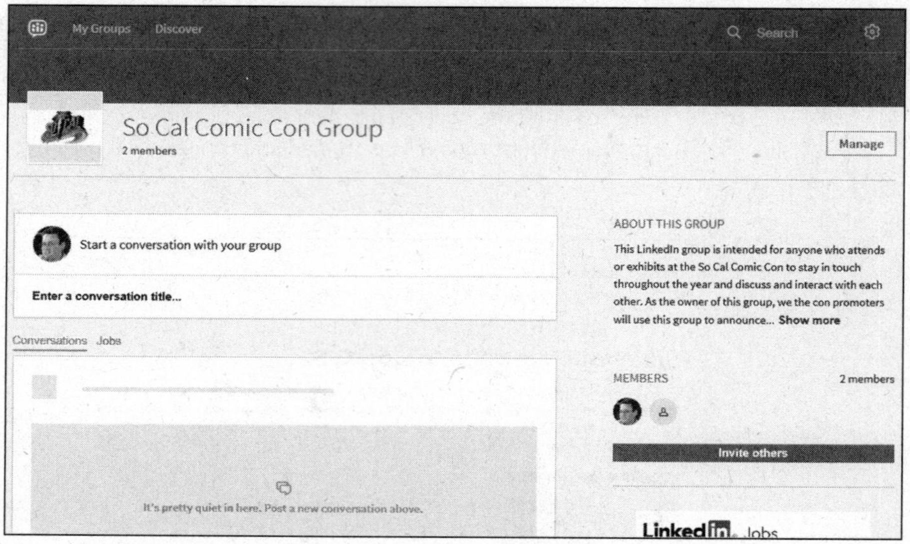

FIGURE 16-8:
Start a
conversation in
your LinkedIn
Group.

2. **Click the Enter a Conversation Title section. Once the cursor appears (and that text disappears), start writing your headline.**

   Here is where you summarize what your post/conversation is about, so write an informative but succinct headline that lets people know what you plan to ask or share. Many people ask a question or include a viewpoint in their headline in order to invite people to comment on the conversation and indicate that you want a real discussion and are not making a fluff announcement.

3. **Click the Add Some Details or Use @ to Mention section. When the cursor appears, start writing the content of your post in the box.**

   Here is where you provide the text to start the conversation. It's recommended to start by asking an open-ended question to generate discussion, instead of the generic "Here's a great article I discovered."

   If you want to pull someone into the conversation, type the @ symbol in the text box and you will see a prompted list of first-degree connections as you type their name, as shown in Figure 16-9. They will be flagged, regardless of whether they are already in the group, and will see this conversation and be able to contribute.

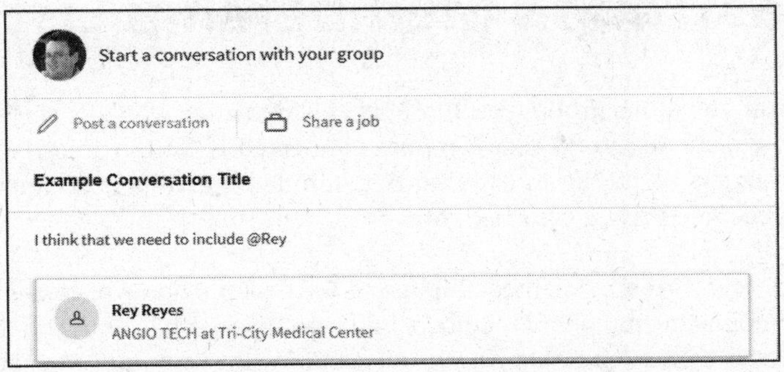

![Start a conversation with your group interface showing Post a conversation and Share a job options, an Example Conversation Title, text reading "I think that we need to include @Rey", and a Rey Reyes, ANGIO TECH at Tri-City Medical Center entry]

FIGURE 16-9:
Tag people to include them in the discussion.

4. **If you are linking to an article or post as part of your discussion, enter the URL for that item in the details section.**

   LinkedIn automatically formats the conversation so people will see a summary of that item in the conversation, and can click that summary to see the rest of the article or post.

5. **(Optional) Use the icon to insert a photo or image into the conversation.**

   In the bottom left corner of the conversation box, there is a graphic representing an image. When you click that graphic, LinkedIn opens a window on your computer, allowing you to select an image file from your computer to upload to the conversation post.

REMEMBER

   You should only upload graphics that will add to the discussion or be useful visual content for the conversation.

6. **Click the blue Post button to start the conversation in the group.**

That's it! Your newly created post will automatically show up at the top of the Conversations tab for the group. Other group members can then click the Like button underneath the conversation or click the Comment link and participate in the discussion, similar to other social media sites.

WARNING

While all conversations are automatically posted, group administrators retain the power to remove any post they consider spam, offensive, or counter-productive to the purpose of the group. Additionally, any group member can report a post and that post is temporarily hidden while the group administrator reviews the report to see if that post should continue or be removed.

Viewing a Group's Membership List

After you join a group, you'll probably want to see who's in the group and find out how or if the group members are connected to you. After all, the point of these groups is to stay in touch with like-minded individuals and perhaps invite them to become part of your network.

To view a group's membership, go to the Group's home page and click the link that contains the number of members in the group, which is found on the right side of the screen next to the Members header. This will bring up a Members List screen, as shown in Figure 16-10. From this list, you can click an individual member's name to go to her profile page and find out if you share any connections with that person.

MEMBERS LIST

Members   Pending   Admins

🔍   Find a member...

Joel Elad
Author, LinkedIn for Dummies; Co-Promoter, So Cal Comic Con
OWNER

Rey Reyes
ANGIO TECH at Tri-City Medical Center

Click this to send the person a message.

When you hover your mouse on any member's name, you will see a Message icon on the right side of that list. You can click that Message icon to send a LinkedIn message directly to that group member. As mentioned earlier, LinkedIn does not want its members to abuse this feature, so each LinkedIn user is limited to a low number of these messages per month.

Creating a Group

When you're ready to create your own group, follow these steps:

1. **From the top navigation bar, hover your mouse over the Interests link and then click the Groups link in the drop-down list that appears.**

   You see your Groups page, with the main section headers of the Highlights icon, the My Groups link and the Discover link.

2. **Click the My Groups link to bring up the web page containing the list of groups you belong to. On the left-hand side, below the My Groups and My Pending Groups headers, click the Create Group button to get started.**

This step brings you to the group creation page, as shown in Figure 16-11. This is where you input all the information about your newly requested group.

FIGURE 16-11:
Enter your
new group
information here.

Logo: Your logo will appear in the Groups Directory and on your group pages.

[Browse...]

Note: PNG, JPEG, or GIF only; max size 100 KB

☐ *I acknowledge and agree that the logo/image I am uploading does not infringe upon any third party copyrights, trademarks, or other proprietary rights or otherwise violate the User Agreement.

* Group Name: [   ]

Note: "LinkedIn" is not allowed to be used in your group name.

* Summary: Enter a brief description about your group and its purpose. Your summary about this group will appear in the Groups Directory.

[   ]

* Description: Your full description of this group will appear on your group pages.

[   ]

Website: [   ]

3. **Upload the logo for your group.**

LinkedIn requires a logo. The file format must be PNG, JPEG, or GIF, and the memory size of the logo cannot exceed 100KB. Click the Browse button (or Choose File if you are using a Mac) next to the logo box. In the Choose File dialog box that opens, locate the logo file on your computer so LinkedIn can upload it, and then click Open.

"But where do I get a logo?" you might ask. Well, you can design your own logo at sites like www.logoworks.com. If a logo already exists, like for an alumni association, ask one of the administrators for a high-resolution copy of the logo, or save a copy of the logo from the group's personal website — as long as you know you have the rights to use that image, of course. If you are not sure if you have the right to use the image, check with the group's administrator.

Your logo can't exceed 100 KB, so watch that file size as you create your logo.

REMEMBER

4. **Provide your group information and settings, including group name, summary, description, website URL, owner e-mail, visibility of the group (whether you want the group visible/Standard or Unlisted), and any e-mail domains of people who are automatically pre-approved to join the group. (See Figures 16-11 and 16-12.)**

You have only 300 characters in your group summary, so choose your words wisely.

TIP

If you're wondering what to write for your group description, search for similar groups using the search box at the top of the page and read through similar groups in your group type. Then go back to the Create a Group page and enter your description. (If you check other group descriptions while writing your description, you'll lose whatever you typed.)

5. **If your group is located in one geographic region, select the Location check box.**

6. **Read through the Terms of Service and then select the Agreement check box.**

At this point, your page should look something like Figure 16-12, where your logos and information are uploaded and ready for review.

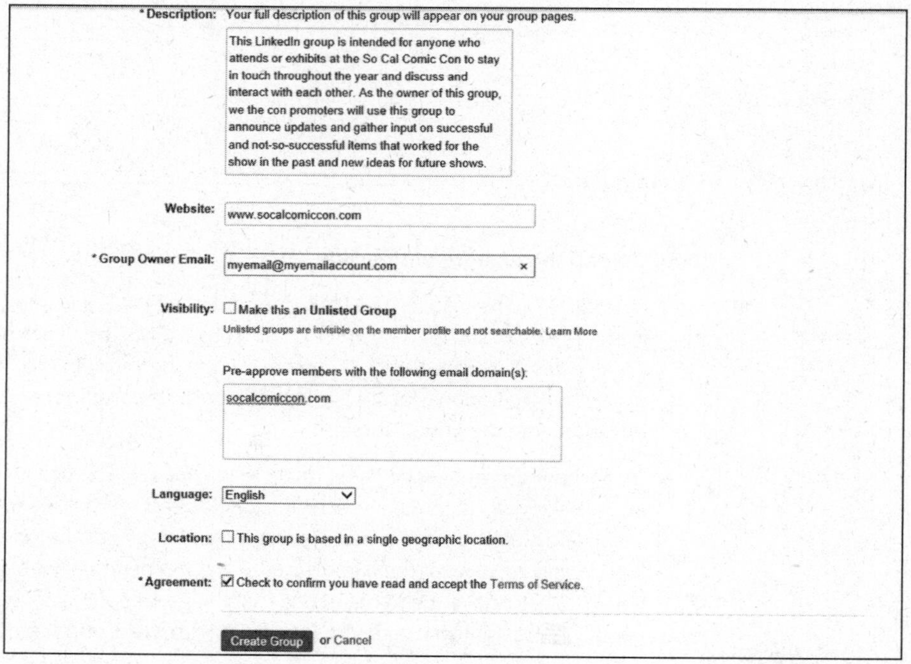

*Description:	Your full description of this group will appear on your group pages.
	This LinkedIn group is intended for anyone who attends or exhibits at the So Cal Comic Con to stay in touch throughout the year and discuss and interact with each other. As the owner of this group, we the con promoters will use this group to announce updates and gather input on successful and not-so-successful items that worked for the show in the past and new ideas for future shows.
Website:	www.socalcomiccon.com
*Group Owner Email:	myemail@myemailaccount.com ✕
Visibility:	☐ Make this an Unlisted Group
	Unlisted groups are invisible on the member profile and not searchable. Learn More
	Pre-approve members with the following email domain(s):
	socalcomiccon.com
Language:	English ⌄
Location:	☐ This group is based in a single geographic location.
*Agreement:	☑ Check to confirm you have read and accept the Terms of Service.
	Create Group or Cancel

FIGURE 16-12:
Your group request is ready to be submitted.

7. **Click the Create Group button to create your group on LinkedIn.**

   After you click that button, you're taken to the newly created home page for your new group, and your request is submitted.

   You should see your newly created group page, as shown in Figure 16-13. Your new group is ready for members!

FIGURE 16-13: Your group has been created.

Setting Up the Group and Inviting Members

After you get your confirmation from LinkedIn that your new group has been created, your next step is to set up the group properly and invite members to be a part of this group. In some cases, LinkedIn prompts you to add people the moment you click the Create Group button, but this is a step you can do at any point after the group is created.

This is actually a multi-part process. Follow these steps:

1. **Review the group settings and information and consider defining rules and automated messages to help run your group more smoothly.**

   You should do this before you send out any invitations or before members start using the group on a regular basis. You can configure your group from these four options on your Manage Group page:

a. *Group Settings:* Here is where you can change your group from Standard (shows up in Group searches) to Unlisted (hidden from all public views) or vice versa.

b. *Group Information:* Here is where you can update your summary, description, website URL, or other information you provided when you created your group.

c. *Group Rules:* Every LinkedIn Group is allowed to write its own rules, which can be recommended rules for conduct, or any specific instructions or guidelines you want to offer your group members (what is acceptable and not acceptable in terms of content, how you will handle abuse or inappropriate comments, and so on).

d. *Templates:* LinkedIn has built-in functionality that allows you to write e-mail templates that can automatically be sent to someone when different actions go out. When you go to the Templates option, as shown in Figure 16-14, you will see how to create and manage custom messages to people interacting with your group. For example, you can write a custom message that will be sent any time someone requests to join the group. By spending some time here writing template messages, it could cut down on administration time down the road.

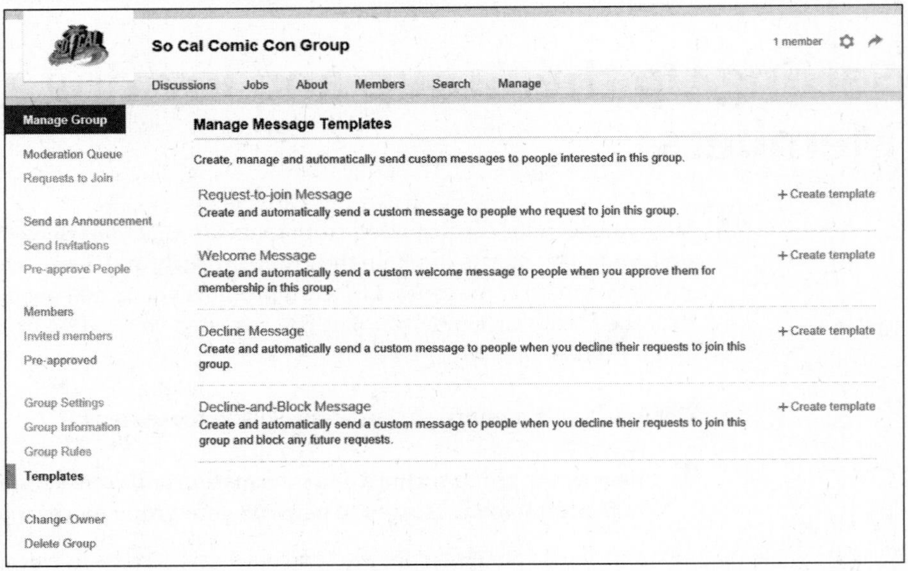

FIGURE 16-14: Use custom templates to inform people as they interact with your group.

2. **You can either invite people directly via LinkedIn to join your group, or you can define a list of pre-approved members, and then directly e-mail these prospective members with an invitation to join your new group.**

LinkedIn provides a web page with a standard Subject line and Welcome message that you can use to send your invitations. You can also pre-approve people and use your own e-mail program to invite people to join your LinkedIn Group.

This method of e-mailing prospective members is recommended because as of this writing, LinkedIn does not allow you to customize the Subject line or Welcome message to protect members from any unauthorized content someone may insert into these group invitations.

3. **When someone clicks the link from her e-mail to join the group, LinkedIn checks to see whether that person is on your pre-approved list.**

If so, she automatically becomes a member. If not, you (the group manager) see a member request in the Manage Group section of your group home page, which you have to manually approve so the person can officially join the group. The person's status shows up as Pending on her My Groups page until you approve her membership request.

Building and managing your member list

When you're ready to build your list of members, just follow these steps:

1. **From the top navigation bar, hover your mouse over the Interests link and then click the Groups link in the drop-down list that appears.**

2. **Click the My Groups link to bring up the web page containing the list of groups you belong to. Scroll down (if necessary) until you see the name and logo of the group you are maintaining, and then click that group name.**

3. **On the right side of the screen, click the Manage button to bring up your Manage Group page.**

You should see something like Figure 16-15. The Manage Group page is your hub for handling any group management duties. Along the left side of this page, you will see the options for controlling the different parts of the group.

4. **Click the Send Invitations option on the left-hand menu to send automated invitations to your group.**

As you type in names of your first-degree connections into the Connections text box, LinkedIn prompts you with possible entries. You can type multiple names into this box, as shown in Figure 16-16. Click the blue Send Invitations button to complete this process.

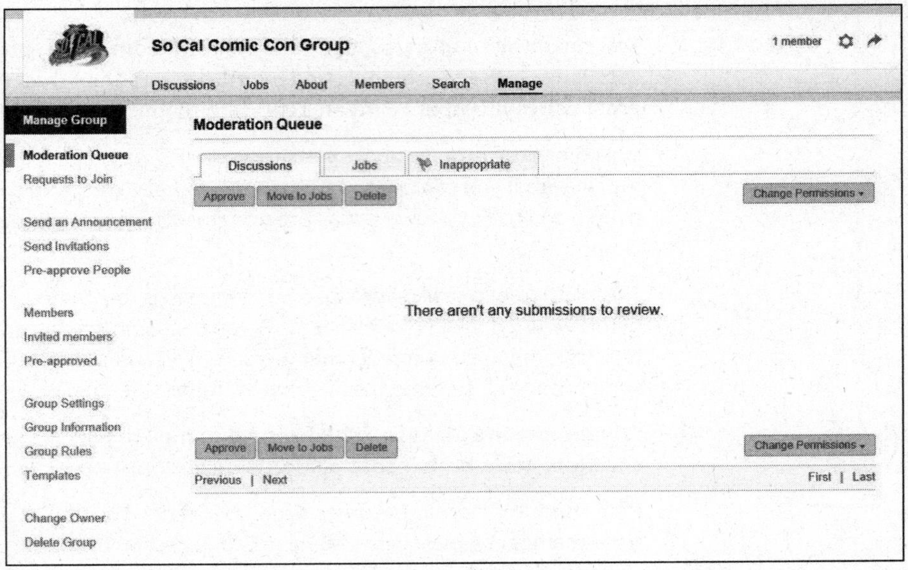

FIGURE 16-15:
Manage your
LinkedIn Group
from this page.

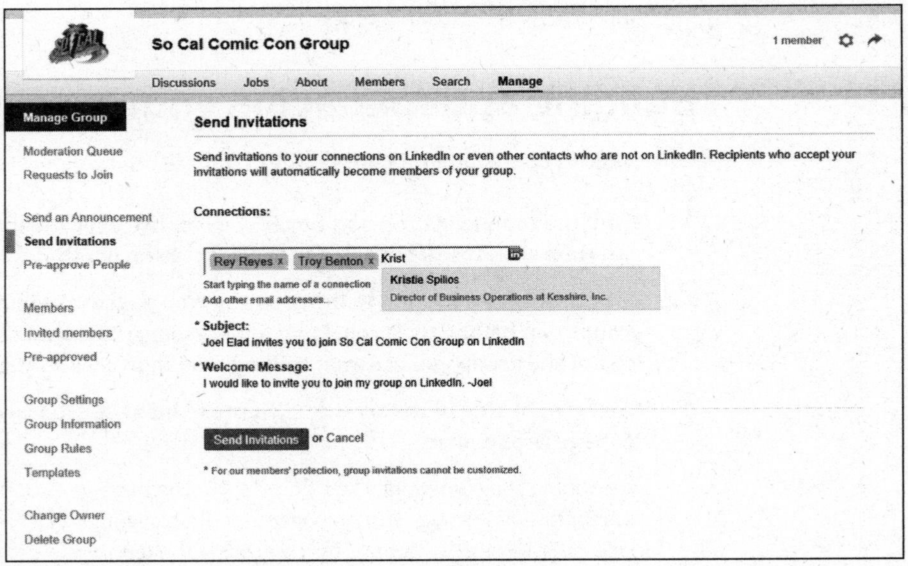

FIGURE 16-16:
You can invite
new people to
your LinkedIn
group here.

5. **Click the Pre-Approve People option on the left-hand menu to set up names of people you want to invite to your group using your own e-mail program.**

When you bring up this option, you see a screen similar to the Send Invitations page, where you can type names into the Connections text box. This time, LinkedIn simply keeps track of which names you enter here, and if any of the names you added end up sending a manual request to join the group, LinkedIn checks this list and pre-approves those people for instant entry into your group.

You can also click the Add Other Email Addresses link and provide LinkedIn with a comma-delimited list of e-mail addresses of people who are not yet LinkedIn members but who you would like to pre-approve for your LinkedIn Group.

WARNING

If the e-mail address of a member's LinkedIn profile is different from the e-mail address you put in the pre-approved list, this member won't be automatically approved when he clicks the link. You have to manually approve him by clicking the Requests to Join link on the left-hand side of the Manage Group page.

You can also define entire domain names that will be pre-approved. This is especially helpful if you create an employee group and you want to automatically approve anyone from your company, for example. This way, you don't have to define individual people, but anyone with an e-mail address containing a domain name you specify will be granted access to the group.

TIP

You can always review your list of pre-approved people by clicking the Pre-Approved link on the left-hand side of the Manage Group page.

Crafting your invitation e-mail

LinkedIn allows you to send group invitations from the Manage Group page because the folks at LinkedIn feel that invitations should come from the group owner — namely, you. At this point, though, LinkedIn provides a standard Subject line and Welcome message to keep things uniform and protect its members. For some of you, these invitations need no extra explanation and the LinkedIn "Send Invitations" function is all you need.

However, if you feel that your invitation needs to come with more information, you will need to pre-approve these members and send them your own invitation from your own e-mail program. Here are a few do's and don'ts to keep in mind as you craft your invitation:

>> **Do relate the purpose and benefits of the group.** People are busy and need to understand why they should join this group. Explain the benefits of being connected to other people, the ability for professional development or advancement, and what you hope to accomplish with this group. Remember, you're sending this to LinkedIn members, so don't worry about explaining LinkedIn — just explain your group.

>> **Don't go on forever.** One or two paragraphs is the maximum this invitation should be. Introduce yourself, introduce the group name, tell people the benefits of joining, encourage them to join, include the link to the LinkedIn Group page, and then sign off. No one will read a long diatribe or laundry list of reasons to join. Use bullet points and short sentences whenever possible.

>> **Don't put other offers in the e-mail.** Some people use this as an opportunity not only to encourage folks to join one group, but to push a second group invitation or highlight a link to the group's non-LinkedIn website. The moment you start presenting multiple options for people, you lose their attention and they are less likely to sign up.

You can use any e-mail program to create an invitation to your group, but don't forget that first, you should click the Manage button from your group's home page and then click the Pre-Approve People link from the options on the left-hand side of the Manage Group screen so that anyone you are e-mailing will be admitted to the group, as discussed in the previous section.

In your e-mail, you should provide a direct link to your LinkedIn Group home page. Simply bring up the page on your computer screen and then copy the URL from the location bar in your web browser. Typically, it will look like this:

    www.linkedin.com/groups/*idnumber*

Where *idnumber* is the numerical ID of your group created by LinkedIn.

After you send out the invitations, as members respond, they're moved from the pre-approved list to the current list of your group, and the small group logo appears on their profiles.

Approving members to your group

As more and more people find out about your new LinkedIn Group and as members start joining, you may find that some of the people who have clicked the link to join aren't on your pre-approved list. Perhaps they are people you didn't realize were on LinkedIn, or you didn't realize they were valid group members, or they clicked the wrong link and/or they don't belong in your group.

REMEMBER

It can be helpful, from an administrative standpoint, to develop criteria or guidelines for people to join your group, so you can evaluate each request as it comes in. Consider talking to any governing members of your group (in case you are just the LinkedIn group administrator, but not the actual "in-person" group administrator) to develop this in the early days of your group, so you don't have to worry about it later on when things get busy.

Regardless, you need to go into LinkedIn and either approve or reject people's membership requests. Follow these steps:

1. **From the top navigation bar, hover your mouse over the Interests link and then click the Groups link in the drop-down list that appears.**

   By default, you should see your Manage Group page, although all your group options are just a click away.

2. **Click the My Groups link to bring up the web page containing the list of groups you belong to. On the page that appears, scroll down (if necessary) until you see the name and logo of the group you are maintaining, and then click that group name.**

   You should see the home page for your Group. Click the Manage button to bring up the Manage tab for your Group.

3. **Click the Requests to Join link below the Manage Group header to bring up the Requests to Join page.**

   This step brings up the list of people waiting to be approved for your group, as shown in Figure 16-17.

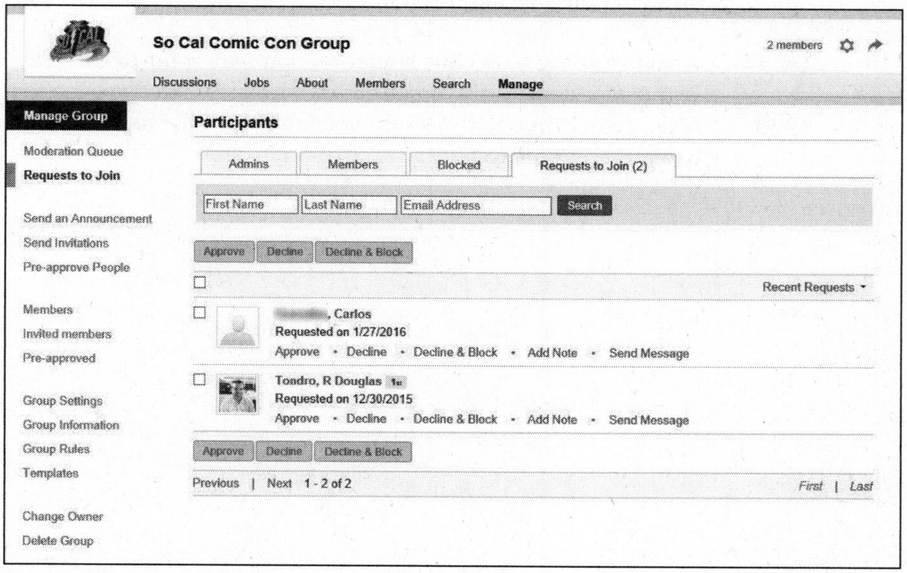

FIGURE 16-17: See who is waiting to be approved to your LinkedIn Group.

4. **To accept people, select the check box next to each person you want to approve to join your LinkedIn Group, and then click the Approve button.**

   You can approve people individually or all at once if you want. You can always select the person's name on the list to read his LinkedIn profile and decide whether he belongs in the group or send him a message through his profile.

5. **To refuse membership, select the check box next to each person you want to decline membership to the group, and then click the Decline button.**

   You can also click the Decline & Block button if you want to permanently block someone from trying to join the group. In addition, you can click the Add Note button to create a note for this entry that is only visible to any group administrator, but not the person in question. This note can be used as an internal reminder or a record-keeping function. Finally, you can click Send Message to send someone a message via LinkedIn.

Similar to the approval process, you can decline people one at a time or all at once. (The easiest way to select everyone is to select the empty check box at the top of the list; the one with no name associated with it.) In either case (approval or decline), the user's name disappears from the Request to Join page. Lastly, remember that you can remove someone from the group membership at any time after you initially approved him.

TIP

If you're going to decline someone, you may want to click the Send Message link first, before declining him, and let him know why you are declining his request. After you decline that person, you won't be able to send him a message without using the InMail system.

Chapter 17

Using Sales and Marketing Techniques for Yourself and Your Business

I n this part of the book, you find out how to start applying everything the previous parts cover about how to use LinkedIn for specific situations and needs. After all, every great invention needs to fulfill some sort of purpose, and LinkedIn is no exception. Its value is not just in how it allows you to network and build your brand, but also in how you can use LinkedIn to handle other tasks more easily and effectively.

In this chapter, I discuss the age-old disciplines of sales and marketing, including how to generate sales and how LinkedIn can affect your entire sales cycle. LinkedIn can help you "spread the gospel" of your business mission by serving as a vehicle for positive and rich marketing messages about both you and your business, whether it's a start-up, personal service provider, or a Fortune 500 company. Part of the power of LinkedIn comes from involving others in your marketing initiatives, so I cover some ways for you to do that as well.

Marketing Yourself Through LinkedIn

When it comes to maximizing the benefit you receive from LinkedIn, you are your biggest advocate. Although your network of connections is instrumental in helping you grow, much of your marketing happens without your being involved. After you create your profile, that and any other LinkedIn activity of yours are read and judged by the community at large — on the other members' own time and for their own purposes. Therefore, you want to make sure you're creating a favorable impression of yourself by marketing the best traits, abilities, and features of you and your business. Because of the nature of LinkedIn, this marketing occurs continually — 24/7. So, you should look at LinkedIn as something to check and update on a continual basis, like a blog. It doesn't mean you have to spend hours each day on LinkedIn, but a little bit of time on a consistent basis can go a long way toward creating a favorable and marketable LinkedIn identity.

The following sections look at the different ways you interact with LinkedIn, and what you can do to create the most polished, effective LinkedIn identity possible to further your marketing message.

Optimizing your profile

In Chapter 3, I discuss building your professional profile on LinkedIn, which is the centerpiece of your LinkedIn identity and your personal brand. I refer to your profile throughout this book, but here, I focus on ways for you to update or enhance your profile with one specific goal in mind: marketing yourself better or more consistently. As always, not every tip or suggestion works for everyone, and you might have already put some of these into action, but it's always good to revisit your profile to make sure it's organized the way you intended.

To make sure your profile is delivering the best marketing message for you, consider these tips:

>> **Use the Professional headline wisely.** Your Professional headline is what other LinkedIn users see below your name even when they're not looking at

your full profile. I've seen some users stuff a lot of text into this field, so you should have enough space to communicate the most important things about yourself. If you have specific keyword phrases you want associated with your name, make them a part of your headline.

A standard headline might read something like "Software Development Manager at XYZ Communications," but you can write entire sentences full of great keywords for your headline. My client Liz Goodgold's headline reads "Branding and Marketing Expert, Author, Coach, and Motivational Speaker." Think about how many people would want to connect with her!

>> **Make sure you use keyword phrases that match popular keywords for you or your business.** The first step, as I just mentioned, is to put these phrases in your headline. The second step is to make sure these phrases are reflected in your Summary, Experiences, and Interests.

WARNING

Be careful not to overuse your main keyword phrases. The search engines call this practice "stuffing," which is cramming as many instances of a phrase into your site as possible in hopes of achieving a higher ranking. If the search engines detect this, you will experience lower ranking results.

>> **If you're available for freelance work, make sure to identify at least one of your current positions as freelance or self-employed.** Remember, people aren't mind readers, so you need to let people know that you're a freelance writer, website designer, dog walker, or whatever. If you look at Cynthia Beale Campbell's profile in Figure 17-1, you can see that she's listed her current position as self-employed.

>> **Use the additional sections in your profile to include any relevant information that reinforces your marketing message.** For example, if you want to be seen as an expert in a given field, add the SlideShare application to upload presentations you've given, or update the Publications section of your profile to include the articles or books you've written, articles you've been quoted in, focus or advisory groups you belong to, and any speaking engagements or discussions you've participated in. LinkedIn has created sections like Projects, Patents, and Certifications for you to display specific accomplishments that are an important part of your professional identity.

>> **Make sure your profile links to your websites, blogs, and any other part of your online identity.** Don't just accept the standard "My Company" text. Instead, select the Other option, and put your own words in the website title box, such as "Joel Elad's E-Commerce Education Website." (See Chapter 3 for more information on linking from your profile to other websites.)

Market yourself as self-employed.

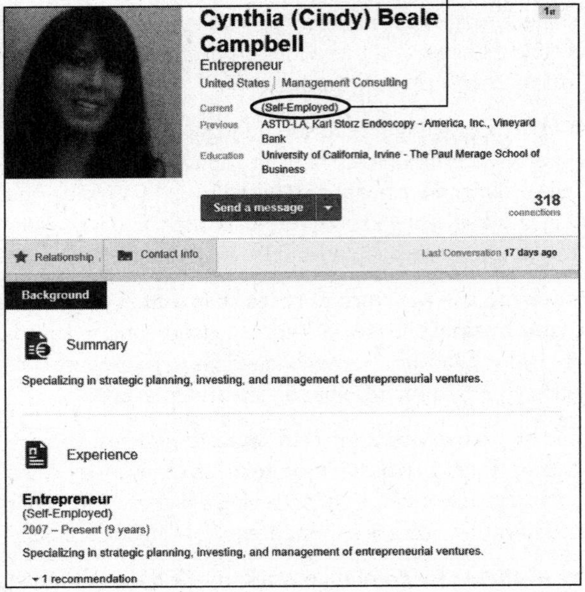

FIGURE 17-1: Make sure to note if you are self-employed or freelance.

For an example of effectively linking your profile to other areas of your online presence, take a look at Scott Allen's profile, shown in Figure 17-2. His website links replace the bland My Company, My Blog, and My Website with his own text — Momentum Factor, Linked Intelligence, and Social Media Is My Middle Name. Not only does this give more information to someone reading his profile, but search engines have a better idea of what those links represent.

Marketing yourself to your network

Optimizing your profile in the ways described in the previous section is one of the best ways to market yourself effectively using LinkedIn. Another is to be alert to how well you're communicating with your LinkedIn connections. Whether it's automatic (like when you update your profile and LinkedIn automatically notifies your network through a network update, assuming you enabled this option in your Settings) or self-generated (when you use LinkedIn InMail or Messages to send a note to someone else, which I cover in Chapter 5), this communication becomes your ongoing message to the members of your network and keeps you in their minds and (you hope!) plans.

FIGURE 17-2:
Give your website
links meaningful
names.

Use meaningful names for your website anchor text.

The most effective marketing occurs when people don't realize you're marketing to them. After all, the average American sees all kinds of marketing messages throughout their day. Your goal is to communicate often but not be overbearing about it so your message subtly sinks into people's minds. If you do that, people will think you're grrrr-*eat*! (Hmm, why am I suddenly hungry for cereal?)

So when you're contemplating how to effectively communicate with your network connections, keep these points in mind:

>> **Update your profile when appropriate.** Updating your profile means that you're sending an update of your newest projects to your network so that your connections can consider involving you in their own current or future projects. You don't need to update your profile as often as you update a blog, but you certainly don't want to leave your profile untouched for months on end, either. Useful times to update your profile include the following:

- Getting a new job or promotion

- Starting a new freelance or contract job

- Launching a new company or venture

- Adding a missing piece of your Experience section, such as adding a new position, updating the description of an existing job, or clarifying the role of a group or interest on your profile

- Receiving an award or honor for your professional, nonprofit, or volunteer work

- Being appointed to a board of directors or elected to a professional association board

- Taking on new responsibilities or duties in any of your endeavors

» **Take advantage of the "Share an Update" feature.** When you specify your current endeavors or share your thoughts or observations, several things happen. Your profile reflects what you enter here, your network connections see what you enter here when they read their network updates about you (see Chapter 10 for more on network updates), and you start to build your own microblog, in a sense, because people can follow your natural progression.

A similar example of a microblog is Twitter. As you update your Twitter profile with 140-character messages, other people can follow your activities and even subscribe to these updates. Tie your Twitter updates to your LinkedIn account, so if you "tweet" on Twitter, those updates are automatically reflected on your LinkedIn profile.

Some people use the "Share an Update" feature to let people know that "Joel is getting ready for his next project" or "Joel is finishing up his fourth edition of *LinkedIn For Dummies.*" Other people use the messages to show progression of a certain task, like "Joel is currently conducting interviews for an Executive Assistant position he is trying to fill," then "Joel is narrowing down his choices for Executive Assistant to two finalists," and finally "Joel has made an offer to his top choice for Executive Assistant." See Chapter 10 for more on how to use this feature.

» **Search for, and join, any relevant LinkedIn Groups that can help you reach your target audience.** It's a good idea to participate in these groups, but whatever you do, don't immediately start conversations just to spam them with LinkedIn messages. When you join the group, you're indicating your interest in that group because your profile now carries that group logo. Membership in such groups gives you access to like-minded people you should be communicating with and adding to your network. Spend some time every week or every month checking out LinkedIn Groups and networking with group members to grow your network. See Chapter 16 for more about LinkedIn Groups.

» **Participate on a regular and consistent basis.** The easiest way to ensure a steady stream of contact with as many people as you can handle is to dedicate a small but fixed amount of time to regularly interact with the LinkedIn community. Some members spend 15 to 30 minutes per day, sending messages to their connections, reading through the Groups and Companies or Influencers page, or finding one to two new people to add to their network. Others spend an hour a week, or as long as it takes to create their set number of recommendations, invite their set number of new contacts, or reconnect with their set number of existing connections. You just need to establish a routine that works with your own schedule.

Marketing Your Business Through LinkedIn

LinkedIn can play a significant role in the effective marketing of your business. LinkedIn's value as a marketing tool gets a lot of buzz from most companies' finance departments, especially because they see LinkedIn as a free way of marketing the business. Although you don't have to pay anything in terms of money to take advantage of most of LinkedIn's functions, you do have to factor in the cost of the time you put in to manage your profile and use LinkedIn to the fullest.

Currently, LinkedIn offers your company promotion through its Company pages section. LinkedIn ties status updates, job titles, and other pertinent information from company employees' profiles directly into the Company page. From each page, you can see those people you know in the company, open career positions, recent updates from their employees, and other pertinent facts.

If you're a small business, you can create your own Company page. You need to have your company e-mail address in your LinkedIn profile and be established as a current employee/manager/owner of that company in your profile as well. I discuss how to build a Company page in Chapter 15.

Using online marketing tactics with LinkedIn

Marketing your business on LinkedIn involves working through your own network, employing both your current list of contacts as well as potential contacts in the greater LinkedIn community. Your efforts should also include making use of links from your online activities to your LinkedIn profile and promoting your business online from your LinkedIn identity. Here are some things to keep in mind as you develop your LinkedIn marketing strategy:

>> **Encourage every employee to have a LinkedIn profile and to link to each other.** Extending your network in this way increases your exposure outside your company. And if anybody in your organization is nervous about preparing

her profile, just tell her that LinkedIn can be an important asset in their professional or career development. You can mention that even Bill Gates has a LinkedIn profile. That should do the trick! (And then buy her a copy of this book to get her started.)

>> **Make sure your business websites and blogs are linked to your LinkedIn profile.** By offering your website visitors a direct view to your LinkedIn profile, you're allowing them to verify you as an employee of the company because they can see your experience and recommendations from other people. They might also realize they share a bond with you and your business that they never would have discovered without LinkedIn.

>> **Make sure your LinkedIn profile links back to your business website and blog.** You not only want your visitors and potential customers to be able to verify who you are, but you also want them to go back to your website and do some business with you! Make sure that you, and every employee of your company who's on LinkedIn, includes a link to your business's website and, if there is one, the company blog.

WARNING

If you have a search engine expert working for you, that person may complain about something called a *two-way link,* which is a link from your LinkedIn profile to your website and a link from your website to your LinkedIn profile. This practice, known as *reciprocal linking,* hurts your search engine ranking. If so, have that person identify which of the two links is more important and implement only that link.

>> **Make sure that your most popular keyword phrases are in your company or personal profile.** Use sites such as Wordtracker (www.wordtracker.com) or Good Keywords (https://.goodkeywords.com) to find the hottest keyword phrases in your field. If your business is doing any online ad campaigns, make sure those keyword phrases are the same as the ones in your profile. Presenting a consistent image to potential customers makes you and your company look more professional.

>> **Develop relationships with key business partners or media contacts.** When you search for someone on LinkedIn, you can be precise about who you want to reach. So, for example, if you know that your business needs to expand into the smartphone market, you can start targeting and reaching out to smartphone companies such as Apple, Samsung (maker of the Galaxy and Note), and HTC (maker of the One). If you want to increase your visibility, start reaching out to media members who cover your industry.

Mining for Clients

It's a big world out there. In terms of clients, you need to ask yourself who you're looking for. Is everyone a potential client, or do you have a specific demographic in mind? A specific skill set? Maybe you've written the greatest plug-in tool for accountants who work in the financial services industry, and you want to sell this tool directly to your likely users. With LinkedIn, you can conduct a search to find people who match your criteria. Then after you locate those people, it's up to you to approach them and close the sale, which I talk about in "Closing the Deal," later in this chapter.

Before you start your search, ask yourself some questions that can help you with generating your leads:

>> Are you looking for people with a specific title or in a particular industry?

>> Are you looking for high-net-worth or well-connected donors for your nonprofit organization?

>> Are you looking for decision makers within a company, or are you seeking a general audience? (That is, are you trying to sell into a company, or directly to people?)

>> Besides your main target industry, can you approach related industries, and if so, what are they?

>> Does the location of your potential contact matter? Does making the sale require an in-person visit (which means that the contact needs to live near you or you have to be willing to travel to this person)?

With your answers to these questions in mind, you're ready to start searching LinkedIn for your leads.

Generating leads with the Advanced People search

When you're ready to start looking for leads, I recommend jumping right in with the LinkedIn Advanced People search, which allows you to search the database consisting of hundreds of millions of LinkedIn members based on the criteria you've established for the leads you want to generate.

To start a search, click the Advanced link next to the Search text box at the top of any LinkedIn page. Say you need accountants who work in the Financial Services industry. To start such a search, you would fill in the Title field and click the Financial Services check box, under the Industry field, of Advanced People search, as shown in Figure 17-3, and then click Search.

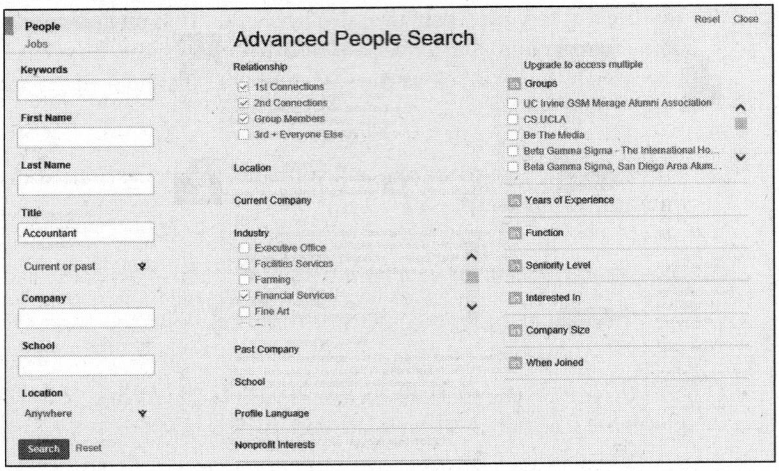

FIGURE 17-3:
Use the Advanced People search to find potential clients.

I also selected the check boxes for 1st Connections, 2nd Connections, and Group Members. Why? When you search the LinkedIn database, your own network can help you identify your *best leads* (people only two or three degrees away from you who you can reach through a first-degree connection introducing you) if you make sure those options are checked. When you see your search results with those options checked, you first see which results are closely connected with you via your connections. You can click each person's name to read his full LinkedIn profile, see how you're connected, and decide whether you have a potential lead. (This method usually gives you much more information than a simple Google search, which would provide only a LinkedIn member's public profile, instead of his full profile.)

After you identify your best leads, you can use LinkedIn to find out what connections you have in common: Simply click the Shared Connections link under the name for each search result. For example, say I click the 1 Shared Connection link for Maria in my search result. I see that my friend Alyssa is the shared connection between me and Maria, as shown in Figure 17-4, and that helps me approach Maria, because I can ask Alyssa for an introduction or for more information about Maria.

FIGURE 17-4:
See who in your
LinkedIn network
is a shared
connection with
your target lead.

When doing general prospecting, surveying the market for that "perfect lead" or, at least, a lead in the right direction, keep these ideas in mind while filling in the appropriate Advanced Search fields for each strategy:

>> **Generalize your search.** If you're looking for your ideal contacts independently of the company they work for, focus primarily on the Title field and the options present under the Industry header to find your leads.

>> **Narrow your search.** Use the Keywords field to narrow your results list when you need to reach people within a certain niche of an industry or job.

>> **Target specific people.** Use either the Company or Keywords field, plus the Title field, to help you find specific employees in your target companies.

>> **Help your product or service sell itself.** Search for the customers of your customers to get those people excited about your product or service, so that they'll demand it from *your* customers! This strategy is also known as *pull marketing.*

Finding the decision maker

Although generating a list of potential leads is a great first step in marketing your product, being an effective salesperson often comes down to finding that "right person" with whom you can present an offer to buy something. This person is the *decision maker* (or the *final authority,* or even just *da boss*). You can talk to as many administrative assistants and receptionists as you'd like, but without the exact name or contact info of the person who makes the purchasing decisions, your sales effort is stalled.

LinkedIn can help you reach that decision maker in the following ways:

>> **Include words like Account Manager, Director, or Vice President in the Keywords field when you perform an advanced search.** If your results show someone who's in your extended network, now you have a specific name to mention when you call the company. I recommend you approach that person via LinkedIn and your mutual connections first, thereby making your first contact with her more of a "warm call" than a cold one.

>> **Access the LinkedIn Company page to find out specific information about your target company.** If you're trying to reach someone within a company, see whether that person shows up as an employee on the Company page. To do so, start typing the name of the company in the top Search box. As LinkedIn generates a drop-down list of options, click the company name in the Companies section of the list. Say, for example, that you need to reach someone within Microsoft. When you bring up Microsoft's Company page, as shown in Figure 17-5, you get some specific information right away.

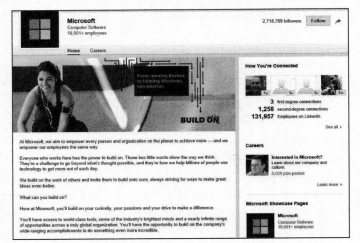

FIGURE 17-5: Get specific information about your target company through its profile.

You immediately see who in your network works for this company, so you know who to approach to pass along your request to the decision maker, or to tell you who that decision maker is. Scroll down the page to view other useful information, such as recent updates from the company, similar companies or topics to this company, and Showcase Pages. You can then follow that company (by clicking the yellow Follow button) to see all its new updates and information as part of your LinkedIn News Feed.

>> **Take advantage of your existing network to ask for an introduction, to seek out advice, or to point you in the right direction.** Using your network in this manner was basically the original intent of LinkedIn: You contact someone who works at your target company and ask that contact to introduce you to the decision maker. The decision maker is much more likely to be receptive to an introduction than a cold call. Your network connection might also recommend you to the decision maker, which carries some weight when you try to close the deal. In addition, you may have a select group of people in

your own network that can provide advice on who to connect with, as well as advice or ideas on selling your product, service, or nonprofit organization.

>> **Use InMail to contact the decision maker (if she is on LinkedIn) or someone close to the decision maker.** You may not have the time or opportunity to get introduced to your decision maker, and if you're using InMail to approach the decision maker, why not just go for the gusto and introduce yourself directly? This is a faster option than waiting or asking for an introduction, but there's the chance the decision maker will ignore your message. (In the case where the decision maker isn't on LinkedIn, use LinkedIn to find the closest person and ask that person for help, for a connection, or for information to help you reach the next level.) You have to decide what's best for your situation.

Closing the Deal

Establishing a connection to the right person (the one who makes the purchasing decisions) is half the battle in getting your product sold. However, you still have to convince the person and close the deal. In this section, I give you some pointers on how to put LinkedIn to work for you for the final phase of a sales effort: completing it successfully!

The key to getting the most out of LinkedIn for closing the deal is knowing that LinkedIn has more than just names — it has detailed profiles of its hundreds of millions of users, millions of Pulse news articles and comments, associations made through LinkedIn Groups, and corporate information through LinkedIn Company pages.

Preparing for the client meeting

Say that your initial conversations with your prospects have gone well and you have been granted a meeting with a potential client to make your pitch. Whereas you may have already used LinkedIn to gain more information about the specific person, you can now get details about the specific industry, the company, and the company's potential response to your business pitch. Here are some tips on gathering information about the people you are meeting and the company:

>> **Read the client's *full* profile to discover all you can about his interests, likes, dislikes, and so on.** You can do far more than simply scan a person's profile looking for past jobs and view her education to see whether she shares an alma mater with you. A person's LinkedIn profile can be a gold mine of

information about that person. For example, people may include links to their own websites, blogs, or company websites. Follow those links, especially to blogs or personal websites, and see what you can find out. In the prospect's profile, look over the Interests section, their status updates, and the Additional Information section. And don't forget the Contact Settings section — here's where you can find out under what circumstances this person wants to be contacted. Be sure to respect those wishes.

>> **Read your client's recommendations for other people.** You can gain a lot of insight by seeing what qualities a person likes to praise in other people, especially if your prospect has left multiple recommendations. In this way, you also gain insight into the people he trusts, so check those people who received a recommendation to see whether you have a connection to any of *them*. If so, ask that person first for an introduction to your prospect.

>> **See the activity your client (and the company) has on LinkedIn.** If you pull up someone's profile, look for a section on his profile page below the summary box called Posts and click the See More link to see posts that the person made and "recent activity" — status updates, articles he liked, commented, or shared, and topics he follows, as shown in Figure 17-6. When you read these items, you might gain some insight into this person's preferences and "hot button issues" — what motivates or annoys him.

FIGURE 17-6: Read through the activity your prospect has created on LinkedIn.

Also, look at the Company page, and pay attention to recent company updates. You will get a sense of what the company is promoting, what its top focuses are, and key company announcements. Doing so gives you more background information and therefore more confidence; also, this type of knowledge helps you identify interests or commonalities to enhance your sense of connection with your buyer (and hers with you).

REMEMBER

All these efforts are meant only to prepare you and get you closer to your prospect or target company so that you can make your pitch. Obviously, to complete the sale, you still need to have a compelling product, pitch, and offer for this company. Have everything ready *before* you approach your prospect. Take the information you've learned; lay it out and organize it around the company, the person you're meeting, and the opportunity you're trying to gain; and prepare any potential questions (along with your answers to those questions) that may come up during the meeting.

Reporting a positive sale

Reporting the completion of a sale is my favorite part of the business sales process. You made the sale, developed the solution, and delivered it to the customer. At this point, many people think, "Whew, I'm done. Nothing to do now but enjoy happy hour!" This is a common and natural response, but as a member of the LinkedIn world, your job isn't really done. You want to demonstrate your growth (and your company's growth) that resulted from handling this project to encourage future contracts to come your way. Here are some actions to consider after you complete the sale and deliver the solution:

» **Invite your customer to join your network.** You worked hard to earn this customer's trust and to meet (or exceed) his expectations by completing the sale. As a result, you should feel comfortable enough to send him an invitation to join your network. Doing so could keep you in contact with this customer for future opportunities. Studies have shown that it's six times cheaper to sell to an existing customer than to acquire a new customer.

» **Leave your customer a recommendation.** After you add a customer to your network, post a recommendation for him on the system if you feel it's deserved. Doing so gives your customer a sense of reward for being a positive contributor, but more important, it informs the community that you did a project for this person, which can help you in the future. Also, the customer may reciprocate by leaving you a recommendation, which strengthens your profile and makes you more appealing to future prospects.

>> **Stay in touch with your customer.** You can keep track of your customer's activities by monitoring your network updates (if he is a part of your network). Routinely keep in touch about the solution you delivered, perhaps to open the conversation for selling additional products or services or maintenance contract work.

>> **Update your profile with the skills you acquired or demonstrated through this sale.** To be ready for future prospects who search the LinkedIn database, it's important to have the right keywords and skill sets on your profile so that these prospects can identify you as someone who can provide a similar solution for them. If you're a consultant or freelance worker, you can add the project you just completed as experience on your profile as well. (See Chapter 3 for tips on how to update your profile.)

>> **Tap the customer's network by asking him for referrals.** After you connect with your customer, keep an eye on his network. If you think you see a future prospect, consider asking your customer for an introduction or a recommendation. Usually, if you provided a quality solution, the customer may readily oblige your request, if they don't feel there is a conflict or a sense of uneasiness.

Chapter 18

Using LinkedIn Ads

With so many options out there on the Internet, even within the LinkedIn website itself, it's easy to wonder how someone can capture a person's attention. There are lots of ways to engage, present, and connect with other professionals, but sometimes, an extra strategy is needed to bring the message home. In LinkedIn's case, it developed an advertising system where people can create targeted messages to reach their community.

LinkedIn Ads allow businesses or consumers to create and manage their own "self-service" advertising and create a targeted, specialized message to reach a portion of the overall LinkedIn network.

In this chapter, I discuss the types of LinkedIn ads and some basic restrictions and guidelines to keep in mind. I walk you through the creation of a LinkedIn ad and go through some of the analytics and reports available for you to judge the efficacy of your ad campaign (especially if you need to go back and make changes for more effective results) on LinkedIn.

Understanding LinkedIn Ads

The first thing you should consider about any advertising system, including LinkedIn Ads, is whether that system can help you reach your target audience. So ask yourself, could you benefit from a network of over 400 million working professionals and business owners around the world? If the answer is no, then perhaps you should flip to the next chapter, but if the answer is yes, keep reading.

One of the powerful aspects of LinkedIn Ads is that you can really target your "target audience." Given that LinkedIn knows a lot about the members who use its site, it can help deliver your ad to a very specific target audience, depending on your needs. Perhaps you're only targeting business owners who live in the Pacific Northwest and have more than 5 years of experience. Maybe you are marketing a financial software package for accountants who work in large companies. Then again, you could be trying to reach all the company presidents or CEO's of small, medium, and/or large companies. With LinkedIn, you can set one or more filters to target only the most relevant audience for your ad, which should increase the participation and effectiveness of your ad.

When you look at your LinkedIn home page (an example is shown in Figure 18-1), you can see the two types of ads that LinkedIn promotes to its members:

>> **Text (and Image) ads:** Just as they sound, LinkedIn Text ads offer you the ability to create a basic ad message, which is typically displayed along the top of the screen or on the right-most column of the LinkedIn home page or your message Inbox, sometimes with a designated image. You can set a specific URL that, when clicked, takes the user to a specific destination or "results" website, either on or off LinkedIn.

>> **Sponsored Updates:** These updates are included in the news feed of a LinkedIn user, but are clearly labeled as "Sponsored" so the user knows it's not coming from one of her connections. These Sponsored updates typically contain a link to an article, destination website, or LinkedIn company page, and give the user the ability to interact with your company through Like and Comment links connected to the update.

These ads allow you to drive qualified professionals to your business or LinkedIn landing page, as LinkedIn offers you a variety of targeting options to pick the right audience. You can control your ad budget and choose between two cost models: Pay-Per-Click (PPC), where you pay every time a potential customer clicks the link in your ad, or Cost-Per-Impression (CPM), where you are billed for every 1,000 times your ad is displayed on a potential customer's screen (that display is also known as an "impression"), regardless of whether the link was clicked.

FIGURE 18-1:
LinkedIn includes Text ads and Sponsored Updates on its pages.

Examples of LinkedIn ads (Text and Sponsored Updates)

TIP

If your ad budget is more than $25,000 per month, you can have access to your own Account Manager and more advertising options like Sponsored InMail. Visit the LinkedIn Business Solutions page for more information at `https://business.linkedin.com/marketing-solutions`.

There are elements of LinkedIn Ads that will seem very familiar to anyone who's engaged in some online advertising, especially if you've used sites like Google AdWords or Facebook Advertising. Beyond the targeting filters, LinkedIn Ads also lets you control the bidding amount you're willing to spend per click or impression; run multiple variations of ads to test for the highest conversion rate; design your ad through its website by picking text, images, and destination URLs; and budget your spending to control daily and total ad expenditures. You get to study the results of your ad campaign to help gauge measurable results, just like with other platforms.

Finding Out About Filtering Options

Other advertising networks allow you to filter your target audience by a few known attributes of the person who will see your ad — age, gender, and location of the audience member. LinkedIn allows you to go one step further by allowing you to search for specific criteria.

You can use filters in LinkedIn Ads to segment your audience by these factors:

» **Company name, industry, and/or size:** While you can make the argument that someone's employer doesn't define who they are as a person, their employer may make a difference in whether your ad (and your product or service, by extension) would be relevant to them. LinkedIn allows you to specify a filter for a company name (let's say you only want companies that include or exclude a particular word), the company's industry (perhaps you only want to target transportation or high-tech companies), or the company's size as defined by the number of employees (this means you could target companies with fewer than 50 employees or 5,001 or more employees).

» **Job title or function:** If you're trying to reach all the software developers or Six Sigma consultants out there, LinkedIn allows you to create a Job title filter and look for specific titles you provide. Going up one level, the Job function filter allows you to target an audience where their job falls under a specific function, like Information Technology, Marketing, Operations, Purchasing, or Sales.

» **Job seniority:** Okay, you've targeted your audience by job title, but is that enough information? After all, someone who's been doing that specific job for 1 or 2 years will have different needs than someone who's been a manager at that job for 10 to 15 years. LinkedIn Ads allows you to specify someone's job seniority (think of it as "years of experience") by different levels, from "Training" and "Entry" (think entry level) to "Senior," "Manager," "Director," "VP," and "CXO" (which is shorthand for any Chief Officer like CEO, CFO, CTO, and so on).

» **Member schools, fields of study, and degrees:** Let's say you are a recruiter and you are trying to reach people based on their higher education. LinkedIn Ads allows you to target your audience by specifying one or more names of schools to include or exclude, as well as specific fields of study or degrees. (For example, maybe you want to reach people with Electrical Engineering degrees, but not people with Mechanical Engineering degrees.)

» **Member skills:** You can specify one or more specific skills that LinkedIn members have identified on their profile, so if you want to reach people who have the same skill, you can do so in LinkedIn Ads.

» **Member groups:** Someone once said that you are judged by the company you keep, and LinkedIn Ads is no exception to that concept. You can target your audience based on the LinkedIn Group memberships that people have. This way, your LinkedIn ad can target people who belong to groups that match the goal of what you have to offer.

The best use of filters comes when you combine two or more elements to really qualify the audience you need to reach. While it may seem that targeting project managers is good enough, for example, you may really need project managers with specific skills, or project managers who have done the job for 5 or more years. Therefore, you should really think about who your target audience is, and that will help you decide which filters to use.

Creating a New Ad Campaign

When you are ready to start a new campaign, follow these steps:

1. **Hover your mouse over the Business Services link on the right side of the top navigation bar, and then click Advertise from the drop-down list that appears.**

   You are taken to LinkedIn's advertising start page (see Figure 18-2), which describes the features and operation of the different ads available.

FIGURE 18-2:
Start building your ad campaign here.

2. **Click the Get Started button in the middle of the page.**

   LinkedIn takes you to its Campaign Manager start page (see Figure 18-3), where you can choose between a Text ad and a Sponsored Update.

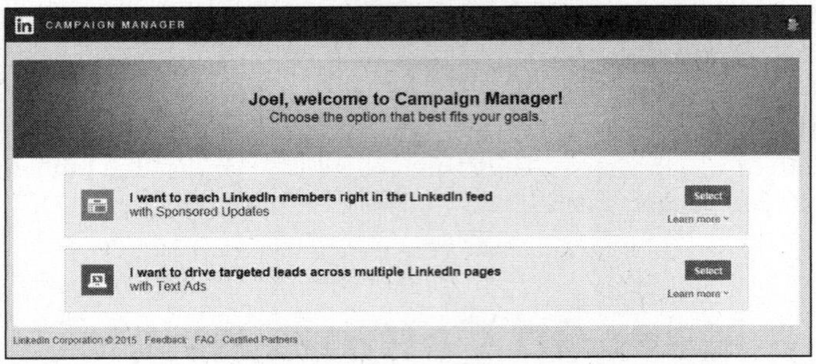

FIGURE 18-3:
Choose the ad
format you
want for your
campaign.

3. **Click the Select button next to the ad type you want to create.**

   For this example, I am going to walk through creating a Text ad. The first time you click either ad product, LinkedIn takes you to an Ad Account creation page, where you define your ad account name, select your currency, and specify if you have a Company or Showcase page to tie to your account. Once you've provided that information, you click the Next button to start building your campaign.

4. **Define a campaign name and, for first-time users, define the language to be used for your campaign.**

   You can use up to 50 characters to define the name of your campaign, so try to create a name that'll summarize the goals or target audience of your ad campaign. Try to add some detail in the name in case you run multiple campaigns to test the effectiveness of your message (for example, Sample Campaign A, B, C, and so on). Enter the name into the box provided (see Figure 18-4) and then click the Next button to proceed.

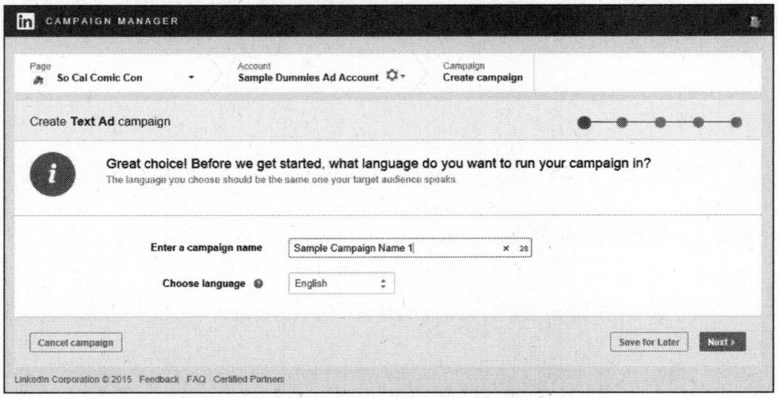

FIGURE 18-4:
Give your
campaign a
meaningful
name.

5. **Define the headline, copy, image, and destination URL of your ad, while seeing a preview of your potential ad as you write it.**

You're taken to the Build Ad page within the LinkedIn Campaign Manager (see Figure 18-5), where you define the meat of your ad, starting with the destination URL. Decide whether the ad will take people to your LinkedIn page (and then define which specific page, like a Company page), or an external website. Define the exact URL in the My Website box provided.

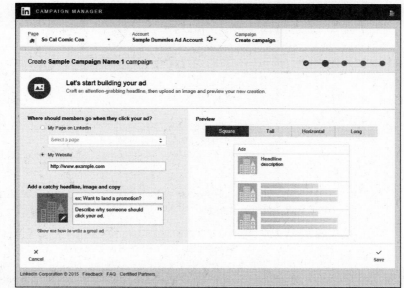

FIGURE 18-5:
Build your ad.

Enter the headline of your ad and the message "copy" in the boxes provided. You are limited to a 25-character headline and a 75-character message for your ad, so choose your words carefully. If you are going to provide an image with your ad, click the pencil icon at the bottom of the sample image provided to load the image from your computer onto LinkedIn.

As you design your ad, along the right side of the screen you see a preview of the finished product (see Figure 18-6 for an example). You can choose different formats for your ad, like Square, Tall, Horizontal, or Long, if you are designing a Text ad.

Once you've defined everything and picked your ideal format, click the Save button at the bottom right of the screen to proceed.

TIP

If you are unsure about whether the content of your ad will be allowed, you can read more about LinkedIn's ad guidelines by going to https://www.linkedin.com/legal/pop/pop-sas-guidelines.

FIGURE 18-6:
See how your ad
will display to
users on-screen.

See a preview of what your ad will look like on-screen.

6. **Make variations of your ad to test out the effectiveness of different text messages and/or images.**

   LinkedIn offers you the ability to create up to 15 variations of the same ad so you can see which combination of text and image is the most effective in gaining attention. Simply click the Create Another Ad link in the middle of the page (see Figure 18-7) and repeat Step 5. Click the Next button when you are satisfied with the number of ad variations for this campaign.

7. **Use the targeting filters to come up with your ideal target audience for your ad.**

   LinkedIn allows you to target potential ad viewers using the information LinkedIn has for their account. You can target based on location, job title, company name/size, and other elements like field of study, skills, degrees, group affiliations, or demographic information like their gender or age. Simply click the particular criteria (see Figure 18-8) to set the desired value. As you add filters, your potential audience number will update along the right side of the screen. Repeat the process until you've defined all your criteria, and then click the Next button to proceed.

WARNING

As of this writing, a location filter is required; you can only target up to 10 regions, sub-regions, or countries; and your ad must be able to target at least 1,000 potential viewers, so you can't use too many precise filters.

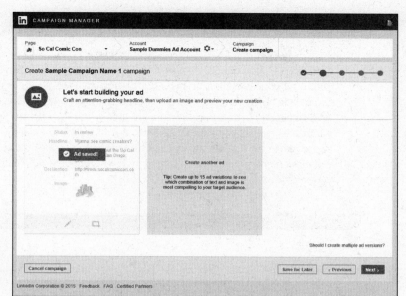

FIGURE 18-7:
Create variations
of your ad to find
the most effective
mix of text
and image.

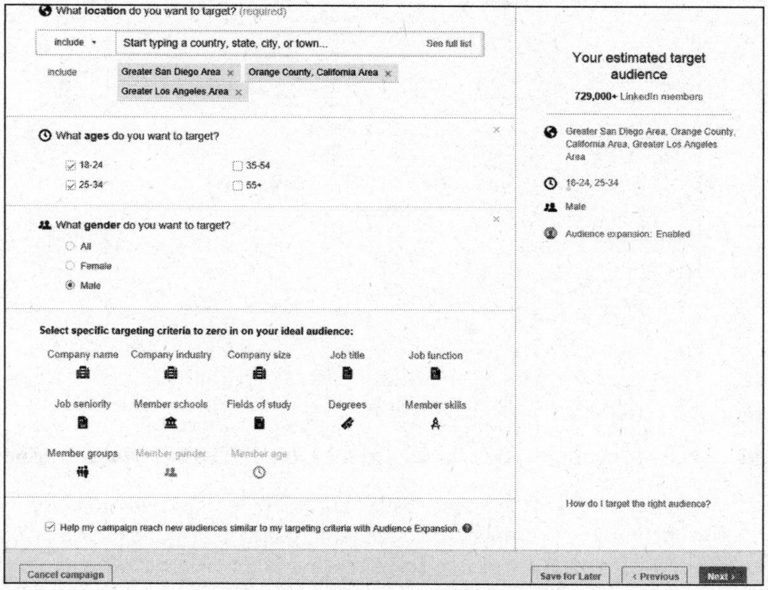

FIGURE 18-8:
Define your
target audience
with built-in
filters such as
location.

8. **Determine your bid type, bid amount, daily budget, and start date for your campaign.**

Once you've defined your ad and your targeting filters, LinkedIn will prompt you to set your spending limits for this campaign, as shown in Figure 18-9. You can decide between cost per click (CPC) and cost per impressions (CPM). Based on that decision, you can set the bid amount and daily budget amount. As for start date, you can choose for the campaign to start immediately after being approved, or set a start date in the future. If you click the Show More link, you can pick an end date for your campaign as well. Click the Next button when you're ready to proceed.

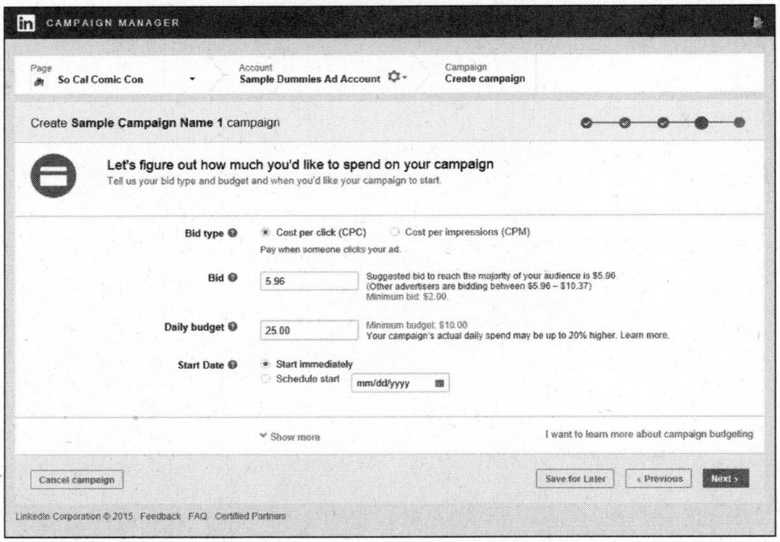

FIGURE 18-9:
Set your spending
limits for your ad.

As of this writing, you must assign a minimum CPC bid of $2 per click and a minimum daily budget of $10.

WARNING

9. **Provide a valid credit card for LinkedIn to bill when your ad campaign is live.**

LinkedIn provides you with a summary and asks you to enter a valid credit card into the prompts provided on the page (see Figure 18-10) so it can bill your card after people start clicking your ad or LinkedIn displays your ad with enough impressions to incur a charge on your ad campaign. After you enter your payment method, scroll down and click the Review Order button so LinkedIn can store that payment information.

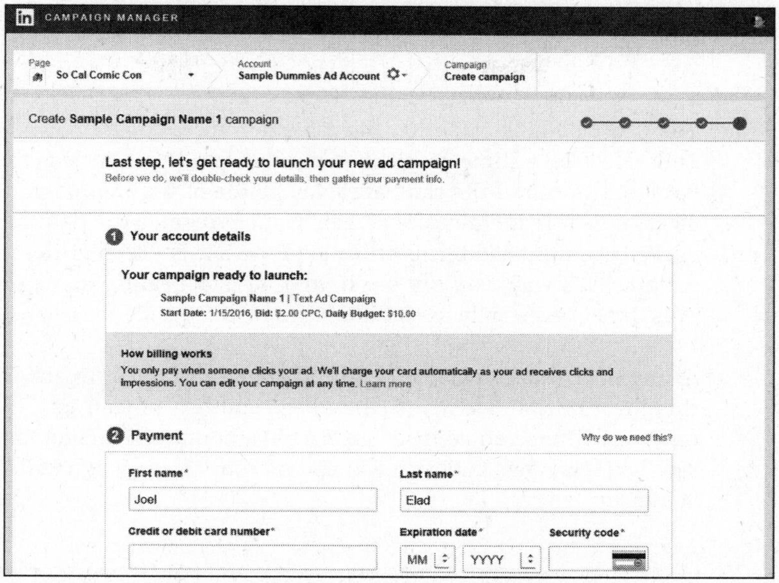

FIGURE 18-10:
Provide LinkedIn
with your billing
information.

10. **Scroll down and click the yellow Launch Campaign button to start your ad campaign.**

That's it! LinkedIn needs to manually review your ad to make sure you are complying with its ad guidelines, but that process usually takes an average of 12 hours or less, depending on what day and time the campaign was submitted to LinkedIn. Once the ad is approved and running, LinkedIn will send you a notification.

Managing Your LinkedIn Ad Campaign

After your ad campaign is approved and starts appearing on your audience's LinkedIn web pages, the LinkedIn Campaign Manager will be able to start displaying relevant information about the performance of your ad campaign.

The Performance page (see Figure 18-11) will summarize the following aspects of your campaign:

» Impressions

» Clicks

>> Social Actions (Likes, Comments, Shares, Follows)

>> $X.XX spent

You can also pick a metric, like Clicks, Impressions, or Average CPC, and have LinkedIn create a line graph showing the data as far back as the most recent day, week, or month of the campaign, or the life of the campaign. LinkedIn also provides a Click Demographics screen that aggregates the data for each person who clicked on your ad in terms of his job function, industry, title, seniority, and other factors. This way, you can see if your ad is appealing to a specific demographic. This data is especially useful if and when you decide to revise your campaign.

At any time, you can go back and edit your existing ad campaign, changing everything from the ad elements (the image and text of your ad), to the audience (the targeting filters you defined), to the bid amount and budget for your ad. Once you save your changes, LinkedIn will update your ad campaign with the newest choices you made.

FIGURE 18-11:
Measure the performance of your LinkedIn ads.

When you look at these metrics and think about how to improve your results, keep these points in mind:

>> **Drop the worst performing variations.** If you created multiple variations of your ad, go back and delete or disable the ones providing the lowest click-through rates. This will raise the effectiveness of your overall campaign and increase the impressions as LinkedIn will be more motivated to serve up a higher-performing campaign so it earns more money for that advertising slot.

>> **Change your destination URL.** The problem may not be with your ad, but with the conversion page the potential customer reaches after clicking your ad. If you use analytic software on your own website, you can see if people are leaving your destination URL after arriving from LinkedIn without acting on your call for action.

>> **Consider using a face as your ad image.** Other advertisers have mentioned that the best-performing ads they've experienced were ads that used a picture of someone's face as opposed to a logo or product image. Since you are limited to a 50 pixels-by- 50 pixels image, you cannot use a complex or text-laden image. You can best connect to your audience with a visual image that's inviting and personal, like someone's face.

>> **Ask for the click.** While you are limited to only 75 characters, you should specify for readers to click the link, not just describe what you are offering. As a bare minimum, give readers a good idea of what they are receiving and/or how your offer can improve their life with a tangible benefit.

>> **Test out new content.** Once you have been running a campaign for a while, try out new content in your ad. It'll catch the attention of people who have already acted or dismissed your previous ad and raise interest and interaction.

>> **If you run a Sponsored Update, pay attention to the comments it receives.** If you want your Sponsored Update to perform better, be sure to Like the update yourself, have your employees engage with the update, and answer any comments from customers that the update may be receiving. That interaction and involvement will raise the update's visibility and hopefully gain you further engagement and a positive brand image.

TIP As you progress with your LinkedIn ad campaigns, you can also utilize tools like AdStage's All in One Advertising platform to help you with all your online ad campaigns. Go to www.adstage.io for more information. You can see AdStage's home page in Figure 18-12.

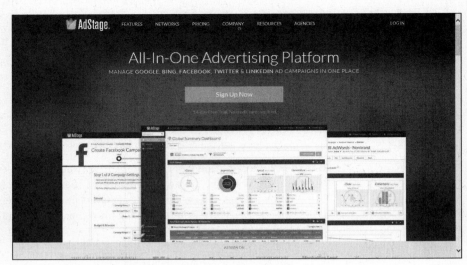

FIGURE 18-12:
You can use advanced tools like AdStage to help manage your ads.

Chapter 19

Miscellaneous Creative Uses of LinkedIn

When you think of a business networking site such as LinkedIn, the most obvious applications spring to mind pretty quickly: finding a job, finding an employee, meeting new people, building a new business, getting funding and partners for that new business, and so on. But LinkedIn has acquired even more uses than the obvious ones. The power of the Internet and hundreds of millions of LinkedIn members have encouraged people to use this large community to accomplish other goals, both close to home and around the world.

In this chapter, I give you a look at some of the creative uses that people have found for LinkedIn. Some people use LinkedIn in combination with other services, such as Google Alerts. Other people use LinkedIn as a gathering place to find recruits to help mold a new venture. Yet others have been using LinkedIn to meet each other in person! I describe these endeavors as well as provide several case studies with some points to keep in mind if you feel like doing something similar.

Mashing LinkedIn with Other Services

One of the trends on the Internet over the years has been the creation of mashups. No, I'm not talking potatoes here. A *mashup* is created when somebody takes data from more than one application and puts that data together into a single new and useful application. For example, say you combine real estate sales data from a database application with the Google Maps application, enabling a search result of the real estate data to be mapped onto a satellite image on Google. The satellite image represents a mashup because it's a new, distinct service that neither application provided on its own.

Something similar to the concept of mashups occurs with creative uses of LinkedIn. As LinkedIn continues to evolve and its members use more and more of LinkedIn's functionality, new uses for LinkedIn continue to emerge, especially as part of a user's Internet exploits. The following sections describe a smattering of these mashups.

LinkedIn and Google Alerts

LinkedIn + Google Alerts = Better-informed communication

I got this tip from Liz Ryan, a workplace expert, author, and speaker, as one of her top ten ways of using LinkedIn. It has to do with using both sites as a business tool when you're trying to reach out to an important potential business contact who you do not know. It works like this:

1. **Click the Advanced link next to the search box on the top of any LinkedIn page to bring up the Advanced People Search page.**

2. **Fill in the appropriate fields to search for the name of a person at a company who is relevant to your situation, and with whom you would like to connect.**

3. **Armed with the name that turned up in the results, set up a Google Alert (by going to** `https://www.google.com/alerts`**) with the person's name and the company name so that Google notifies you when that person is quoted or in the news.**

When you go to Google's Alerts page (as shown in Figure 19-1), you simply enter the person's name and company name in the search query box, and then configure how you want Google to alert you by clicking the Show Options link and then setting the How Often, Sources, Language, Regions, and How Many filters below the search query box. Finally, you set the e-mail address you want the alerts to be sent to with the Deliver To drop-down list option. Click the Create Alert button, and you're good to go!

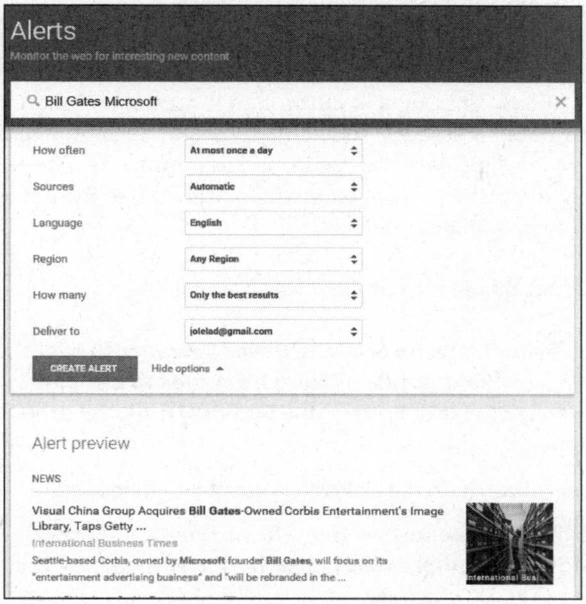

FIGURE 19-1:
Google can
automatically
send you
specific alerts.

When you receive a notice from Google Alerts, you have a much better idea of what the person is working on as well as his impact at the company. This knowledge gives you an icebreaker you can use to strike up a conversation. Rather than send a random connection request, you can reference the person's speech at the last XYZ Summit or agree with his last blog post. You show initiative by doing the research, which can impress or flatter the contact and give you something to refer to when you talk about his accomplishments or innovations.

Don't overuse all this information you get when you contact the person, or, as Liz Ryan warns, he might think you're a business stalker.

WARNING

LinkedIn Archives and Data Syncing

LinkedIn Archives + Data Syncing = Ready to build Rolodex

There is a wealth of information contained in your LinkedIn account — from your list of connections to your experience, education, skills, and other profile information, to your status updates, long-form publisher posts, and publications posted through LinkedIn, and much more. As time goes on, the information from this account may contain more up to date info than your e-mail or contact information systems. If you're in a sales position, in particular, your contacts and daily information is your lifeblood, and that data is crucial to your ongoing survival. Today, there's an easy way to capture that data and use it for other programs to help you manage your life.

LinkedIn allows you to request an archive of your data, which means you can download files that contain all your account activity from the moment you joined LinkedIn to today. This means all of your connections and contacts, as well as your profile data, messages sent and received, recommendations written and given, and so on. This data is downloaded as Comma Separated Value files, which can be easily imported to a data syncing platform like Evernote, so your data can be available across all your devices.

To benefit from this feature, follow these steps:

1. **Log in to your LinkedIn account. Hover your mouse over the Account & Settings icon (your profile picture) from the top navigation bar, and then click Manage (next to Privacy and Settings) from the drop-down list that appears.**

   Doing so takes you to the LinkedIn Account & Settings page.

2. **Click the Account category from the bottom left side of the Settings box, below Groups/Companies/Applications, and then click the Request an Archive of Your Data link.**

   When you click the Account category, you will see the account settings page, as shown in Figure 19-2. The Request an Archive of Your Data link is on the bottom right of the screen.

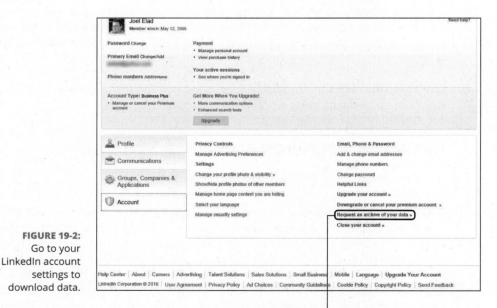

FIGURE 19-2:
Go to your LinkedIn account settings to download data.

Request an Archive of Your Data link

3. **Click the Request an Archive of Your Data link to bring up the Request Your Data Archive page, as shown in Figure 19-3.**

   The Request Your Data Archive page contains links to the LinkedIn Help center's overview of what comes with your archive.

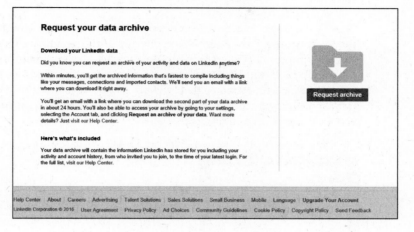

4. **Click the Request Archive button to start the LinkedIn data download process.**

   The data archive will come in two pieces. A short time after you click the button, you will get a file with the easier-to-collect parts of your data archive, like messages, connections, and any contacts you imported to LinkedIn. Within 24 hours, on average, you will get an e-mail with instructions on how to download a second file containing the rest of your LinkedIn data.

Once the data is all downloaded to your computer, use your favorite information storage program, like Evernote, to upload this archive and keep track of your LinkedIn connections and activity.

LinkedIn and Evernote work together

LinkedIn + Evernote = Automated networking processes

If you use Evernote to help control all the information you record and access on a constant basis, now you can benefit from an official integration between Evernote Premium and LinkedIn to help make your networking life much easier. Evernote has a feature in its mobile app that allows you to photograph a business card and Evernote will parse that picture to pull out all the key contact information. More importantly, it will use the e-mail address from the card and scan LinkedIn to see if that person is already on LinkedIn. If so, Evernote will display his LinkedIn profile information within Evernote and allow you to instantly send an Invitation to Connect. This way, you can meet someone, get his business card, instantly add this person's information to your contact program, and send him a LinkedIn invitation while you're still in front of him!

Figure 19-4 shows an example of how a business card looks after it's been scanned into Evernote using the Evernote mobile app. If the person is a LinkedIn user, then Evernote imports that person's profile photo, name, company, and title from his LinkedIn profile and assigns him to the corresponding fields within the Evernote record, which is indicated by the LinkedIn icon next to those fields. Once this integration has occurred, Evernote helps you send a LinkedIn invitation to this new contact from the Evernote screen.

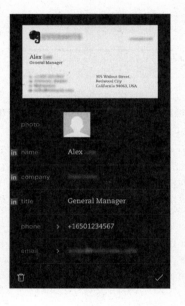

FIGURE 19-4:
Evernote integrates LinkedIn information when you meet someone new.

WARNING

As of this writing, you are not able to send customized invitations with this feature, so the person will be getting a generic invitation message. However, if you inform the person of this incoming invitation when you are face-to-face, it mitigates the impersonal nature of the invitation.

Beyond the business card feature, Evernote allows you to store templates you can use when you send out customized invitations, invitation responses, or responses you make commonly when interacting with people. However, any storage program can hold your templates, whereas Evernote is currently the only app that integrates with business card scanning. When you want to add this functionality to your Evernote app, follow these steps:

1. **Go to the Evernote app and click Settings. Scroll down until you see the section on Camera and click the Camera heading.**

   You see the settings page for Evernote using your mobile device's camera, including a link for Business Cards.

2. **Click Business Cards. You are asked to log into LinkedIn (see Figure 19-5) and give your authorization to connect your LinkedIn account with your Evernote account.**

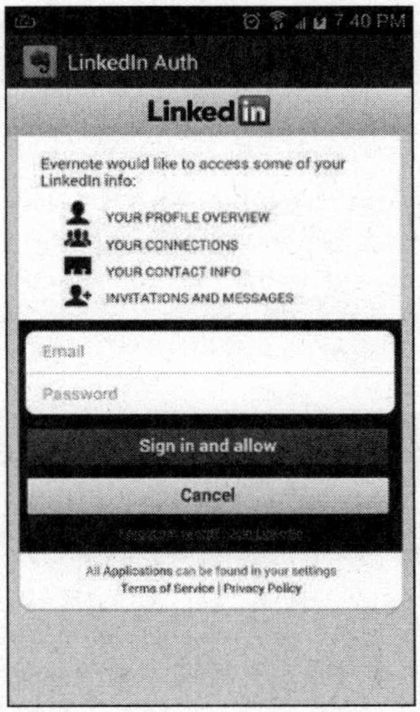

FIGURE 19-5: Give Evernote authorization to interface with your LinkedIn account.

Congratulations! Your Evernote and LinkedIn accounts are now connected. The next time you take a picture of a business card, you should see the LinkedIn integration at work.

Building Your Focus Group

In other chapters, I tell you about the potential for finding qualified employees and customers using LinkedIn, and how LinkedIn can help you perform market research and gauge reactions to a product using advertising. Here, I want to take these ideas one step further and discuss how LinkedIn can help you build a focus group for your new or next project.

Here are some ideas to keep in mind if you want to build your own focus group using LinkedIn:

>> **Start by building your network.** Your best participants in this group are first-degree connections of yours (or of another employee of your company) because those people are most likely to join based on your recommendation and how well they fit your group's purpose. Try to network and invite potential candidates right away.

>> **Build your accompanying website before building the group.** Your focus group participants will want to see something before deciding to join and participate, so make sure you've spent some time building an informational web page, e-mail, FAQ, or other system that is available for viewing before you start to build your group.

>> **Use your first-degree connections to expand your network.** After you've rustled up some involvement there, expand your group by asking for referrals or introductions to potential second- and third-degree network members or general LinkedIn members who might add some value and insight to your process.

REMEMBER

Odds are your focus group will be Closed, or invisible to searches, so you will need to rely on invitations or word of mouth to gain a targeted and screened audience for your focus group.

>> **Continually send out updates.** You should always be sending out some form of update, whether you do so by filling out the status update option, using LinkedIn Messages, or going through your own e-mail system. Don't deluge people with messages — but also don't ask them to sign up and then be silent for weeks or months at a time. Keep your group members informed and ask for input when needed.

>> **Ask for recommendations.** As group members get introduced to your product, ask them for a recommendation on your profile if they liked or approve of the product. Getting their feedback or recommendations helps build future involvement when your product is live and ready for the mass market.

Using Location-Based LinkedIn Ideas

It's easy to forget the importance of location when you have easy access to such a resource-rich community as LinkedIn. After all, you can communicate with your contacts through LinkedIn Messages, send recommendation requests or post questions, or grow your network without leaving your computer. When you're done using your computer, however, you need to interact in the real world, whether your interaction amounts to shoveling snow or catching a plane to a far-flung convention. When it comes to what I call "location-based" situations, meaning that the problem or situation is tied to a physical spot, you can discover solutions with the help of LinkedIn.

The best use of LinkedIn for location-based problems is this: Your network is typically spread out across the country and across the world. Therefore, not only can you tap someone's professional experience, you can also tap his knowledge or presence in a specific geographical area to help you solve a problem. Take a look at three different location-based situations.

Building your network before moving to a new city

These days, when you have to move to a new city, you can do a lot of planning for it on the Internet. You can research the neighborhoods, look into the school systems, and shop for homes online. You can take this one step further if you plan to move to a different country, and you need information on local customs, cultures, and practices. But what about the questions you can't seem to answer through a web browser? What about the "local knowledge" of where to go and where to avoid? LinkedIn can help.

Every LinkedIn user has defined her location, so you can do a search and figure out which LinkedIn users live in your target area. If nobody in your network is from your target area, start networking and expand that network to include people who reside (or used to reside) in that area who can help.

HELLO? ANY OPPORTUNITIES OUT EAST?

Chuck Hester had a problem. He had to relocate his family from California to Raleigh, North Carolina, and he didn't have a job for himself when he would arrive. In fact, he didn't know anyone in Raleigh — but what he *did* have was a rich LinkedIn network. Hester quickly saw the value of LinkedIn and started contacting people and building relationships, driving his number of connections into the thousands.

Hester started networking with everyone he could who was located in Raleigh. He tapped his existing network to put him in touch with like-minded individuals who lived in the area and kept searching for contacts. One of the contacts he made was the chief executive of iContact, an e-mail marketing company. Hester turned this contact into a job interview, and he became the corporate communications manager for iContact. Even virtual persistence can pay off! Today, Hester continues to grow his LinkedIn network, and he even encourages his local contacts to network "Live," or use LinkedIn Live, to be specific — a feature that I cover later in this chapter.

Here are some specific actions you can take through LinkedIn to help you with the big move:

>> **Use LinkedIn Groups to find your community.** Not every group on LinkedIn is directly related to software development or venture capital. You can look for specific groups of people who share a common skill through LinkedIn Groups (see Chapter 16 for more information on how to do this), join the group and start a discussion topic with your question, and see what the community says in response. Take a look at Figure 19-6, which shows how a search for a specific city, such as New York City, yields thousands of possible groups. You can narrow your search by adding a specific profession or interest, then click Join to access the group.

>> **Start as early as possible.** Building a region-specific network takes time as you recruit new members, ask your existing contacts for referrals, and search for specific people who match the location and either an industry or job title. As soon as you sense that a move is necessary, or maybe when you're mulling over whether to move, start building your network so that you can tap those people for location-specific information before you actually move.

>> **Consider Chamber of Commerce groups.** Do an Internet search for Chamber of Commerce groups in your new area and see if they have a LinkedIn Group or their own website. These groups often have excellent resources for people who are relocating and looking to learn more about the area, especially for local business needs.

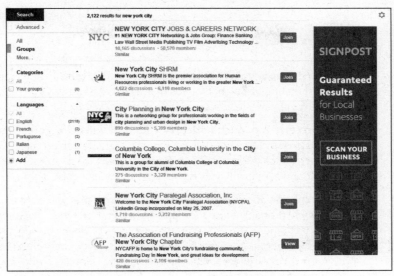

>> **Look for contacts who used to live in your new city.** You might try entering the location of your new city in the Keyword search field rather than the Location field. By doing so, you might find first-degree connections or second-degree network members who used to live in your target area but have since moved; they might reference their past locations in their profiles. Contact those people and see whether they can introduce you to any contacts they may still have in that target area, regardless of whether those contacts are on or off LinkedIn.

Arranging face-to-face meetings when traveling

LinkedIn can serve as a wonderful resource even when you're not moving to another city but simply traveling for business or personal reasons. Say that you know you have some extra time on your trip, or you want to make some local connections to reinforce your business trip. Why not tap your LinkedIn network and visit your contacts in person?

A growing practice of busy LinkedIn professionals who travel is to arrange face-to-face visits with other LinkedIn members during a business trip. This way, the traveler can meet with someone she is familiar with who could share similar interests and goals. Also, both people get a chance to expand their networks by creating a stronger connection. To bring about in-person meetings, most people either post something to LinkedIn Groups or send a message to targeted members of their networks.

If you're interested in making your next trip more of a LinkedIn adventure, keep these tips in mind:

>> **Provide enough notice to attract people's attention.** If you're putting up a post on Monday night that you're available for Tuesday lunch, you probably won't get many responses in time to set up anything meaningful.

>> **Don't give too much notice, or your visit will be forgotten by the time you arrive.** Some notice is necessary to get on people's calendars, but too much notice will make people forget as your visit gets closer. More than two to four weeks in advance is probably too much notice.

>> **Be specific about your availability.** It's great that you want to get together, but you probably have other plans when you're visiting. Therefore, when you contact other members, offer a few choices of when you can get together — and be specific. For example, you could say, "Hey, I'm going to be in San Jose for most of next week. Who's available either Monday night or Wednesday lunchtime to get together?"

>> **Use your get-together to help prepare for business.** Your get-togethers with people in other cities don't have to be purely social. Say that you know you're traveling to that city for an interview. Perhaps you want to send a targeted message to a few contacts who used to work for your target company and ask to meet them in person before your interview so that they can help you prepare. Or maybe you want to practice your sales presentation on a knowledgeable person before you go into someone's office to do the real thing.

Networking with LinkedIn . . . in person!

Social networking is a great way to stay connected, grow your personal and professional contacts list, and learn about new opportunities. But after lots of e-mails, Instant Messages, and discussion boards, sometimes you just want the experience of meeting someone face to face. Many LinkedIn members feel this way and use the virtual power of LinkedIn to bring together people in the real world. Although online methods can expedite the process of finding the right people, they can't replace the power of face-to-face networking.

You can find all sorts of "chapters" of in-person networking groups inspired by people first meeting on LinkedIn and then connecting in-person with people from their network at a live event. Besides Linking the Triangle in North Carolina, I've discovered LinkedIn Live or LinkedIn Face-to-Face events in Miami, Dallas, and Denver — and there may well be more.

LINKEDIN LIVE

If you use LinkedIn and you're in the Raleigh-Durham area of North Carolina, odds are you've heard of Chuck Hester. "I'm known as the Kevin Bacon of Raleigh," he smiles. "If I don't know a person, I probably know someone who does." He's the creator of LinkedIn Live Raleigh, an informal networking group formed years ago and dedicated to having Hester's virtual connections meet each other in person so they can increase their own networking. By that time, Hester had built up more than 700 connections in the Raleigh area alone, so he sent out an invitation, and 50 people showed up to the event. The event was such a success that meetings were held every other month, and attendance grew exponentially, more than tripling in the first six months. In fact, Hester doesn't have to worry about the costs because he gets sponsors to donate the food, meeting space, and even door prizes! He expanded this group to the larger region in North Carolina by forming a LinkedIn Group called Linking the Triangle.

Hester receives calls from more than a dozen other similar LinkedIn Groups, each asking for advice on how to set up and maintain these live networking events. He's proud of the results from all this live networking, saying "At least 20–30 people have found new jobs from meeting someone at a LinkedIn Live." Of course, he used the opportunity to build brand recognition for his employer at the time, iContact, which he found by networking on LinkedIn. (See the "Hello? Any opportunities out east?" sidebar earlier in this chapter.) The LinkedIn Live Raleigh networking has also earned him mentions in the Fast Company blog, *The Wall Street Journal, Inc.* magazine, and *The New York Times*. You can find out more by reading Hester's blog at www.chuckhester.com.

To find or organize a LinkedIn Group from your network, keep these tips in mind:

>> **Search your LinkedIn connections to see if they are involved with any local groups.** Do an Advanced People search to see which of your connections are located in the city you want to relocate to, for example, and scroll down their profile page to see which groups they belong to. You might find someone like Chuck Hester, who, besides starting Linking the Triangle near Raleigh, has helped others start LinkedIn Groups in cities such as London and Miami. You can see these and other groups by going to the Groups section of his profile, as shown in Figure 19-7.

>> **Search LinkedIn Groups to see whether a group exists in your area.** Click Groups and then do a search for terms like "LinkedIn Live" (don't forget the quotes) to see what kinds of groups of LinkedIn members show up. For example, when I searched for "LinkedIn Live," I saw LinkedIn Groups in places like Houston, Rhode Island, and Toronto, as shown in Figure 19-8.

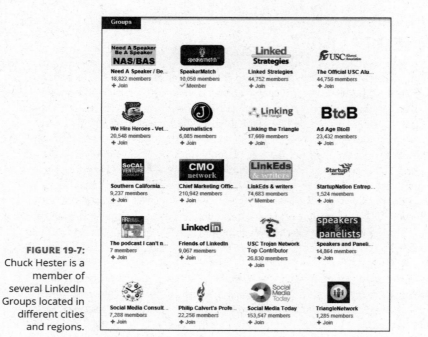

FIGURE 19-7:
Chuck Hester is a member of several LinkedIn Groups located in different cities and regions.

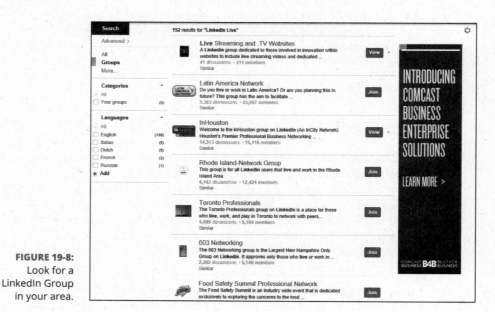

FIGURE 19-8:
Look for a LinkedIn Group in your area.

>> **Use the Internet to look for social networking meetings.** You may have to go outside LinkedIn to find an eager group of LinkedIn members. If you do a search with a networking site like Meetup.com, you will find a number of LinkedIn Groups already established in cities around the world, as shown in Figure 19-9.

>> **If nothing exists, start your own live group.** Create something on LinkedIn Groups and build a core group for the first event. Send an update or message to your network members who live in the area and encourage them to pass along the message to their local friends who are LinkedIn members.

One of my connections, Andrew, turned to LinkedIn to help find interest for a regular get-together of technology folks, for which companies involved in newer web-based technologies open their doors to hungry technology workers who then learn about their host company over lunch. He posted a question on LinkedIn to find a host company and got several responses, which led to some great meetings!

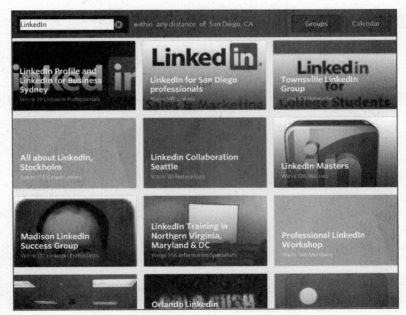

FIGURE 19-9:
Read about LinkedIn in-person groups on the Internet.

6

The Part of Tens

Discover ten essential do's and don'ts for getting the most value out of LinkedIn.

Find ten popular online resources to help you with your LinkedIn activity.

Chapter 20

Ten LinkedIn Do's and Don'ts

I cover a lot of ground in this book — so much that it might be hard to remember it all as you're going about your daily use of LinkedIn. So here are ten essential do's and don'ts to help you build relationships and get the most value out of LinkedIn.

Do Keep Your Profile Complete and Current

Even though LinkedIn has many features, your profile is still one of the most compelling reasons to use the website, which is why LinkedIn is one of the best searchable databases of businesspeople available. And if you want other people to find you, you need to make sure that your data is complete and current. Here are a few ways to do that:

>> **List all your former employers and schools.** Several features help users find and connect with former colleagues and classmates (see Chapter 6). Including your complete work and educational background in your profile can help you reconnect.

If you've had a lengthy career, you don't necessarily need to include details about positions early in your career — just the companies and titles will suffice. A good guideline is to include details on just the past 7 to 10 years. Additionally, consider including only those positions relevant to your current work. I seriously doubt that my first job at a McDonald's is relevant to my current work as an author (unless I want to write the sequel to *Fast Food Nation*). I've also grouped a lot of my contract work under one experience heading with my own consulting company name, because many of the consulting jobs were similar in nature. It's up to you how you want to present your experience to the LinkedIn community.

>> **Take advantage of the rich sections you can add to your profile.** In the early versions of LinkedIn, you could highlight your work experience and education and a few other elements of your identity. Today, LinkedIn allows you to add many sections that could apply to your overall work experience, whether it's posting presentations or publications that you wrote, courses that you've taken, patents that you've earned, or projects that you're working on. In addition, you can add documents, videos, photos, web links, or presentations to any job you list in your Experience section.

>> **Update your profile (and headline) any time you achieve a new position, complete a major side project, or receive a special award or recognition.** Your direct connections will be notified (assuming they haven't turned off the feature) of the change. This is a subtle, unobtrusive way to notify your network of your career changes. And you never know when someone is going to be looking for what you have to offer. Make sure that if you have a new position, you update your e-mail address with your new corporate e-mail address so people can still reach and invite you. You should also provide status updates that go out to your network. Many people share their status update but forget to go back and update their profile, so be sure to do both tasks on a regular basis.

Don't Use Canned Invitations

There is never a good situation in which to use one of the default invitation text messages LinkedIn provides when you send someone an invitation to join your network on LinkedIn. Nothing says "You're not really worth a few extra seconds of my time" quite like the all-too-familiar "I'd like to add you to my professional network" message.

That doesn't mean every invitation has to be a lengthy personal epistle. Here are a few tips for keeping invitations efficient but personal:

>> **Keep it short when you can.** With people you know well and have been in recent contact with, the canned messages are actually too long. The message can be as simple as "Great to see you last night, Jerry — let's connect."

>> **Make sure to mention how you know the person, especially for contacts you haven't spoken to recently.** While you may remember the person you are hoping to connect with very well, that person may not have the same recollection. If it's a contact you haven't spoken to in a while, start the invitation with some sort of indirect reminder or reference of the last time you two interacted. For example, "Hey, I know it's been 10 years since we went to UCLA and had Computer Science classes together, but I thought we could stay connected via LinkedIn."

>> **If the contact isn't already a member of LinkedIn, offer to help with the registration process.** You can try to explain the benefits of joining LinkedIn in an e-mail, but no matter what you do, it's going to come across as a sales pitch, or at least a bit evangelistic. The best way to persuade people is to offer to spend a few minutes on the phone explaining LinkedIn and how you're using it. That also turns the invitation into an opportunity to strengthen your relationship with that person by offering your time to bring her something of value.

>> **You can still personalize a batch of invitations.** You can give the invitation a personal touch even if you're sending it to multiple people. For example, you can send the same invitation to all the people you met or ran into at an event. Or you can send one invitation to everyone in your chamber of commerce. Just remember to write it as if it were going to one person, not the whole group.

For more on invitations, see Chapter 6.

Don't Expect Everyone to Network Like You Do

Setting rigid networking expectations can be a source of needless frustration and can actually prevent you from building relationships with some pretty great people. Here are some of the common issues that arise:

>> **Different people have different standards for connecting.** Some people use LinkedIn to connect only with people they know very well. Some connect

only with people with whom they share some common points of interest. Others connect with anybody. None of these approaches is wrong. If some people don't have the same standard for a connection that you do, don't take it personally, and don't judge them — they're doing what's right for them.

>> **People might have perfectly good reasons not to allow other people to browse their LinkedIn connections list.** Don't hold anything against people who don't enable it. People may be concerned about client confidentiality, and thus be required to keep their connections private. Or they may be connected to a competitor and not want their bosses and co-workers to know about it. Or they may just be concerned about their time commitments and not want to handle a growing number of requests to meet other people in their network, if all their friends see their long list of connections. However, even if a person has disabled connections browsing, you can still ask for introductions to people that person knows. Frankly, if you're just browsing other people's networks, maybe you should think about a more focused approach.

>> **Not everyone responds in a timely manner.** If your request doesn't get forwarded or you haven't gotten a reply to your InMail after a couple of weeks, don't take it personally. It doesn't mean that you're unimportant; it just means the people you're trying to contact are busy, or infrequent users of LinkedIn. If it's really urgent, pick up the phone, or consider sending another e-mail acknowledging that the other person is likely very busy but you were checking in one more time to see if he or she would be willing to set up a time to talk or converse online. Don't underestimate the power that a friendly and under-standing note can have on the other party.

>> **Some people are bad with names.** Just because you remember somebody's name doesn't mean that she remembers yours. Unless you're 100 percent certain that she will recognize your invitation, contact her via e-mail or phone or a LinkedIn message before sending a connection request. Otherwise, don't be surprised when she declines your invitation or clicks the I Don't Know This Person link.

>> **Relationships aren't always reciprocal.** For example, if you were someone's client, you might be able to provide a great recommendation for him. That doesn't mean he can do the same for you, so don't expect it.

>> **Not everyone networks just to network.** Some people are extremely busy and not receptive to "I'd just like to meet you" requests. It's nothing personal, and it doesn't mean they're bad networkers. It just means that the demands on their time exceed the supply.

Do Your Homework

People provide you with all kinds of guidance, both direct and implicit, regarding what to contact them about and how. If you're the one initiating the communication, it's your responsibility to communicate on their terms. And showing that you took the time to do your homework about them demonstrates a certain level of commitment to the relationship right from the outset.

The most basic rule of good conversation is to listen. In the context of LinkedIn, that rule means simply this: Pay attention to what's on a person's profile. Any time you contact somebody, review her profile first as well as any "Advice for Contacting" that person has in the Additional Info section of the profile. Respect what you see in her profile and advice section.

When you send an introduction request message or an invitation to someone you don't know very well, don't put the burden on her to figure out what the common areas of interest or potential opportunities are. You took the time to read her profile and determine that it's a worthwhile connection. Save her the trouble of figuring out what you already know and put your common areas of interest in your introduction request or invitation.

Do Give LinkedIn Messages Equal Importance

Many people have a tendency to treat LinkedIn communications as less important or less time-sensitive than an official e-mail or phone call.

Nothing could be further from the truth. People get jobs, hire employees, gain clients, and make deals as a result of LinkedIn-based communications. They are every bit as much a part of your essential business correspondence as the rest of your e-mail. (If they're not, you're connecting with the wrong people!)

Here are some tips for managing your LinkedIn communications:

>> **Don't turn off e-mail notifications.** Missing time-sensitive communications is one of the worst things you can do. If the volume of e-mail seems overwhelming, you can use e-mail rules to move LinkedIn requests into a separate folder, but as a general productivity practice, you want as few different Inboxes as possible.

To make sure you have e-mail notifications set up correctly, log in to your LinkedIn account and either visit the Communications section of the settings page, or go to www.linkedin.com/settings/email-frequency.

You see the Email Frequency screen, as shown in Figure 20-1. By clicking each category, such as Messages from Other Members (see Figure 20-2), you can set up what comes to you as an individual e-mail, a weekly digest e-mail, or no e-mail so you can decide what is most important. (In some categories, a daily digest e-mail option is also available.)

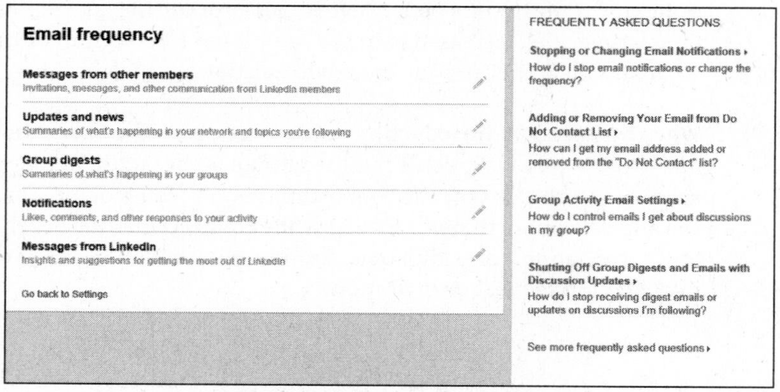

FIGURE 20-1:
Set your e-mail notification frequency so you don't miss an important message.

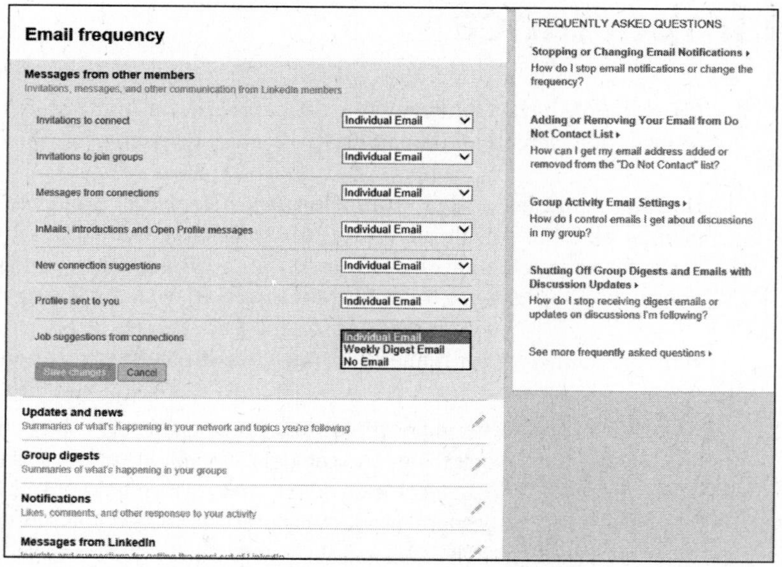

FIGURE 20-2:
Decide for each category how often you wish to be contacted.

>> **Check your LinkedIn Inbox every day.** Or at least every couple of days. You wouldn't go a week without checking your e-mail at work — don't treat LinkedIn messages any differently. (See Chapter 10 for more on how to manage your LinkedIn Inbox.)

>> **Do it, delegate it, defer it, or delete it.** This technique from David Allen's book *Getting Things Done: The Art of Stress-Free Productivity* (Penguin, 2015) will help you keep your Inbox organized. As you're going through your Inbox, if you can handle a request in under two minutes, go ahead and do it. Or you can delegate it by sending on the introduction request or recommending one of your contacts as an expert to answer the person's question. If something in your Inbox takes a little more time, you can defer it by putting it into your work queue to handle later.

For additional tips on e-mail organization and productivity, check out David Allen's book *Getting Things Done*, and also take a look at 43 Folders' Inbox Zero collection at www.43folders.com/izero.

Don't Spam

One person's networking is another person's spam. Better to err on the side of caution. There are plenty of ways to use LinkedIn productively without getting a bad rep as a spammer. Here are some basic rules of etiquette:

>> **Don't post marketing messages or connection-seeking messages as your status updates.** All these will get your message flagged and fairly quickly removed. Don't waste your effort. There's a fine line between market or product research that calls attention to your company and an advertisement.

>> **Don't automatically subscribe your connections to your newsletter.** This is admittedly a gray area. Connecting with someone indicates a certain level of receptivity to receiving communication from that person, and it's reasonable to assume that should include something more than just LinkedIn messages. After all, he's supposed to be someone you know and trust, right? Well, that's not necessarily the same thing as signing up for a regular bulk newsletter.

I think it's better to be safe than sorry, so I don't recommend auto-subscribing folks to your newsletter. People can get ticked off if they suddenly start getting some newsletter they didn't subscribe to.

The best approach is simply to ask permission to subscribe your individual contacts to your newsletter. If you get their permission, even if they do complain later, you can politely point out that you asked first.

>> **Don't send connection requests to people you don't know.** Unless they've given some kind of explicit indication that they're open to receiving invitations (for example, announcing it in a LinkedIn Group, stating it in their profiles, or being a member of an open networking group), you have to assume that most people don't want to receive LinkedIn connection invitations from strangers. LinkedIn has taken measures to curb such rampant inviting behavior, and it will get you suspended soon enough. Again, there's a simple solution: *Ask permission first.* Send a message to get introduced through a common connection, or contact the person via e-mail or his website, and ask whether it would be okay for you to send him a connection invitation.

Do Be Proactive About Making New Connections

If you just set up a profile, connect with a few of your contacts, and then expect business to come your way, you're setting yourself up for disappointment. That's not to say that it can't happen, but being a little bit proactive goes a long way:

>> **Search for people who can help you with your goals.** If you want to meet people in a particular city, industry, or target market, search for them specifically and send messages to request an introduction. Some people are receptive to corresponding or talking just for networking purposes, but you'll get a better response if you have a specific need or opportunity as the basis of your contact.

>> **Introduce people to each other.** LinkedIn's basic introduction paradigm is reactive. For example, an introduction is made when person A wants to connect with person C via person B. But an essential practice of a good networker is identifying possible connections between people in your network and introducing them to each other. You can do this by sharing one person's profile with the other and copying in the first person (see Chapter 5). You can send a LinkedIn message to both connections introducing them and telling them why you think they should get to know each other.

>> **Get involved.** The Groups section is the main form of public group interaction on LinkedIn. You can come together with other people to talk about a shared interest, or as alumni of a school or university, or as former or current employees of a given company. After you join a LinkedIn Group, you have access to the other group members just as you do a first-degree connection or second-degree network member on LinkedIn, and group involvement is a great way to expand your network and further your education.

Do Cross-Promote

Your LinkedIn profile is just one web page of your total web presence. It should connect people to your other points of presence, and you probably want to direct people to your LinkedIn profile from other venues as well. Here are some good cross-promotion practices:

>> **Customize your LinkedIn profile links.** As described in Chapter 3, you can create up to three links on your profile that you can use to lead people to your business site(s), personal site, blog, book, event, and so on.

>> **Include a link to your LinkedIn profile in your signature.** You can use this both in your e-mail signature and also on discussion forums. If you don't have a centralized personal professional website, your LinkedIn profile is a good alternative.

>> **Link to your LinkedIn profile in your blog's About page.** Why rehash your entire bio? Put a couple of paragraphs that are relevant to the blog and then refer people to your LinkedIn profile for more details.

>> **Install the LinkedIn app for your smartphone.** LinkedIn has added a lot of functionality to their mobile app, which is available for the iPhone or Android operating system. Using the various LinkedIn mobile apps will allow you to access the site when you're out and about, networking in person. I cover the different LinkedIn apps in Chapter 12.

>> **Put your LinkedIn URL on your business card.** More and more people are starting to do this, as your LinkedIn profile is a good "home page" for business contacts. You can put contact information, your experience history, and many other vital details on your LinkedIn profile. Once someone connects with you via LinkedIn, that person will always be able to reach you. While phone numbers and e-mail addresses can change, your LinkedIn connection will never change unless you want to remove someone as a connection.

Do Add Value to the Process

LinkedIn is based on the idea that existing relationships add value to the process of people meeting each other. If all you're doing is just passing the introduction "bucket" down the virtual bucket brigade, you're actually getting in the way of communication, not adding value.

To add value, you have to give those request messages for an introduction some thought. Is it an appropriate fit for the recipient? Is the timing good?

Add your comments to any message you forward to help facilitate an introduction. How well do you know the sender? Saying "I worked with Michael Bellomo for several years as a co-author, and he was hard-working, trust-worthy, and ambitious" goes a lot further than saying "Hey, Francine, here's this guy Michael to check out." For additional guidance on how to handle this tactfully, see Chapter 5.

Don't Confuse Quantity with Quality

Just because you're doing a lot of something doesn't mean you're doing something well. And when you think about it, is *more networking activity* what you really want? Or do you really want *more results with less activity?*

If you want to track your real progress using LinkedIn, don't measure it by meaningless metrics like number of connections, endorsements, or questions answered. Use metrics that you know directly tie to business results, such as these:

>> Leads generated

>> Joint venture/strategic partner prospects generated

>> Qualified job candidates contacted

>> Potential employers successfully contacted

>> Interviews scheduled

>> Speaking opportunities garnered

>> Publicity opportunities created

These dos and don'ts are a basic list for you to keep in mind as you use LinkedIn. The best rule to consider is the Golden Rule: "Do unto others as you would have them do unto you." Be open, accommodating, honest, and respectful, and the power of LinkedIn should become more evident every day you use it.

IN THIS CHAPTER
Useful blogs and networking sites
Helpful webinar and video channels
Information repositories and podcasts
Aggregation and smartphone tools

Chapter 21

Ten LinkedIn Resources

A s you continue building your LinkedIn presence, you might want to take advantage of additional websites that keep you up to date on new features and possibilities on LinkedIn. These sites explore common and uncommon uses for the website and make you think about how to take advantage and enjoy the benefits of LinkedIn and social networking in general. I've rounded up a list of ten Internet resources that can provide extra information or functionality regarding your LinkedIn activities. Most of these resources are completely free, but Buffer and Evernote offer more powerful features for a monthly fee. Whether you use one or use them all, I'm sure you can find the resources that best match the way you like to learn and grow online.

The Official LinkedIn Blog

blog.linkedin.com

Years ago, Mario Sundar, previously a LinkedIn "evangelist" who promoted the company on his own blog, was hired by LinkedIn to start its official company blog. Today, various LinkedIn employees put up fun, informative, and timely blog posts about new functions or changes to the site as well as success stories, case studies, and practical information to make your LinkedIn experience that much more rewarding.

In addition, the blog posts live on forever, and you can search them to find out valuable information or post your own comments to give feedback!

TIP

You can also follow the official LinkedIn Twitter feed (@LinkedIn), the LinkedIn Help Desk Twitter feed (@LinkedInHelp), or follow LinkedIn on Facebook at https://www.facebook.com/linkedin.

LinkedIn Instagram

    https://www.instagram.com/linkedin

While LinkedIn maintains an active Facebook and Twitter account, its Instagram page is an up-and-coming way for LinkedIn to share visual data with its ever-growing audience. LinkedIn uses the Instagram account to share lots of information, including its new "Top Voices" initiative, where leading writers from different industries come together to inspire people with new ideas in hopes of sparking conversations about core skills. LinkedIn also shares fun and timely content through photos, videos, and infographics, whether it's "Do's and Don'ts," a company event like "Bring Your Parents to Work" day, or a recent poll that applies to its target audience.

When you click each tile on LinkedIn's Instagram page, you'll be able to read more comments attached to that item, click Like, or add your own comment to it. When you follow LinkedIn's Instagram page, you can stay up to date on all its new postings.

LinkedIn Learning Webinars

    https://www.linkedin.com/company/webinar

LinkedIn launched a set of webinars designed to help you use your LinkedIn account more effectively and to introduce you to LinkedIn's newest features and functionalities. These webinars and training videos are available from the LinkedIn Help Center. You can register for new webinars, which are typically held weekly.

The Sophisticated Marketer

```
www.slideshare.net/LImarketingsolutions/
```

In 2012, LinkedIn acquired a company called SlideShare, which allowed people to store, display, and collaborate on their presentations using the SlideShare website. LinkedIn then incorporated SlideShare into its overall business, allowing people to display SlideShare presentations from their LinkedIn profile. The Marketing Solutions team has created a hub of fascinating presentations on the SlideShare website, grouping together actual presentations they give at industry conferences, case studies of companies and people who use LinkedIn and their various marketing elements, and insights and infographics that LinkedIn has generated.

The result is the "Sophisticated Marketer" hub on SlideShare, which has, as of this writing, hundreds of presentations and thousands of followers. You can follow this account to be notified of the newest uploads, and watch videos and download presentations in a number of areas, with the primary focus being LinkedIn's different Marketing Solutions.

LinkedIn YouTube Channel

```
https://www.youtube.com/LinkedIn
```

The explosion of video clips available on the Internet is best signified by looking at one of the most popular websites on the Internet — YouTube. Today, people use YouTube as a search engine, looking for a video clip that can answer their question instead of a text result from a search engine like Google. Because of this, companies such as LinkedIn have their own "channels," or collections of videos about their subject matter, that are easily organized and cataloged for quick viewing.

LinkedIn's YouTube channel offers a wealth of information, from the informational videos about products like LinkedIn Mobile or Company Pages, to LinkedIn Influencers who share their knowledge with the worldwide community, to a LinkedIn Speaker Series that shares knowledge catering to working professionals who use LinkedIn. You can subscribe to this channel to be informed of any new additions to the channel, as new content is always being added.

Linked Intelligence Blog

`http://linkedintelligence.com`

When LinkedIn was growing in size and popularity during its early days, blogger Scott Allen put together the Linked Intelligence site to cover LinkedIn and its many uses. Over the years, he built up a healthy amount of blog posts, links, and valuable information from himself and other bloggers regarding LinkedIn and how to use it.

One of his more ambitious projects is simply dubbed 100+ Ways to Use LinkedIn. Allen had bloggers compete to provide valuable information and tips across all of LinkedIn's functions, and he created a table of contents of the best entries on his blog site. You can still find this handy resource at `http://www.linkedintelligence.com/smart-ways-to-use-linkedin`.

The large repository of links and information can be helpful to new, intermediate, or power users of the site. The blog posts are divided into topics such as LinkedIn News and Networking Skills.

Linked Conversations — Podcast

`http://firpodcastnetwork.com/linked-conversations/`

The staggering popularity of the Apple iPod gave rise to a new way of broadcasting audio information to eager listeners — the podcast. Think of the podcast as a recorded audio broadcast that you can download to your iPod, smartphone, iPad, computer, MP3 player, or other device. You can subscribe to engaging and unique podcasts, regardless of where in the world they're recorded and played.

At Linked Conversations, host Chuck Hester talks about different ways you can use LinkedIn and brings in guest speakers to share their experiences, tips, and tricks with LinkedIn. This podcast also has a wealth of archived shows that are available for download, so you can listen to success stories and get all sorts of tips. You can subscribe to this show and hear great interviews, tips, and stories of how other people and companies connect online.

Digsby Social Networking/IM/E-Mail Tool

`www.digsby.com`

As you monitor your LinkedIn activity, you're most likely using other tools and networks as part of your overall experience, such as Facebook and Twitter. Rather than go to each site individually, you can use an *aggregator* — a special software tool you use to group all the information generated in all your social networks — and then present them in one tool.

One such application is Digsby, which promises to integrate your e-mail, Instant Messaging, and social networking accounts in one clean interface. After you download and set up Digsby, you can view a live newsfeed of all your friends and connections based on their events or activities on sites like LinkedIn, as well as manage chat sessions and see e-mail notifications. In the era of information overload, a tool like Digsby can help you make sense of all the messages and updates zooming to your computer screen.

Turn Business Cards into LinkedIn Contacts with Evernote

`https://evernote.com`

If you're like many people who collect business cards at a networking event or conference, and you never get around to cataloging or responding to these new contacts, then Evernote is for you. Evernote's mobile smartphone app allows you to scan in a business card and then directly connect with that person on LinkedIn. You will see the profile photo, job title, and company information of the new contact's LinkedIn profile in the notes section of Evernote where you scanned in the business card.

One Update for Multiple Sites with Buffer

`https://buffer.com`

If you're active on LinkedIn and other social networking sites (Facebook, Twitter, Pinterest, and others), you probably hop from site to site to provide up-to-the-minute information about what you're doing and what you want others to know.

Well, instead of site hopping, you can use one function to update your status across all your social networking pages and microblogs: Buffer.

It works like this: You log on to the site and enter your message into the dashboard. You then select the sites you want to update with your new status message, pick the day(s) and time you want the updates to be posted, and Buffer does the rest, reaching out to your various pages to add your new status message. It's a great centralized way to keep all your various profiles as up to date as possible, and it's designed to update your LinkedIn status by answering the question, "What are you working on?" As of this writing, Buffer offers a free plan that allows you to schedule up to 10 posts at one time.

Index

publishers, as source of LinkedIn Pulse content, 150, 152

Pulse app, 147, 148, 153, 154, 207, 209

Q

quality *versus* quantity, 102–103, 342

quotation marks, use of in advanced searches, 75, 82

R

Recent Conversation (sort option in LinkedIn Contacts), 128

reciprocal linking, 292

reciprocated recommendations, 163

recommendations

  Ask for Changes button (Recommendations feature), 176

  Ask for Changes link (Recommendations feature), 177

  Ask for Recommendations page, 170

  asking for from group members, 322

  choosing who to request from, 169–170

  collecting of, 241

  creating, 166–169

  creating polite recommendation request, 170

  customized recommendation request, 172

  deciding who to recommend, 164–165

  declining of or request for, 172–173

  editing or removing of ones you've made, 174–175

  examples of, 161

  exploring power of, 161–177

  Give (person) a Recommendation page, 166, 167

  handling new ones, 176

  importance of quality of, 164

  making them stand out, 165–166

  managing of, 174–175

  posting of when adding customer to network, 299

  reciprocated recommendations, 163

  Recommendations feature, 134, 162, 163, 167, 180

  Recommendations header, 174

  Recommendations page, 170, 174, 177

  Recommendations section, 174, 177

  Recommendations You've Received page, 177

  removing of or requesting revision of, 176–177

  requested recommendations, 163

  requesting of, 169–172

  as shown on profile, 163

  understanding of, 162–164

  unsolicited recommendations, 162, 169

  View Profile As button (Recommendations feature), 62, 170

  What's Your Relationship? section (Recommendations feature), 168

  Who Do You Want to Ask? page (Recommendations feature), 170

  Write a Recommendation text box, 167

  writing of, 164–169

  Your Connections text field (Recommendations feature), 170–171

Recommendations feature, 134, 162, 163, 167, 180

Recommendations header, 174

Recommendations page, 170, 174, 177

Recommendations section, 174, 177

Recommendations You've Received page, 177

Recommended for You, 151, 152

Recruiter functions, 20

Reference Search function, 221

referrals

  asking customer for, 300

  asking existing contacts for, 324

  asking first-degree connections for, 322

  asking for whenever possible, 245

  encouraging former managers/bosses, co-workers, and partners to provide, 240, 241

  finding target company referrals, 247–248

  LinkedIn as business referral system, 173

Relationship box, 132

Relationship filter, 76, 251

Relationship tab, 130, 131

Relationships Matter (LinkedIn slogan), 7

Reminder link (LinkedIn Contacts), 132

About the Author

Joel Elad, MBA, is the head of Real Method Consulting, a company dedicated to educating people through training seminars, DVDs, books, and other media. He holds a master's degree in Business from UC Irvine, and has a bachelor's degree in Computer Science and Engineering from UCLA. He also operates several online businesses and co-founded the So Cal Comic Con.

Joel has written seven books about various online topics, including *Facebook Advertising For Dummies, Starting an Online Business All-In-One For Dummies, Starting an iPhone Application Business For Dummies,* and *Wiley Pathways: E-business.* He has contributed to *Entrepreneur* magazine and Smartbiz.com, and has taught at institutions such as the University of California, Irvine, and the University of San Diego. He is an Educational Specialist trained by eBay and a former Internet instructor for the Learning Annex in New York City, Los Angeles, San Diego, and San Francisco.

Joel lives in San Diego, California. In his spare time, he hones his skills in creative writing, Texas Hold 'Em poker, and finance. He is an avid traveler who enjoys seeing the sights both near and far, whether it's the Las Vegas Strip or the ruins of Machu Picchu. He spends his weekends scouring eBay and local conventions for the best deals, catching the latest movies with friends or family, and enjoying a lazy Sunday.

Dedication

To my best friend Magda, who faces life and adversity as strongly as she values our friendship. You amaze and inspire me, and I hope you never give up on anything! Friends Forever — Joel

Author's Acknowledgments

First and foremost, I have to give the BIGGEST thanks to the great team at Wiley who made this book project possible. Thanks to Amy Fandrei for pushing this project forward and keeping me in place. An absolute, huge, bear-hug thanks to Lynn Northrup for putting up with my fast and furious submissions; she definitely kept me on track to make this book happen. And where would I be without my copy editor, who makes me sound so clear and grammatically correct!

I have to give a special thanks to Scott Allen, who was instrumental in getting this book project started. Scott, I appreciate your help and support, as well as your infinite knowledge on the subject.

Thanks, as always, go out to my friends and new LinkedIn contacts who provided me with stories, examples, and endless encouragement. I especially want to thank Troy Benton, Cynthia Beale Campbell, Michael Bellomo, Anthony Choi, Lynn Dralle, Jun Goeku, Greg Goldstein, Stacey Harmon, Steve Hayes, Chuck Hester, Doug Johnson, Sarah Lundy, Kyle Looper, David Nakayama, Blair Pottenger, Kristie Spilios, Doug Tondro, Jan Utstein, and Michael Wellman. I even need to thank Lestat's Coffee House in North Park, San Diego, for being open 24 hours a day to help me with my late-late-night writing sessions.

Lastly, thanks to my family for putting up with my late-late-night writing sessions and frequent seclusion to get this book ready for publication. Your support is always invaluable.

Publisher's Acknowledgments

We're proud of this book; please send us your comments at http://dummies.custhelp.com. For other comments, please contact our Customer Care Department within the U.S. at 877-762-2974, outside the U.S. at 317-572-3993, or fax 317-572-4002.

Some of the people who helped bring this book to market include the following:

Acquisitions Editor: Amy Fandrei

Project Editor: Lynn Northrup

Copy Editor: Lynn Northrup

Technical Editor: Michelle Krasniak

Production Editor: Kumar Chellappan

Editorial Assistant: Matthew Lowe

Sr. Editorial Assistant: Cherie Case

Cover Image: ©BackgroundStore/Shutterstock